ROLLS-ROYCE
AND
BENTLEY

THE CREWE YEARS

The above latin motto means: 'Whatever is rightly done, however humble, is noble.' – Royce, 1924.

ROLLS-ROYCE
AND
BENTLEY

THE CREWE YEARS

Martin Bennett

Foulis

Haynes

First published in 1995
Reprinted in 1996

A catalogue record for this book is available from the British Library.

ISBN 0 85429 908 4

Library of Congress catalog card number 94-73831

G. T. Foulis & Co.
is an imprint of Haynes Publishing,
Sparkford, near Yeovil, Somerset, BA22 7JJ

Printed in Great Britain by Butler & Tanner Ltd, London and Frome.

Typeset in Times by Character Graphics, Taunton, Somerset.

Acknowledgements

The vast majority of illustrations in this book have been supplied over several decades by Rolls-Royce Ltd and their successors Rolls-Royce Motors Ltd and Rolls-Royce Motor Cars Ltd. For this generous contribution and for information given readily, access to the Crewe factory and other Company facilities, I am deeply indebted and mention in particular Dennis Miller-Williams, David Preston and John Bodie.

Of particular significance and for which I am especially grateful are the superb drawings of John Bull (R.R.O.C.A.) which are seen throughout this book. John also generously loaned a number of Hooper photographs from his collection.

During the final preparation of the book a pleasant couple of days were spent with Tom Solley (R.R.E.C.) who very kindly allowed access to his photographic files and supplied a number of photographs of inestimable value to the finished work. Likewise Richard Mann (R.R.E.C.) has allowed me to plunder his photographic files on several occasions, as well as supplying many invaluable recollections of his years at Mulliner Park Ward as Senior Quality Engineer. Thanks are also due to Klaus-Josef Roßfeldt (R.R.E.C.) who, in addition to supplying a number of his excellent photographs, provided information on the coachbuilt Bentley Mk VI cars. Tom Clarke (R.R.E.C.), a great Rolls-Royce enthusiast, author and researcher of enormous talent, has my gratitude for his kind encouragement, advice and assistance with the manuscript.

I also record my thanks to the following for providing the illustrations indicated:

The Autocar – 12 (bottom), 41 (top), 124 (centre, bottom), 309 (bottom), 311 (bottom); Jack Barclay Ltd – 43 (bottom), 44 (bottom right), 54 (centre, bottom), 57 (bottom), 107, 108, 109 (bottom), 121 (top, bottom), 122 (top left), 132, 134 (top, bottom), 169, 175 (centre bottom), 177 (top), 178 (top), 181 (top, centre), 199 (middle), 202 (top), 204 (middle), 219 (top, middle), 234, 235 (top right, bottom), 236 (top, middle); Michael Bull – 172 (centre); Tom Clarke (R.R.E.C.) – 120 (centre, bottom left), 233 (middle); Bill Coburn (R.R.O.C.A.) – 126 (bottom left), 133 (upper centre, bottom), 160 (bottom right), 170 (centre), 274 (centre); Commonwealth Government of Australia – 216 (bottom); Tony Davidson (R.R.O.C.A.) – 90 (bottom), Greater London Council Photographic Library – 232; Russell P. Herrold Jnr. (R.R.O.C. Inc) – 12 (top); A.R. Illingworth (R.R.E.C.) – 59 (bottom left); Brian McDonald (R.R.O.C.A.) – 31 (bottom right); Brian McMillan (R.R.O.C.A.) – 196 (top, centre); Roger Morrison (R.R.O.C. Inc) – 51 (top); R.R.E.C. Photo Library – 59 (top, centre right), 105 (top, centre), 191 (bottom), 255, 256; Klaus-Josef Roßfeldt (R.R.E.C.) – 61 (centre right), 79 (centre, bottom), 99 (upper centre), 113 (top), 120 (top, bottom right), 129 (bottom right), 136 (top), 137 (top), 168 (bottom), 215 (middle); David Scott-Moncrieff – 50 (bottom), 55 (top); Dr C. S. (Sam) Shoup (R.R.O.C.) – 167 (bottom); Thomas T. Solley (R.R.E.C.) – 58 (lower centre, bottom), 64, 103, 115 (bottom), 118 (bottom), 119, 131 (bottom), 136 (bottom), 175 (top), 205 (bottom), 213 (bottom), 283 (bottom); Matthew Sysak (R.R.O.C. Inc) – 56; Roger Thiedeman (R.R.O.C.A.) – 270 (bottom); Vintage Autos – 70 (centre right); Gary Wales (R.R.O.C. Inc) – 118 (centre right), 125 (top, centre), 127, 128; Western Australian Newspapers Ltd – 217 (top); York Motors (Sales) Pty Ltd – 261 (bottom).

A small number of photographs are of unknown origin and I trust the photographers concerned will forgive the absence of acknowledgement.

Martin Bennett

Contents

Preface

Of the 120,000 or so motor cars built by Rolls-Royce since 1904, some 95,000 have been produced since the Car Division's post-World War II move to Crewe, Cheshire.

The early post-war years saw the advent of standardised steel saloon bodies which were supplied by the Pressed Steel Company and assembled, mounted on their chassis, trimmed, painted and finished at the Crewe factory. Meanwhile, the traditional coach-builders also flourished briefly, building individual bespoke coachwork for a decreasing number of customers still willing and able to pay for such luxuries.

While their maker's claim comes under much closer and increasingly sceptical scrutiny nowadays, in the early post-war years it was more or less an article of faith that the Rolls-Royce was 'The Best Car in the World' – which of course it unquestionably was. Now Rolls-Royce Motor Cars Ltd more often make that claim for their superb Bentley Turbo R, which for sheer performance in a large, luxurious and good-looking saloon must be very difficult indeed to equal. Whether or not Rolls-Royce and Bentley cars continue to justify being called the world's best, and it is the considered opinion of this author that they do, it is certain that for the priceless aura of prestige that they bring to Great Britain they remain un-equalled.

The mystique of the Rolls-Royce car is such that older models consistently out-perform their rivals in retained value and later appreciation, while the remarkable revival in the Bentley marque's fortunes has meant that some models are now more valu-able than their Rolls-Royce counterparts and the period when Bentley cars were sometimes 'converted' to take on Rolls-Royce appearance is remembered with embarrassment. The survival rate, too, of Rolls-Royce and Bentley cars is incomparably higher than that of even their nearest rivals. It has been esti-mated that around 70 per cent of all the cars ever made by Rolls-Royce are still in use. When one considers the numbers of quite usable cars that were lost to war-time scrap drives this figure is all the more remarkable.

The marques, too, have given rise to a large and thriving club movement, of which the Rolls-Royce Enthusiasts' Club in Great Britain with some 7,000 members world-wide, the similar-sized Rolls-Royce Owners' Club Inc. in North America, the smaller but nonetheless enthusiastic Rolls-Royce Owners' Club of Australia with more than 1,000 members and, of course, the Bentley Drivers' Club, are the main components. Owners of cars illustrated in this book have the initials of their main Club affiliation in brackets after their names.

Rolls-Royce & Bentley: the Crewe Years provides detailed, complete, and above all, accurate coverage of all aspects, technical and coachwork, of the post-war Rolls-Royce and Bentley cars. If the reader gains half as much enjoyment as I did from research-ing and writing it, I will have succeeded in my aim.

Martin Bennett,
Goulburn, New South Wales,
1994

Chapter One

Post-War Resurgence and a New Factory

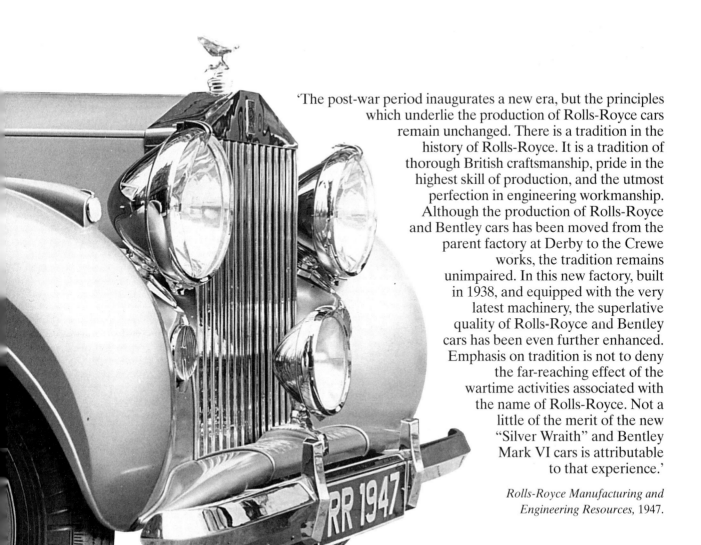

'The post-war period inaugurates a new era, but the principles which underlie the production of Rolls-Royce cars remain unchanged. There is a tradition in the history of Rolls-Royce. It is a tradition of thorough British craftsmanship, pride in the highest skill of production, and the utmost perfection in engineering workmanship. Although the production of Rolls-Royce and Bentley cars has been moved from the parent factory at Derby to the Crewe works, the tradition remains unimpaired. In this new factory, built in 1938, and equipped with the very latest machinery, the superlative quality of Rolls-Royce and Bentley cars has been even further enhanced. Emphasis on tradition is not to deny the far-reaching effect of the wartime activities associated with the name of Rolls-Royce. Not a little of the merit of the new "Silver Wraith" and Bentley Mark VI cars is attributable to that experience.'

Rolls-Royce Manufacturing and Engineering Resources, 1947.

Firms like Rolls-Royce Ltd, producing very high quality and necessarily high priced, luxury motor cars, were faced with seemingly insurmountable difficulties in the immediate post-World War II period. The prevailing economic and social climate favoured manufacturers of small mass produced cars, whose all too often depressingly mediocre products, hurriedly built from poor quality materials to basically pre-war designs, practically sold themselves. The same climate, however, did not augur well for makers of large luxury motor cars and certainly mitigated against the bespoke coachbuilt car traditionally associated with Rolls-Royce Ltd. The truth is that although the reasons had changed, the Company's difficulties in selling its cars for a reasonable return on investment had not suddenly manifested themselves when the War ended. The Rolls-Royce and Bentley range of the 1930s did not sell particularly well and never showed a profit for the Company. The fault did not lay with the actual cars, for the $4\frac{1}{4}$ Litre Bentley, the newly introduced Wraith and above all the Phantom III were all splendid cars by any standard. The problem was that although each was designed and built in accordance with proven Rolls-Royce philosophy which ensured that the end product was the best possible, they shared few common components and while not quite built regardless of cost, certainly embodied avoidable cost elements. While the six cylinder Bentley and Wraith were not overly difficult or expensive to maintain, the dauntingly complex Phantom III with its 7.34 litre V-12 engine was demonstrably guilty on both counts. After the War, with these problems largely solved, punitive rates of income tax meant that vast sums needed to be earned by a potential purchaser in order to have the price of a new Rolls-Royce or Bentley car, which itself was inflated by a similarly punitive purchase tax, the rate of which was *doubled* to 66$\frac{2}{3}$% in the 1947 Budget.

A decision taken in 1937 to 'rationalise' the motor car range made the cars cheaper to build without in any way compromising their quality. This programme called for the development of a standard chassis frame design (variable in length) for all cars in the range, a standard range of engines with 90% interchangeability of components and simplified chassis details including new independent front suspension.

The first car to show the influence of the developing rationalisation programme was the Mk V Bentley, introduced just as war broke out in 1939. All the main elements of the programme were evident with the exception of the engine, which was basically a twin S.U. carburetter version of the Wraith unit. However, a new engine with overhead inlet and side exhaust valves, and belt drive for the water pump and dynamo, had already been developed and tested in experimental cars. Some of these experimental cars were fitted with Park Ward 'standard' saloon bodies of patented all-metal construction which could be seen as the forerunners of what eventually became the second cornerstone of post-war Rolls-Royce motor car policy – the use of standardized pressed steel saloon bodies.

It was intended to introduce the complete Rationalised Range of cars at the 1940 Olympia Motor Show. The Bentley Mk V was to have received the new engine and pressed steel disc wheels, the Wraith was to have been replaced by a new model closely approximating that which emerged after the War as the Silver Wraith and the PIII was to have given way to the Phantom IV, with the in-line eight cylinder version of the new F-head power unit. This, of course, was not to be. War intervened and all motor car production was halted. The Rationalised Range had to await the end of hostilities.

An even more far-reaching plan, proposed by W. A. Robotham whilst he was in charge of chassis design, to market a 2.8 litre car using a four cylinder version of the rationalised engine, never came to fruition beyond the experimental prototype stage. Active consideration was even given to cars with engines as small as 1.5 litres, to sell as complete cars for as little as £400, which if proceeded with would have so altered the basic concept of the Rolls-Royce and Bentley car that the marques would almost certainly either have gone the way of Armstrong Siddeley and Alvis or become so mundane that they could never have inspired the writing of books such as this! Instead, the 1938 motor car output of 563 cars was doubled in 1949 and tripled in 1951, figures which leave little room for doubt about the commercial soundness of the rationalisation decision. All this was achieved in a climate heavily loaded against car makers like Rolls-Royce re-entering the motor car business at all. Moreover, it was achieved without in any way lowering the legendary standards for which the marques Rolls-Royce and Bentley are renowned and without entering the unfamiliar territory of the small 4-cylinder car market.

This post-war success could largely be attributed firstly to range rationalisation, which reined in manufacturing costs (and as a bonus, also simplified servicing) and secondly to a reliance on standardised steel coachwork for the bulk of output. The advent of the standard steel saloon dramatically reduced the cost of producing complete cars, at first only on the Bentley chassis but later, with its success firmly established, in Rolls-Royce guise too. These all-steel bodies were produced by the Pressed Steel Company (now Pressed Steel Fisher) of Oxford with the fitting to the chassis, finishing and trimming carried out at the Crewe factory. Without the standard steel saloon the Company would have remained entirely dependent on the surviving coach-builders. After the War there were only five major firms still engaged in that trade, one of which (Park Ward) was owned by Rolls-Royce Ltd. There could never have been any question of reliance on these firms or their methods for the volume anticipated.

The quality of the all-steel bodies left little to be desired in terms of elegance, finish and interior luxury. The materials used and the stan-dard of craftsmanship lavished on the interior furnishings were in every way comparable with those of the specialist coachbuilders' products. The only area of doubt lay in the quality of early post-war sheet steel. It should not be left unsaid that considerable numbers of standard steel saloons succumbed to a serious rust prob-lem which had still not been completely overcome by the time the second generation of standard saloon bodies was introduced in 1955, with aluminium bonnet, boot lid and doors. Unfortunately many were neglected to the point where in the late 1960s and early '70s steel Mk VI Bentleys could be purchased for a couple of hundred pounds or so. Such was the durabil-ity of the chassis and mechanical parts, however, that a thriving industry grew up around the rebodying of Mk VI, and to a lesser extent R- and S-type Bentleys as vintage-style open sports cars. In fairness to the steel bodies it should also be pointed out that many well maintained early standard steel saloons have survived in excellent condition.

Enthusiasts of the pre-war cars could be forgiven for bemoaning the passing of such elegant features as wire wheels with centre-lock hubs and the beautifully made gear trains that once drove the water pump and dynamo, now that they had to settle for ordinary bolt-on steel disc wheels and vee-belts. Perhaps they should be thankful for the fact that Rolls-Royce have never used chain drives for their valve gear and that some pre-war features were retained. One of these was the 'ride control', which was retained in a rather simplified form. On the Phantom III and Wraith all four dampers were auto-matically and progressively stiff-ened as the road speed increased and an over-riding hand control on the steering wheel centre. For the post-war cars the ride control was arranged to operate on the rear dampers only. Other simplifica-tions included the independent front suspension which incorpo-rated exposed coil springs, where those of the PIII and Wraith had been enclosed in oil-filled hous-ings.

The standard post-war power unit was the 4,257cc six cylinder unit from the Rationalised Range of cars developed before the war for planned introduction at the 1940 Motor Show. These engines were used successfully during the war in both military and civilian applications, as well as in experi-mental Rolls-Royce and Bentley cars. The straight-eight from the same range was eventually to power that most exclusive of Rolls-Royce motor cars the Phantom IV, which was originally envisaged as a replacement for the Phantom III in the Rationalised Range but which never went into production beyond eighteen examples, of which seventeen were sold – to royalty and heads of state only. Each of the Rationalised Range engines had three important dimensions in common with that of the pre-war Wraith engine. These were: the bore at $3^1/2$ inches, the stroke at $4^1/2$ inches and the centre-to-centre dimension between neighbouring bores (except number three to four) at 4.15 inches. The stroke and centre-to-centre can be traced in an unbroken line back to the 20 h.p. of 1922. The bore, which started at 3 inches for the Twenty, had been increased progressively, firstly to $3^1/4$ inches for the 20/25 and $3^1/2$ Litre Bentley and then to $3^1/2$ inches for the 25/30, $4^1/4$ Litre Bentley, Wraith and Mk V Bentley. The $4^1/2$ inch stroke crops up even more, having been used for the Phantom III and even the very early Silver Ghost. After the war, the bore was increased still further, at the expense of water spaces between the cylinders, firstly to $3^5/8$ inches in 1951 then to $3^3/4$ inches in 1954, initially only for the Bentley Continental.

In addition to their use in the post-war Rolls-Royce and Bentley motor cars, the Rationalised Range engines were made avail-able from 1948, in less refined form, for commercial and military use. This was the B-range, comprising the B40 four cylinder, B60 six cylinder and B80 eight cylinder of 2,838, 4,257 and 5,675cc respectively. By 1973 more than 40,000 B-range engines were in use in more than 75 countries and were standard in all wheeled combat vehicles of the British Army, as well as being used by the defence forces of 27 other nations. Civilian uses included emergency vehicles such as airport crash tenders and fire appliances – applications in which power and reliability are vital attributes. Later B-range variants were designed to operate on alternative fuels such as natural gas and liqui-fied petroleum gas.

The overhead valve layout of the pre-war six cylinder engines imposed severe limits on the growth of the valves, so to improve 'breathing' without increasing the overall length of the engine a change was made to the overhead inlet, side exhaust valve ('F-head') layout, which eventually allowed the inlet valves to grow to two inches diameter. Not that there was anything new about the F-head layout – it had been used by Royce for his first motor cars in 1904 and the Rolls-Royce derivatives, produced in two, three, four and six cylinder configurations, followed suit and thus demonstrated that Royce had an intuitive understanding not only of good internal combustion engine 'breathing' but also of range rationalisation!

The use of an iron monobloc cylinder block and crankcase, together with the reduction in the gear train from three gears to two almost halved the manufacturing cost of the six cylinder engine, and by adding a cylinder at each end, still using standardised reciprocating parts, a powerful eight cylinder unit could be produced at a fraction of the cost of the V-12 Phantom III engine.

It was the intention of the makers that the post-war engines should have a life of at least 100,000 miles between overhauls. An interesting feature aimed towards this end but which failed to achieve the hoped-for results was the 'Flashchroming' of the upper half (i.e. $2\frac{1}{4}$ inches) of the cylinders to minimise bore wear. Short pressed-in high chromium content liners were quickly substituted with greater success. However, after very high mileages a 'step' tended to develop where the iron of the cylinder block met the harder material of the liner, so for the Silver Cloud and Bentley S Series of 1955 full-length liners were introduced.

At one time Rolls-Royce manufactured not only their own carburetters but also most of their own electrical equipment. When Silver Ghosts, and later Phantom Is, were built in the United States (in Springfield, Massachusetts) there was a move away from that policy with the use of certain proprietary items of equipment. This process was extended to Derby-built cars with the fitting of S.U. carburetters to the $3\frac{1}{2}$ Litre Bentley of 1933 (and most subsequent Bentleys) and continued after Royce's death with the adoption of Stromberg carburetters for the 25/30, Phantom III and Wraith. The use of proprietary equipment, in all cases specially manufactured for Rolls-Royce to special specifi-

cations, gathered momentum after 1945 with twin S.U. carburetters for right-hand drive Bentleys, a Stromberg for the Silver Wraith and left-hand drive Bentleys, Lucas Special Equipment starter, dynamo and other electrical equipment, Delco-Remy distributor, Girling brakes with Lockheed hydraulic master cylinder and other items of bought-out equipment common to both models.

For the Rationalised Range Chief Project Engineer Ivan Evernden devised dies to produce pressed steel chassis frames in varying lengths. These frames were immensely strong structures of deep channel section steel with two long, curved bracing members extending from below the scuttle, meeting in the centre where they were riveted together between two substantial steel plates, and rejoining the side members at the upsweep over the rear axle – thus forming a 'cruciform' bracing. A huge box-section pan at the front supported the front suspension components and contributed to the strength and rigidity of the frame. The same basic frame design eventually appeared in no fewer than five wheelbases (including one of 10ft 4in for the pre-war Mk V Bentley, its first production application.) The shortest was that for the Mk VI/R Bentleys and Silver Dawn, with a 10ft wheelbase. Extra length at the point where the two members of the cruciform met gave 10ft 7in wheelbase for the original Silver Wraith, 11ft 1in for the long wheelbase Silver Wraith and a massive 12ft 1in for the rare Phantom IV, the frame for which was further lengthened ahead of the dashboard to accommodate the straight-eight engine. Cost savings were considerable. The manufacturing cost of the post-war chassis frames was only 40% of that of the Phantom III and Wraith frames.

Before the war, partially welded construction had been used for the frame of the Wraith, whereas

previous Rolls-Royce chassis had been painstakingly assembled using square-headed tapered bolts. This system had been proved to be the best by means of the famous 'bump test' – using a machine devised by Royce that was said to crowd 'ten years into a day'. The Company's own publicity on the bump test stated unambiguously that 'one of the lessons of the bump test was to show that ordinary rivets were useless' (for chassis frame construction.) Despite this, however, Crewe at first opted for riveting, only making a change to fully welded construction in 1953. The welded frames were much more satisfactory and eliminated the problems encountered in countries with rough road conditions, of rivets working loose and frames cracking. One such territory was Australia, where modifications to overcome these problems were devised by York Motors Ltd of Sydney, the Rolls-Royce and Bentley distributors for New South Wales and Queensland. The late Bert Ward, York Motors' service manager from 1946 until his retirement in 1967, recalled that modifications very similar to theirs were incorporated when the welded frames appeared in 1953.

The post-war home of the Motor Car Division (later Rolls-Royce Motors Ltd then Rolls-Royce Motor Cars Ltd) is located in the town of Crewe, in the county of Cheshire, some forty miles north west of Derby. Before Rolls-Royce, Crewe's main claim to fame was as a major rail junction on the important main line from London to Glasgow and the north west of England. The main employer of the town's 46,000 inhabitants was the London Midland and Scottish Railway company, whose locomotive and rolling stock construction and maintenance workshops were among the biggest in the country, if not the world. The choice of Crewe as a site for a Rolls-Royce factory was made not by the Company but by the Air Ministry and the

Ministry of Labour, and its function was to build not cars but Merlin aero engines in preparation for the war that was then regarded as inevitable. This was 1938, and motor car construction at Derby had just one year left to run.

The site chosen was Merrill's Farm, Pym's Lane, a sixty acre site on the outskirts of the town. Levelling of the site commenced on June 6th, 1938 and by the end of the month the first structure had been built. By the middle of September the framework for the 1,050ft by 240ft main shop had been erected. Installation of the machinery commenced bay by bay as construction progressed.

Managing Director E. W. Hives* had for some years wanted to

* Ernest Walter Hives, Managing Director from January 1946. Company Chairman 1950–57. Elevated to the Peerage in 1950 to become Lord Hives of Hazeldene. Died April 24th, 1965.

move motor car production out of Derby and at one stage Burton-on-Trent was considered. After the war ended the Crewe factory became the obvious choice of a new location for the Motor Car Division and so the move was made and car production resumed in time for a small number of Silver Wraith chassis and Mk VI Bentley cars to be delivered before the end of 1946. Not all aspects of motor car work were immediately transferred to Crewe. Most of the design work for the early post-war cars was carried out at Derby, or more specifically Belper, 7½ miles north on the A6 road, including the styling of the standard steel saloon body for the Mk VI Bentley. Ivan Evernden and Bill Allen were largely responsible for this, but when John Blatchley, who had come to Rolls-Royce from Gurney Nutting, was appointed chief Styling Engineer in 1950 his functions were transferred to Crewe. It is worth noting

that the very exclusive Phantom IV chassis were built at Belper.

Crewe has produced more than three quarters of the Rolls-Royce and Bentley motor cars built to date. An indication of the inherent strength of the car business is that in 1971, when problems with the RB211 jet engines for the Lockheed Tristar airliner forced Rolls-Royce Ltd into receivership, the Motor Car Division at Crewe continued without interruption and by May 1973 had become an independent company – Rolls-Royce Motors Ltd. An October 1980 merger saw the thriving Rolls-Royce Motors become part of the Vickers plc group. Many top Rolls-Royce people went to the Vickers board, including David (later Sir David) Plastow, who became Chief Executive of Vickers, being succeeded as Chief Executive of the Motor Car Group by George Fenn. Today, Peter Ward is Chairman and Chief Executive of Rolls-Royce Motor Cars Ltd.

Below left *The first post-war Managing Director of the Motor Car Division, Dr F. Llewellyn Smith, who steered the Company from the resumption of car production and the advent of complete cars with standard steel saloon bodies, through to the Silver Shadow era.* **Below right** *Sir David Plastow who, as first Managing Director of Rolls-Royce Motors Ltd after the Motor Car Division was separated from the aero engine business in 1971, presided over the outstanding success of the newly independent car manufacturer, culminating in the introduction of the Silver Spirit range of cars in 1980 and the merger with Vickers, of which group Sir David then became Chairman and Managing Director.*

Left *The Wraith was the last of the pre-war 'small horsepower' models. The wheelbase, at 136 inches, was 11 inches longer than that of the first post-war Rolls-Royce, the Silver Wraith. However, there was more room for coachwork on the Silver Wraith chassis due to the radiator, and everything from that point back, being further forward. For the same reason, unfortunately, this also meant that the Silver Wraith never achieved the excellent visual balance of a pre-war car Wraith with good coachwork. The sidemount spare wheel on this Wraith was a most satisfactory feature from the points of view of both appearance and practicalities. On the post-war cars the limited space between the front wheel and the scuttle meant that a sidemount spare had to be mounted higher than aesthetic considerations alone would have dictated, so it is perhaps fortunate that few Silver Wraiths were so fitted. The centre-lock wire wheels of the Wraith (usually concealed by discs as seen here) were a casualty of post-war economies.*

Above *The bore and stroke dimensions of the pre-war Wraith engine, seen here, were perpetuated after the War for the Silver Wraith and Mk VI Bentley (and from 1949 for the Silver Dawn). However, there was practically nothing else in common. The Wraith engine was an all-overhead valve unit with separate crankcase and cylinder block and as such was a direct descendant of the 1922 20 h.p. engine.*

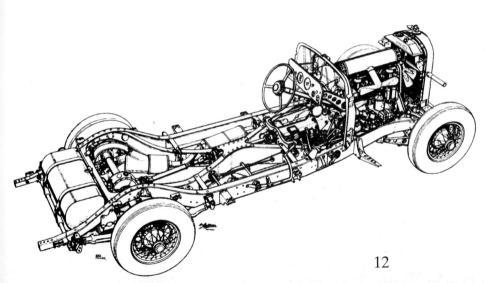

Below left *The last pre-war Bentley was the Mk V, which had been developed barely in time for fewer than twenty production chassis to be built before the outbreak of World War II. The Mk V was a design leader in that its frame and other details of the chassis, including a new design of independent front suspension, were to have formed the basis of the 'Rationalised Range' using a common chassis design (though in various lengths) for all Rolls-Royce and Bentley models. This scheme had to await the resumption of motor car production after the War and the similarity between the Mk V chassis and that of the early post-war models is very much in evidence.*

Right *The Experimental Department based at Belper, near Derby, installed the 5.3 litre in-line eight cylinder version of the range of engines then under development for the Rationalised Range into a Bentley V chassis. This was experimental chassis 11BV, fitted with Park Ward saloon coachwork and called 'Comet' – though its performance gave rise to the colourfully descriptive but unofficial name 'Scalded Cat.' Pressed steel wheels of the type envisaged for the Rationalised Range were fitted.*

Right *The first post-war Rolls-Royce was this experimental Silver Wraith. Its chassis number was at first 34GVIII, in the experimental 'Goshawk' series, but the number 1SWI was quickly substituted. Though experimental, 1SWI represented the Silver Wraith design in its all but finalised form. The power-operated built-in hydraulic jacks, one of which can be seen inboard of the offside rear wheel, were deleted for production. Other than that, the only changes were details such as the steering column finish which was changed from chromium plate to black enamel and the rather cheap looking proprietary handbrake which was changed to a better, chrome plated fitting. This chassis went to Hoopers for saloon coachwork.*

Left *The main office block at the Crewe factory, the post-war home of Rolls-Royce Ltd, Motor Car Division – later Rolls-Royce Motors Ltd and now Rolls-Royce Motor Cars Ltd. The Silver Cloud III and Bentley S3 cars place the photograph in the early-to mid-1960s, though the building appears exactly as built in 1938 for aircraft engine production. A new reception area was added in front of the centre entrance portico in 1989.*

Above *The first post-war Bentley was experimental chassis 1BVI. Though the handsome H. J. Mulliner saloon coachwork gave way to new designs for production by that coachbuilder, the chassis design represented by this experimental car was given over to production unchanged. In fact, 1BVI was subsequently given a production chassis number, B256AK, and sold.*

Left *The second post-war Bentley was experimental chassis 2BVI. It was the first to receive the newly developed standard steel saloon coachwork. Note the absence of a chrome waist moulding, rear spats and other detail refinements that came later. The wheel trim discs were changed for production.*

Left *The Silver Wraith was a larger and more imposing car than the companion Bentley Mk VI. Its 17 inch wheels and huge Lucas R.100 headlamps made it appear even more so. The front wheel centre-line was well rearward of the radiator, which shortened the wheelbase and improved handling but somewhat marred the visual balance. The divided bonnet side seen here was a feature of the earliest cars.*

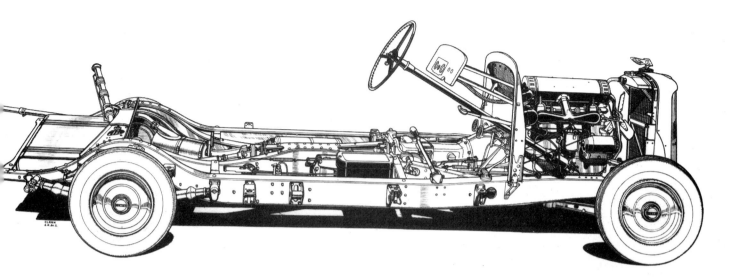

Above *A very early Bentley Mk VI chassis, was the subject of this superbly detailed drawing. Note the two long, curved frame members meeting in the middle of the chassis to form the cruciform section of the immensely strong frame.*

Right *A close-up view of 1SWI, showing some of the early post-war chassis detail. Note the beautifully made exhaust system with its lagged silencers and bolted flanged joints, the divided propeller shaft, the twin S.U. petrol pump on the frame side member and the battery, which was accessible through a covered hatch in the floor under the driver's seat.*

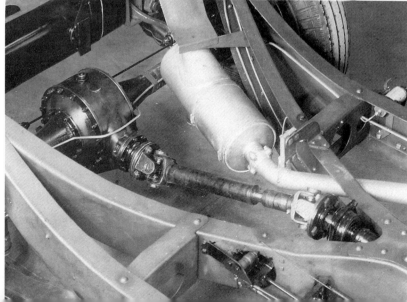

Bottom right *The front half of the divided propeller shaft was supported by a bearing in the frame and the rear half had a sliding joint to compensate for rear axle movement.*

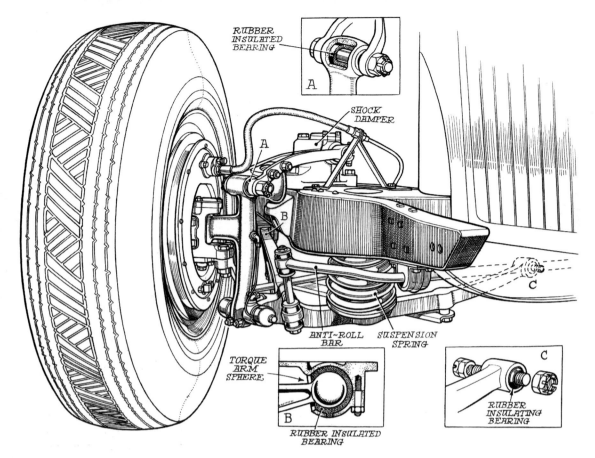

RUBBER INSULATED BEARING

A

SHOCK DAMPER

B

C

TORQUE ARM SPHERE

B

RUBBER INSULATED BEARING

ANTI-ROLL BAR

SUSPENSION SPRING

C

RUBBER INSULATING BEARING

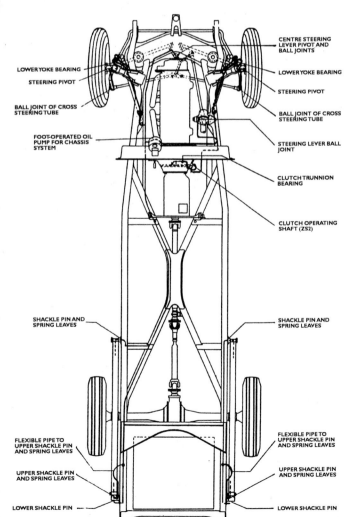

CENTRE STEERING LEVER PIVOT AND BALL JOINTS

LOWER YOKE BEARING

STEERING PIVOT

BALL JOINT OF CROSS STEERING TUBE

FOOT-OPERATED OIL PUMP FOR CHASSIS SYSTEM

LOWER YOKE BEARING

STEERING PIVOT

BALL JOINT OF CROSS STEERING TUBE

STEERING LEVER BALL JOINT

CLUTCH TRUNNION BEARING

CLUTCH OPERATING SHAFT (ZS2)

SHACKLE PIN AND SPRING LEAVES

SHACKLE PIN AND SPRING LEAVES

FLEXIBLE PIPE TO UPPER SHACKLE PIN AND SPRING LEAVES

FLEXIBLE PIPE TO UPPER SHACKLE PIN AND SPRING LEAVES

UPPER SHACKLE PIN AND SPRING LEAVES

UPPER SHACKLE PIN AND SPRING LEAVES

LOWER SHACKLE PIN

LOWER SHACKLE PIN

Above *This drawing shows the details of the independent front suspension system of the Silver Wraith and Bentley Mk VI – and later the Silver Dawn, Phantom IV and Bentley R-type. The design was borrowed from Packard.*

Left & right *An early post-war chassis in plan view showing the points lubricated by the centralised lubrication system. The combined oil reservoir and pump was mounted on the firewall under the bonnet with the pedal projecting into the car under the fascia.*

Below *A later Mk VI chassis. The Rolls-Royce Silver Dawn, as introduced in 1949, was similar except for its radiator shell and Silver Wraith-type single carburetter engine.*

Right *The Bentley Mk VI engine and gearbox, nearside. This is a very early engine. The crankcase breather, below the dip-stick, was replaced by a longer pipe on the front of the rocker cover from chassis B198BH and the double-ended air silencer was replaced from chassis B2BH by an A.C. fitting with a mesh filter at the front only. For export, an oil-bath air cleaner was made available to cope with dusty conditions. A 'Y' piece linked the two halves of the exhaust manifold to the single exhaust system on 4,257cc cars, while the 4,566cc cars, with the exception of left-hand drive cars, had a dual exhaust system. The round fitting at the rear of the gearbox is the ride control pump, the curved lever being connected via linkages to the control on the steering wheel boss.*

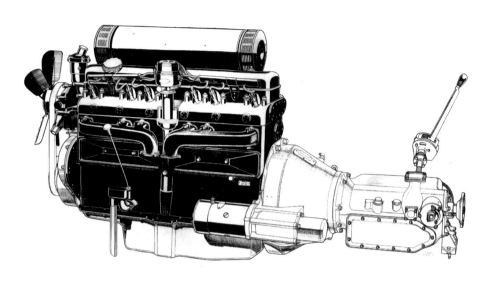

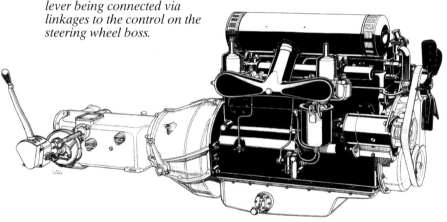

Left *The offside view shows the 1½ inch S.U. carburetters. These gave way to 1¾ inch S.U.s from chassis B83HP, while the by-pass oil filter was a rather inefficient feature of the 4,257cc engine, the later 4,566cc version having a full-flow filter. The pair of pressure relief valves below the oil filter regulated the oil pressure to the crankshaft and connecting rod bearings to 25 lb/sq. inch and at a reduced pressure to the inlet rocker shaft. The device on the side of the gearbox behind the gear lever gate is the friction disc servo for the brake system. The 4½ inch dynamo shown proved inadequate and was replaced by a larger (5 inch) type from chassis B426CF. The early Silver Wraith engine was similar except for its single Stromberg downdraught carburetter and underwent similar changes.*

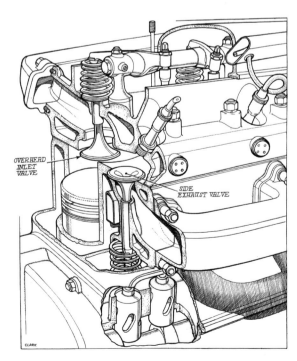

OVERHEAD INLET VALVE

SIDE EXHAUST VALVE

CLARK

Lower left *A feature of the post-war in-line engines was the overhead inlet, side exhaust valve layout, admirably shown in detail in this drawing. Note the double inlet valve springs.*

Above *Checking gear tooth profiles. The profile was reproduced on the indicator diagram in the centre of the picture.*

Left *Gear grinding machine for finishing tooth profile to ensure oil retention on the friction surfaces.*

Below *Precision cutting of gears for engines and gearboxes.*

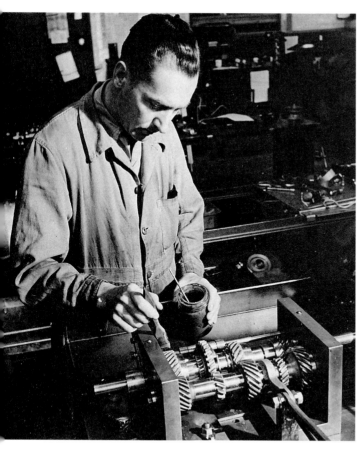

Above left *Lapping gears prior to assembly in gearbox.*

Above right *Checking concentricity of spigot relative to casing, early post-war gearbox.*

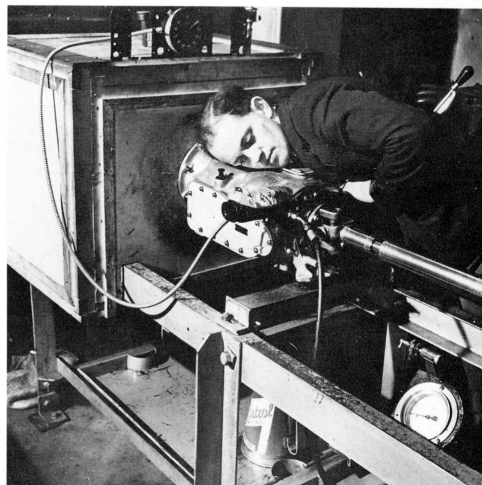

Right *Inspector sound-testing gearbox in a specially built silent room. He has not fallen asleep, nor has he been stabbed in the back with the gear lever! Note the speedometer on top of the soundproof box housing the electric motor used to drive the gearbox.*

Right & below left *Special purpose machines for crankshaft turning, early post-war six cylinder crankshafts and (below) crankshafts entering an electric furnace in the heat treatment department.*

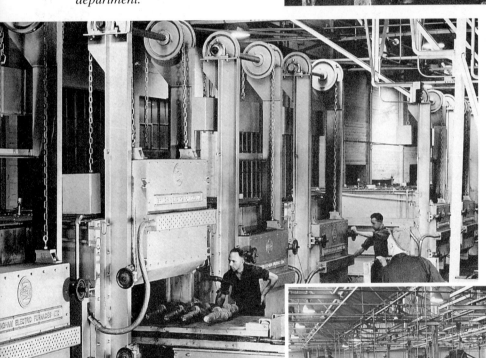

Right *Cylinder head and wheelcase machining, early post-war six cylinder engines.*

Above *Engine test department. Bentley Mk VI and Silver Wraith engines on test. The valve rocker covers were apparently fitted only temporarily in this view, as the Bentley engine in the right foreground (note the S.U. carburetters) has a Rolls-Royce cover!* **Right** *a Mk VI engine being mounted for testing. All engines were run for a minimum of 7½ hours using town gas for fuel. The exhausts were piped outside the building. Further testing after installation in the chassis or car took 7 days.*

Top *Bentley Mk VI chassis assembly line. They did not have white steering wheels! They appear so because they were wrapped in protective tape during assembly. The chassis at right are nearly ready for the next stage – the fitting of the body. Most would have gone on to the Crewe body fitting line but about 20% went out to coachbuilders for custom coachwork, as did all the Silver Wraith chassis.*

Above *Components being fitted to the firewall – early Bentley Mk VI. Note the very early (Berkshire) windscreen wiper motor, the Bijur chassis lubrication reservoir/pump and the twin coils (one was a stand-by).*

Left *Sound-amplifying test-rig body fitted to a Silver Wraith chassis for testing. Elegance was not an important consideration in the design of these test bodies!*

Above right & left *Mk VI standard steel saloon bodies receiving their initial primer coats in the purpose-built spray booth at Crewe and (above right) being fitted up in the body fitting shop prior to uniting with the chassis and finishing.*

Right *Very early Mk VI Bentleys (note the absence of chrome waistline strips) receiving their final polish. After being fitted with wheel trims and radiator mascots the next and final stage was the final rectification bay.*

Below *Body assembly line. Bodies mounted on their chassis being fitted with front wings, bonnets and radiator shells. These are all Bentleys, but from 1949 the Rolls-Royce Silver Dawn was assembled on the same line.*

Left *Final rectification bay with early Mk VI standard steel saloons being made ready for transport to dealers. Note the early rearward-leaning mascots, which needed to be turned 90 degrees before opening the bonnet.*

Below left *This view of the final rectification bay is a little later than the previous photograph, as witnessed by the Silver Dawn nearest the camera and the forward-leaning mascots of the Bentleys.*

Below *Upholstery shop. Hides being cut and seats made for long boot Silver Dawns and Bentley R-types, circa 1953.*

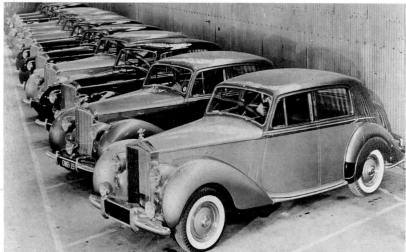

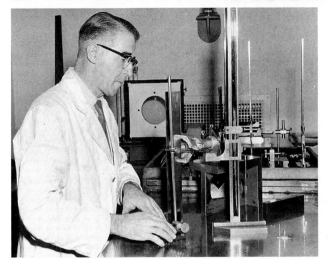

Above left & right *Standards room. Checking cam forms of camshaft.*

Right *Wadkin belt sanding machine being used to prepare Silver Cloud/S Series stainless steel door window frames for final polishing.*

Below left *Checking for axle whine on road test, Silver Cloud II.*

Below right *The drop test – particularly brutal test for experimental Silver Cloud II 30-B. One of many rigorous tests for developing shock absorbers and front suspension to ensure the highest standards of service and reliability. This car was subsequently sold as chassis SAE687.*

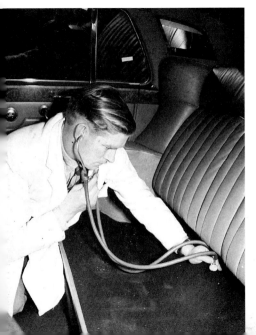

Above *Silver Cloud III and Bentley S3 standard saloons nearing completion, 1963.*

Below *Inspector, using a highly trained and experienced ear and a dipstick to listen for untoward noises in a Silver Shadow engine. Needless to say, few are ever detected!*

Above *Silver Cloud III chassis, ready for specialised coachwork, under test on the Crewe roller rig.*

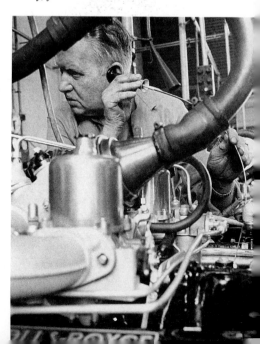

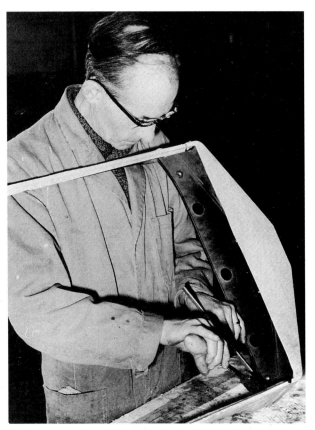

This page *A time-honoured practice at Crewe is the hand soldering of the Rolls-Royce radiator shell from stainless steel sheet, in this instance for a Silver Shadow. The Bentley shell is a chrome plated brass pressing.*

Above *Fitting the finished radiator shell to the car in the finishing shop.*

Left *Craftsman admiring his work – a pair of book-matched picnic tables for an early Silver Shadow or Bentley T Series.*

Below *A long-haired brush called a fiche, a steady hand and lots of skill were the main ingredients for applying the coachlines, in this case on a Silver Shadow. This was one of the last jobs before the car was passed out.*

Right & below right *The final rectification bay again, this time some two decades later. Early Silver Shadow and Bentley T Series Saloons receiving their final inspection and grooming prior to delivery to their fortunate owners.*

Below *Crewe today. Final hand attention to a crankshaft.*

Below right *John Elliott (RROCA) with Bentley Turbo engines during a 1989 visit to Crewe.*

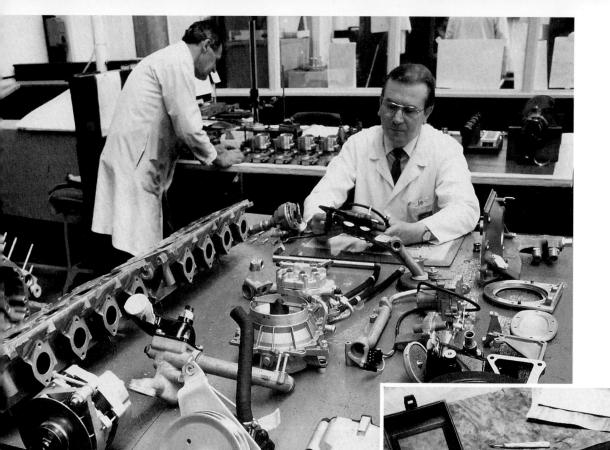

Above *Quality control is paramount at Rolls-Royce Motor Cars Ltd, Crewe. This photograph shows engine components laid out for inspection after a rigorous test to which one in every hundred engines is subjected.* **Right** *Testing burr walnut veneer for moisture content.*

Left *Silver Spirit, Silver Spur and Bentley Eight, Mulsanne S and Turbo R motor cars in the finishing shop, 1989.*

Chapter Two

The Silver Wraith

'…the Silver Wraith has an indefinable something about it, a delicacy of behaviour, which escapes definition in written words… Perhaps the particular charm of the Silver Wraith lies in the effectiveness with which all the undesirable manifestations incidental to the development of power by machinery have been skilfully exorcised. The result is a car which is a sentient being and is like a living thing. An imaginative person might easily believe that the (Silver) Wraith's feelings could be hurt by a carelessly casual or definitely dangerous driver. Offended dignity might cause it of its own volition to move quietly off to more congenial company! Perhaps such imaginings arise from the extraordinary responsiveness of the car. All the controls work beautifully smoothly and easily: it obeys instantly the slightest wish of the driver, and it obeys exactly. And yet underneath that willingness one senses power.'

The Autocar, April, 1946.

The first post-war Rolls-Royce, despite its name, had little other than engine bore and stroke – and the significant centre-line to centreline dimension between bores – in common with its predecessor the Wraith. The Silver Wraith was in all respects a new model, the culmination of rigorous testing of prototype chassis before and during the War, with engines having been tested in lorries and other commercial vehicles as well as in cars.

As related in the previous chapter, the most notable departure from established pre-war practice was in the use of the overhead inlet, side exhaust valve layout. This rather unusual choice was influenced by a number of factors. Valve size in the overhead valve six cylinder engines had reached its practical limit with the Wraith and the F-head configuration allowed the use of much larger inlet valves without increasing the overall length of the engine, while avoiding the noise and maintenance problems – both anathema to Rolls-Royce – inherent in alternative solutions such as double overhead camshafts. As well as improving 'breathing' the inlet over exhaust layout made for better and more even cooling of the valve and spark plug seats and simplified maintenance. The compression ratio was of necessity kept low (6.4:1) in order to cope with the very low octane 'Pool' petrol of the early post-war years and the need to preserve the characteristic Rolls-Royce qualities of smoothness, silence and flexibility. The improved 'breathing' in any case rendered a higher compression ratio largely unnecessary.

The carburetter fitted to the early Silver Wraith engine was a Stromberg duplex downdraught type with an automatic cold starting device including provision for a suitably fast idle when starting from cold, allowing the hand mixture control to be eliminated. To start from cold it was merely necessary to fully depress the accelerator pedal once then release it, to allow the throttle stop to reposition itself on the fast idle cam in accordance with engine temperature sensed by a thermostat, which also controlled mixture strength, located in the water jacketed centre portion of the inlet manifold. Engine coolant temperature regulation by means of thermostatically-operated radiator shutters was a pre-war feature that was, curiously enough, retained unchanged. In the event of faulty operation of the thermostat it was a straightforward operation to disconnect it and leave the shutters open.

The power output of the Silver Wraith engine in its early 4,257cc form was about 125 bhp as installed and silenced in the car. In today's context this may seem modest for an engine of over four litres capacity, but it was sufficient to endow the large and heavy car with a top speed in the region of 90mph with good acceleration capabilities. The makers' description of the power output as 'adequate' was perfectly justified. As the engine capacity grew, firstly to 4,566cc in 1951 then to 4,887cc in 1956, the power output increased significantly. By 1957, with large bore S.U. carburetters, the brake horsepower was up to around 160, though with automatic transmission, power assisted steering, refrigerated air conditioning and the heavier coachwork that the intervening decade had spawned, the road performance did not see a corresponding increase.

Another pre-war feature to survive was the delightful 'hot knife through butter' right-hand gearchange – with the practical improvement that the lever was now biased towards the right of the gate by spring action rather than to the centre. This meant that the lever no longer had to be moved against spring pressure when passing through the gate to engage third and top gears. As with previous models, the handbook pointed out that first gear was unnecessary except for starting from rest on a gradient. The origin of this extra-low first gear may be traced to the 'Alpine Eagle' Silver Ghost variant which saved Rolls-Royce the embarrassment of a repetition of the 1912 Austrian Alpine Trials incident in which one of the Rolls-Royce cars entered failed to climb a steep pass before unloading passengers. On the Silver Wraith, perfect synchromesh was provided on second, third and top gears.

Front suspension was independent by coil springs and piston type double-acting hydraulic shock dampers of Rolls-Royce design and manufacture. The levers of the dampers doubled as the upper suspension radius arms. The large exposed coil springs were mounted vertically between a seat formed as an integral part of the chassis frame and the forward lower radius arms, which were pivoted in rubber bushes near the centre of the front pan. The rearward lower links extended from the lower ends of the vertical yokes on which the stub axles were pivoted, to rubber-bushed joints on the underside of the frame side members below the dash. The first application of this suspension layout had been the Mk V Bentley of 1939 and the design is known to have been derived from the contemporary Packard, the chief attraction being that it dispensed with the expensive and potentially troublesome oil baths which enclosed the horizontal coil springs and dampers of the earlier General Motors-derived 'knee-action' design used on the pre-war Phantom III and Wraith.

The leaves of the semi-elliptic rear springs, in the finest Rolls-Royce tradition, were ground all over, cadmium plated, enclosed in leather gaiters and fed with oil from the centralised chassis lubrication system. The rear dampers, like their fellows at the front, were of Rolls-Royce design and manufacture but differed in having a horizontal piston instead of a pair of vertical ones and in being controllable from the ride control lever on the steering wheel centre. A small pump carried in a casing bolted to the back of the gearbox maintained oil pressure in a system of piping connected to the rear dampers. This pressure was variable, being controlled through a relief valve operated by the aforementioned lever. This oil did not provide the actual damping medium but instead controlled the loading of the valves past which the damper oil was forced by the action of the damper piston. This system remained a feature of the Silver Wraith until the 'F' series long wheelbase cars with power assisted steering received the contemporary Silver Cloud's electrically controlled dampers. Unlike that of the pre-war Wraith, the post-war rear suspension lacked a torsion bar stabiliser. The wheelbase, at 10ft 7in, was nine inches shorter than that of the Wraith but the overall length of the car was up by three inches.

Steering was by Marles-type cam and roller connected by a fore-and-aft drag link ('side steering tube' in Rolls-Royce parlance) to a divided track rod ('cross steering tube') the ends of which passed through apertures in the rearward lower suspension links.

The braking system was the subject of much rethinking. While the rear brakes remained mechanically operated, hydraulics were employed, for the first time on a Rolls-Royce, to operate the front brakes. The classic friction-disc mechanical servo, mounted on and driven by the gearbox, was retained and coupled to a Lockheed hydraulic master cylinder mounted in the chassis below the driver's seat as well as by mechanical linkage to the rear brakes. The footbrake applied the rear brakes directly and engaged the servo, which in turn applied the front brakes hydraulically and assisted the application of the rear brakes. Because there was no direct connection between the pedal and the master cylinder a loss of hydraulic fluid or accidental entry of air to the hydraulic system left the pedal travel unchanged and the rear brakes unaffected. The servo was moved from the left side of the gearbox, where it had been on the Wraith, to the right, just below the gear-change cross-shaft. This change, like so many of the post-war chassis details, was pioneered by the 1939 Mk V Bentley and allowed considerable simplification of the linkages – though some complexity was re-introduced when construction of left-hand drive chassis commenced in 1949. The design of the servo itself also differed quite substantially from that of the pre-war Wraith, largely with a view to simplifying adjustment and maintenance. A pistol-grip, or umbrella-handle type pull-out handbrake connected to the rear brakes through a cable was a less than enthusiastically received development and it must be said that it was very inferior to the beautifully made pull-up lever and linkage used on the Phantom III, Wraith and Mk V Bentley. However, it persisted, at least on right-hand drive cars, to the end of Silver Wraith production.

It was originally intended to fit the Silver Wraith with permanent hydraulic jacks, but this was not proceeded with. The Phantom III and Wraith had been so equipped as was the prototype Silver Wraith 1SWI which was the subject of early Silver Wraith press releases. In fact there was to have been an improvement over the pre-war system in that the jacking pump was to have been powered by an electric motor, as opposed to hand-operated, but it was not to be and when the production Silver Wraiths appeared they were simply equipped with a Dunlop portable screw-type jack carried in the spare wheel compartment and jacking points on either side of the chassis below the centre pillars of the body. A feature that did not fall victim to post-war economies, however, was the centralised chassis lubrication or 'one shot' system by means of which the moving parts of the front suspension, steering and rear road springs and their shackles were fed with oil from an oil reservoir and pump mounted at the rear of the engine compartment with the operating pedal in the driver's compartment under the fascia.

The table on the following page summarises the respects in which the Silver Wraith differed from its pre-war counterpart.

Prior to World War II, at least since 1922, it had been Rolls-Royce policy to offer 'large' and 'small' models. The Silver Wraith would have fitted into the latter category had the eight cylinder Phantom IV gone into series production and been offered to the general public. The Silver Wraith was, after all, identical in engine capacity, of similar overall size and in fact the direct successor to the Wraith, which had been the 'small' model of the pre-war range. As it happened, however, the Silver Wraith was the only Rolls-Royce model offered until 1949 when the Silver Dawn was introduced – at first for export only – from which time the Silver Wraith, which was seven inches longer in the wheelbase, with larger wheels and conspicuously more massive in overall bulk, became effectively the 'large' model, though the two models shared the same engine. Thus the 1922 two model policy was still operating in essence, though it had become much less clearly defined.

The Silver Wraith chassis carried a far greater variety of coachwork than any other post-war chassis type. Most of the old coachbuilding houses were still in business and eager to return to their traditional role after six years of war related work, though in the main their resurgence was to be short lived. Most Silver Wraiths were bodied by Park Ward, H. J. Mulliner, Hooper, James Young or Freestone & Webb, though a number of smaller coachbuilders, including some foreign ones, contributed to a lesser degree for the first few years. The majority of bodies were saloons or limousines, though Mulliners offered a number of sedanca de ville designs and even coupés, fixed head and drop-head, were not unknown on the Silver Wraith chassis. The early coachwork designs were largely of basically pre-war appearance and shared fundamentally similar razor-edge or semi razor-edge styling with the large, characteristic Lucas R.100 headlamps, long front wings swept back to meet the rear wings at a very low point and short luggage boots.

The first radical departure from pre-war styling was the practice of concealing the running boards beneath the doors, with the front wings swept across the actual door skins. H. J. Mulliner and James Young were the first coachbuilders to adopt this feature, though the very early Park Ward saloons also had concealed running boards, but with front wings that stopped short of the front doors. Since it was not now necessary to drop the front wings very low to accommodate running boards, this cleared the way for increasingly higher winglines with the front wings meeting the rear wings quite high on the body-side on many designs by the mid 'fifties. Another innovation, devised by Hooper's Chief Designer Osmond Rivers, was the elimination of the rear wings as separate entities with the front wings sweeping right back to the base of the tail. Mr Rivers referred to this as his 'new look', though it has since become erroneously known as 'Empress line', after the Daimler Empress which had similar Hooper styling. Although Freestone & Webb, as was their wont, copied the 'new look' they never achieved the crisp razor-edge appearance of most of the Hooper efforts.

In 1951 the cylinder bore was increased to $3^5/8$ inches, raising the swept volume from 4,257cc to 4,566cc. A strengthened crank-shaft and full-flow (in lieu of by-pass) oil filtration system were introduced with the bigger engine,

which produced around 140bhp. Shortly after, the Stromberg dual choke carburetter gave way to a single downdraught Zenith.

The introduction of the 'big bore' engine also saw the offering of an alternative 11ft 1in wheelbase chassis. Since most Silver Wraith purchasers opted for the Long Wheelbase chassis the original 10ft 7in version was dropped in 1952. Very large 7-seater limousine coachwork was not easily accom-modated on the shorter chassis and styling always seemed to suffer as a result, particularly around the rear quarters. The longer wheelbase did not entirely abolish this problem, but it did enable the coachbuilders to offer even more commodious limousines while reducing the need to sacrifice graceful styling. Even so, in pursuit of rear compartment spaciousness some placed the rear seat so far rearward that the provision of anything more than a diminutive, almost vestigial luggage boot was all but impossible. The

ideal limousine combination of a really large rear compartment, ample luggage space and hand-somely balanced styling had to await the advent of the Phantom V in 1959. Most Silver Wraiths, however, were possessed of exceed-ingly handsome lines for so large a car, with an excellent compromise having been reached between the conflicting customer requirements of spaciousness, useful luggage capacity and elegant lines.

The Autocar, in its April 1946 description of the then still to be introduced Silver Wraith, waxed lyrical on the unique qualities of the car, describing it as follows:

'...the Silver Wraith has an inde-finable something about it, a delicacy of behaviour, which escapes definition in written words....Perhaps the particular charm of the Silver Wraith lies in the effectiveness with which all the undesirable manifestations incidental to the development of

1939 Wraith	1946 Silver Wraith
Chassis	*Chassis*
Partially welded box-section frame.	Riveted channel-section frame of simpler construction.
136" wheelbase.	127" wheelbase.
Front suspension by horizontal coil springs enclosed in oil baths.	Front suspension by exposed vertical coil springs.
Fully floating rear axle.	Semi floating rear axle.
Rear anti-roll bar.	No rear anti-roll bar.
Wire wheels with centre-lock hubs.	Bolt-on pressed steel wheels.
DWS built-in hydraulic jacking system.	Dunlop portable jack in toolkit.
Mechanical brakes assisted by friction-disc servo on left-hand side of gearbox.	Hydraulic front, mechanical rear brakes, with simplified servo on right-hand side of gearbox.
Automatic ride control, with manual over-ride, on all four dampers.	Manually operated ride control on rear dampers only.
Engine	*Engine*
Separate alloy crankcase and cast iron cylinder block.	Cast iron monobloc cylinder block and crankcase.
Cast iron cylinder head.	Aluminium alloy cylinder head.
All overhead valves operated by pushrods.	Overhead inlet valves, operated by pushrods; side exhaust valves.
Gear driven water pump and dynamo.	Water pump and dynamo driven by fan belt.

power by machinery have been skilfully exorcised. The result is a car which is a sentient being and is like a living thing. An imaginative person might easily believe that the (Silver) Wraith's feelings could be hurt by a carelessly casual or definitely dangerous driver. Offended dignity might cause it of its own volition to move quietly off to more congenial company! Perhaps such imaginings arise from the extraordinary responsiveness of the car. All the controls work beautifully smoothly and easily: it obeys instantly the slightest wish of the driver, and it obeys exactly. And yet underneath that willingness one senses power.'

For all that, however, there were those who believed, and still believe, that the post-war Rolls-Royce was inferior to its forebears. In fact, nothing could be further from the truth. The whole essence of Company policy towards motor car design, build quality and the unremitting pursuit of excellence rendered this impossible. With the possible exception of the Phantom III, Rolls-Royce cars were never built without regard to cost. This is made abundantly clear in John Fasal's superb book *The Rolls-Royce Twenty* in which communications between the Derby factory and Royce's homes at West Wittering and Le Canadel are reproduced. These contain numerous references to the need for cost containment in designs adopted for production. However, where cost savings and quality were in conflict, the latter invariably won out. This was in no sense less true after the War than before. After driving a good Silver Wraith (or Silver Dawn) even the most enthusiastic adherent of the pre-war cars would be hard pressed to deny that the Crewe car is superior in practically every respect to, say, a 25/30 or even a pre-war Wraith – a model in which the

traditional Rolls-Royce attributes of smoothness and silence had attained a very high level of development indeed. To do so, in fact, would be to do less than justice to the talented and dedicated engineers charged with carrying out the Company's unchanging policy of meticulous attention to detail, both in design and workmanship – a policy followed as closely in 1946, and indeed today, as it was in the days of Sir Henry Royce.

Interestingly, the Silver Wraith owner's handbook contained, unchanged from that of its direct ancestor the Twenty Horsepower, the following prescription for successful running:

'THE SECRET OF SUCCESSFUL RUNNING
Before a Rolls-Royce chassis is sold, it is very carefully tested and adjusted by experts. It will run best if no attempt is made to interfere unnecessarily with adjustments.

An owner would do well to instruct his driver as follows:-Lubricate effectively, in strict accordance with the advice given in this book, and do not neglect any part.

Inspect all parts regularly, but take care not to alter any adjustments unless really necessary.'

And:

'Our interest in your Rolls-Royce car does not cease when you take delivery of the car. It is our ambition that every purchaser of a Rolls-Royce car shall continue to be more than satisfied.'

This latter pledge was meant completely sincerely. It served as an assurance that the Company's attitude towards fine engineering and quality design was unchanged and that the desire that their customers should receive excellent long term value for their money remained utterly undiminished.

After the Silver Dawn and its Bentley equivalent the R-type were superseded in the Spring of

1955 by the Silver Cloud and Bentley S Series, the Silver Wraith remained in production in relatively small numbers to cater for the coachbuilt carriage trade. At first the Silver Wraith remained mechanically uninfluenced by the Cloud, but when power assisted steering and refrigerated air conditioning were offered in 1956 the latter's engine capacity of 4,887cc was adopted for the Silver Wraith. By 1957 the twin S.U. carburetters of the Silver Cloud had also found their way onto the Silver Wraith.

Apart from the new engine and the introduction of the two important developments referred to above – power assisted steering and refrigerated air conditioning – the Silver Wraith chassis remained fundamentally unchanged during the period the six cylinder Silver Cloud was in production. The power assisted steering was a valuable adjunct to handling the large and heavy car the Silver Wraith had become, while the efficiency of the air conditioning was such that even the overheated interior of a large black limousine left out in the sun could be cooled to a comfortable temperature in three or four minutes. These optional features are described more fully in Chapter Five.

The later Silver Wraiths, (i.e. those with the 4,887cc engine) may normally be recognised by their heavy and distinctive Silver Cloud-pattern bumpers and overriders and their 'standing' type Spirit of Ecstasy. Built-in headlights of the Silver Dawn pattern were optional from 1949 and the smaller Silver Cloud type had become standard by 1956. However, a few examples continued to appear with Lucas R.100s, despite production of these magnificent fittings, which were designed and made exclusively for Rolls-Royce, having been discontinued by their manufacturer.

By 1958 the Silver Wraith had reached the limit of its development, the last chassis having been delivered to the coachbuilder in October of that year. The Silver Cloud and Bentley S Series were about to receive the new 6,230cc V-8 power unit and a prototype of the replacement for the Silver Wraith, using the same aluminium V-8 engine, was bodied and running by mid-1957. This was the Phantom V, the largest and most luxurious Rolls-Royce ever. The Silver Wraith had for twelve years provided the basis for the most fascinating variety of bespoke luxury motor cars seen in the post-war era. The fact that so many of the 1,883 cars built are still giving pleasure to their owners amply testifies to the strength, durability and soundness of design of this earliest post-war Rolls-Royce.

TECHNICAL SPECIFICATION

Rolls-Royce Silver Wraith

Engine

Dimensions
Six cylinders in line.
Short wheelbase A to E series: Bore 3.5 inches (89mm), stroke 4.5 inches (114mm), cubic capacity 260 cu. in. (4,257cc)
Short wheelbase F series onwards and long wheelbase A series to chassis DLW162: Bore 3.625 inches (92mm), stroke 4.5 inches (114mm), cubic capacity 278.6 cu. in. (4,566cc)
Long wheelbase from chassis LDLW163: Bore 3.75 inches (95.25mm), stroke 4.5 inches (114mm), cubic capacity 298.2 cu. in. (4,887cc)
Compression ratio 6.4:1 (6.75:1 available from short wheelbase H series and long wheelbase B series and standard from long wheelbase C series. 8:1 from chassis FLW60).

Cylinder block/Crankcase
Iron monobloc casting. 1948: with 30% chrome iron liners at tops of bores.

Crankshaft
1% chrome molybdenum steel (EN.19) nitrided. Bolt-on balance weights. Seven main bearings of copper-lead-indium.

Pistons
Aluminium alloy (RR.53) tin plated. Granodised piston rings, one compression, one L-section and one slotted oil control ring.

Cylinder head
Aluminium alloy (RR.50) with inserted valve seats.

Valve gear
Overhead inlet, side exhaust valves. Exhaust valves in KE.965. Stellite coated seats and tips. Camshaft driven by helical gears.

Carburetter
Short wheelbase to chassis WSG6: Stromberg dual downdraught carburetter with accelerator pump and automatic choke.
Short wheelbase from chassis WSG7 onwards and long wheelbase A to chassis LFLW19: single Zenith downdraught carburetter with accelerator pump and automatic choke.
Long wheelbase chassis FLW20 to LFLW59: twin S.U. HD.6 (1¾" bore) carburetters with automatic choke.
Chassis FLW60 onwards: twin S.U. HD.8 (2" bore) carburetters with automatic choke.
Water heated hot spot. Short wheelbase cars had a hand throttle control on steering wheel boss (except automatic gearbox cars and all left-hand drive cars from H series). Air intake silencer incorporating mesh air filter element (oil bath type air cleaner on cars for use in dusty conditions).

Ignition system
Ignition by high tension coil and Delco-Remy distributor with twin contact breaker points. Early cars were fitted with a spare coil for emergency use. Firing order 1,4,2,6,3,5.

Lubrication system
Helical gear oil pump in crankcase

driven by skew gear from camshaft. Floating oil intake in sump incorporating gauze strainer. By-pass filter on side of cylinder block. Pressure relief valve incorporating high and low pressure feeds. High pressure to the main and big-end bearings, camshaft bearings and skew gear drive to oil pump and distributor, low pressure to valve gear and timing gears. Sump capacity 16 pints (2.4 U.S. gallons, 9 litres). Short wheelbase F series onwards and all long wheelbase, full-flow oil filter.

Cooling system
Radiator shutters controlled by thermostat in header tank. Auxiliary thermostat in cylinder head to give quickest possible warm-up from cold. Belt driven centrifugal coolant pump and fan.

Chassis

Dimensions
Overall length, short wheelbase 17' 2" (5,232mm)
Overall length, long wheelbase 17' 9½" (5,423mm)
Wheelbase, short 10' 7" (3,226mm)
Wheelbase, long 11' 1" (3,378mm)
Front track 4' 10" (1,486mm)
Rear track, short wheelbase 4' 11½" (1,511mm)
Rear track, long wheelbase 5' 4" (1,626mm)

Frame
Channel section frame of riveted (from chassis BLW48 onwards, welded) construction with cruciform centre bracing. Additional crossmember either side of cruciform on long wheelbase chassis. Box section pan to support front suspension components.

Suspension
Front: independent by coil springs and rubber bushed wishbones, double acting hydraulic dampers and anti-roll bar.
Rear: semi-elliptic leaf springs protected by leather gaiters. Controllable hydraulic dampers by an oil pump mounted on the gearbox

and an overriding control on the steering wheel boss. Long wheelbase cars with power-assisted steering had electrically operated controllable dampers operated from a switch on the side of the steering column.

Steering
Marles type cam and roller. Fore and aft side steering tube (drag link) to centre steering lever pivoted on front chassis cross member and two-piece cross steering tube (track rod). Turns lock to lock, 3½.
Power assisted steering was offered as an option from the long wheelbase F series onwards.

Transmission
Four forward speeds and reverse. Right-hand change (column change on left-hand drive cars). Synchromesh on second, third and top gears.
Ratios: Top 1:1, Third 1.343:1, Second 2.02:1, First 2.985:1, Reverse 3.15:1.
Single dry-plate, centrifugally assisted clutch.

Optional from short wheelbase H series and standard from late long wheelbase D series: Rolls-Royce 4-speed automatic gearbox and fluid coupling, with selector mounted on the right of the steering column. Ratios: Top 1:1, Third 1.45:1, Second 2.63:1, First 3.82:1, Reverse 3.15:1.

Two-piece propeller shaft with needle roller bearing universal joints and centre bearing.

Rear axle: semi-floating type with hypoid gears. Ratio, short wheelbase 3.727:1 (3.416:1 available for certain export markets from F series onwards). Ratio, long wheelbase 3.727:1 (3.416:1 optional. From E series onwards 4.25:1, from F series onwards 4.375:1).

Brakes
Hydraulic front, mechanical rear. Operation by means of friction disc servo on the offside of the gearbox, which applies the front brakes through a Lockheed master cylinder and assists the application of the rear brakes. Handbrake on rear wheels by pull-out handle under right side of fascia through a cable and mechanical linkage.

Exhaust system
Single pipe system with two lagged expansion boxes.

Centralised lubrication system
All bearings in the steering and suspension systems, including the rear spring main leaf and shackles, fed with oil from a reservoir and pump mounted on the bulkhead in the engine compartment. Pump operated by a pedal under the fascia, to be operated once every 100 miles (160 km).

Fuel system
Rear mounted petrol tank, capacity 18 gallons (21.6 U.S. gallons, 81.8 litres). S.U. dual fuel pump mounted in the frame. Filter between tank and pump.

Electrical system
12 volt positive earth system with 55 amp/hour battery. Lucas special equipment dynamo and starter motor with reduction gearing and gentle-engagement pinion. Lucas R.100 headlamps. Lucas built-in headlamps began to appear on Silver Wraiths in 1948. Lucas centre lamp (twin Lucas fog lamps began to appear on export cars from 1948 and were standard by late 1951). Medium wave/Long wave Radiomobile radio with push-button tuning and two speakers. Direction indicator switch on the fascia capping rail. Hot water type interior heater under the front passenger's seat with electric blower.

Other accessories
Trico vacuum operated windscreen washer.

Road wheels and tyres
17 inch steel disc well-base wheels, on five studs, carrying 6.50 x 17 Dunlop Fort tyres. Certain export cars from short wheelbase F series onwards and all long wheelbase cars had 16 inch wheels with 7.50 x 16 tyres. Tyre pressures, 17 inch, front 24 lb/sq. in., rear 35 lb/sq. in., 16 inch, front 19 lb/sq. in., rear 27 lb/sq. in.

Milestones and modifications

	Chassis	Year
First (10' 7" wheelbase) chassis	WTA1	1947
Aluminium bonnet	WVA16	1947
5" dynamo	WZB1	1948
Crankcase breather and rocker cover	WZB15	1948
Pressed-in short cylinder liners	WCB31	1948
Radiator heated demister	WFC1	1949
Provision of hand inspection lamp	WFC63	1949
First left-hand drive Silver Wraith	LWGC58	1949
3⅝" bore (4,566cc) engine, Full Flow oil filter	WOF1	1951
7.50 x 16 tyres for certain export cars	WOF37	1951
Zenith single choke carburetter	WSG7	1952
2-speed wipers, separately housed main fuse	WVH1	1952
3-position heater & demister switches	WSG45	1952
First long wheelbase (11' 1") chassis	ALW1	1952
Hot/cold demister	WVH1, ALW27	1952
Last 10' 7" wheelbase chassis	LWVH116	1953
Radiator 4" further forward	BLW39	1953
Welded chassis frame	BLW48	1953
Bentley Continental type demister system	DLW80	1954
3¾" bore (4,887cc) engine	LDLW163	1955
Twin S.U. type HD.6 (1¾" bore) carburetters	FLW20	1956
HD.8 (2" bore) carburetters, 8:1 compression ratio	FLW60	1957

Coachwork

All bodies built by the following outside coachbuilders to owners' specifications:

Coachbuilder	Short Wheelbase	Long Wheelbase
Park Ward	313	164
H. J. Mulliner	335	182
Hooper	323	146
James Young	105	100
Freestone & Webb	81	39
Scottish C.W.S.	27	–
Gurney Nutting	12	–
Vincents	7	–
Rippon Bros	5	–
Franay	4	4
Windovers	4	–
Alpe & Saunders	3	1
Cooper	2	–
Jones Bros	2	–
Inskip	2	–
Woodhall Nicholson	2	–
Denby	2	–
E. D. Abbott	2	–
Saoutchik	1	–
Van den Plas (Brussels)	1	–
Epps Bros	1	–
Brewster	1	–
Harwood	1	–
Simpson & Slater	1	–
J. Cairns	1	–
Ghia	1	–
Gustaf Nordbergs	–	1
Vignale	–	1
Reals	–	1
Unknown	5	–
Totals	1,244	639

Chassis and engine numbers

Silver Wraith chassis are numbered consecutively. The number 13 was omitted from chassis numbering but not from engine numbering.

Short Wheelbase

Series	Chassis numbers	Engine numbers
A	WTA1-85	W2A-W252A
	WVA1-81	
	WYA1-87	
B	WZB1-65	W1B-W201B
	WAB1-65	
	WCB1-73	
C	WDC1-101	W1C-W300C
	WFC1-101	
	WGC1-101	
D	WHD1-101	W1D-W100D
E	WLE1-35	W1E-W129E
	WME1-96	

F	WOF1-76	W1F-W75F
G	WSG1-76	W1G-W75G
H	WVH1-116	W1H-W115H

Total: 1,244 cars.

Long Wheelbase

Series	Chassis numbers	Engine numbers
A	ALW1-51	L1A-L50A
B	BLW1-101	L1B-L100B
C	CLW1-43	L1C-L42C
D	DLW1-172	L1D-L171D
E	ELW1-101	L1E-L100E
F	FLW1-101	L1F-L100F
G	GLW1-26	L1G-L25G
H	HLW1-52	L1H-L51H

Total: 639 cars.

Total Silver Wraiths built: 1,883.

Right *The 10ft 7in Silver Wraith chassis used the longer of the two rationalised frames introduced immediately after the War. This drawing by John Ferguson of* The Autocar, *was based upon the first Silver Wraith chassis built, experimental car 34GVIII (later renumbered 1-SW-I). This chassis was equipped with built-in hydraulic jacks – a feature not retained for production. The jacks can be seen below the steering box and on the leading edge of the rear axle. At the beginning of 1952 a long wheelbase (11ft 1in) version of the Silver Wraith chassis was offered optionally and by the end of the following year the original 10ft 7in chassis had been discontinued.*

Middle *The original 4,257cc Silver Wraith engine used a single dual choke Stromberg carburetter and by-pass oil filter. Note the knurled bakelite oil filler cap on these early cars. Far right is an offside view of the same engine showing the linkage from the bi-metal heat sensor in the inlet manifold to the cold-start arrangement, which incorporated a fast idle cam for reliable tick-over after starting from cold. Note also the vacuum-operated windscreen washing equipment, fuse box, centralised chassis lubrication reservoir and pump and the inspection lamp with its neatly coiled lead, stowed in its clips. Chassis WME18.*

Bottom *The 4,566cc engine, introduced at the start of the 'F' series in October 1951, used the same carburetter as the 4,257cc engine at first, but with full-flow oil filtration and a satin nickel-plated brass quick action oil filler cap like that of the late pre-war cars. From chassis WSG7 and on the Long Wheelbase chassis from its inception, a single choke Zenith carburetter, as seen here, was substituted for the original Stromberg. The photograph of the engine as installed in the car is of chassis ALW28.*

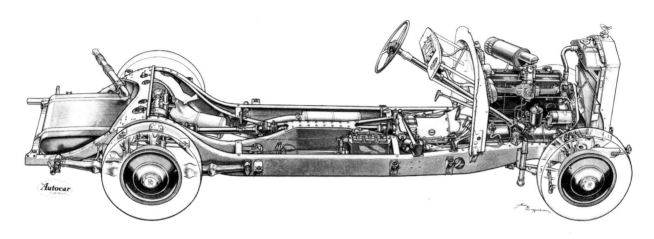

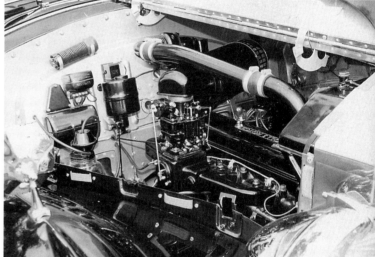

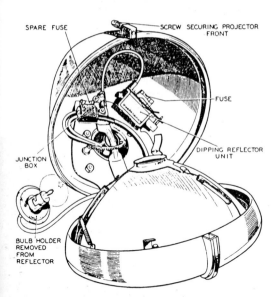

SPARE FUSE

SCREW SECURING PROJECTOR FRONT

FUSE

JUNCTION BOX

DIPPING REFLECTOR UNIT

BULB HOLDER REMOVED FROM REFLECTOR

Above *R.100 sealed-beam headlamp fitted to a U.S.-delivered Silver Wraith.*

Above *The early Silver Wraiths were fitted with the magnificent Lucas R.100 headlamps, as had been the late Phantom III and the Wraith before the War. This design of headlamp was made exclusively for Rolls-Royce and Bentley cars. The cheaper P.100-L, fitted to early post-war Jaguars and one or two other makes, was never used by Rolls-Royce. Dipping was by means of a swivelling reflector operated by a solenoid in the standard R.100 headlamp, but there were other variants to meet various export requirements. These included the R.100-EF (Export France) with right dipping and yellow diffusers and a special sealed-beam R.100 for certain States of the U.S.A. The Silver Dawn type built-in headlamps began to appear on some Silver Wraiths from 1949, and the smaller Silver Cloud type, which never really suited the Silver Wraith, were standard from the Long Wheelbase 'E' series of October 1955 onwards. However, R.100s continued to feature on a few cars after that date, though by then they were no longer manufactured and would have come from stock.*

Below *The lofty driving position and controls of a Silver Wraith, in this instance a limousine by H. J. Mulliner. Note the controls on the steering wheel boss for the hand throttle (open/closed) and ride control (normal/hard), and the short, right-hand gear lever, pistol-grip handbrake and the classic 'switchbox' on the fascia to the right of the steering column. The long lever on the driver's door is the 'quick-lift' window control, the smaller crank-type winder being for the quarter-pane. The 'quick-lift' device lost favour after the driver's right hand was freed from gear changing by the introduction of the automatic gearbox. Chassis ALW28.*

Top right *The earliest saloon coachwork offered for the Silver Wraith chassis by Rolls-Royce Ltd's own coachbuilder Park Ward was design number 13. A significant departure from pre-war styling was the pronounced out-sweep of the bottoms of the doors to conceal the running boards, with short front wings ending rather abruptly at the scuttle. Park Ward records indicate that 25 bodies to this design were built, including one for experimental car 2-SW-I, plus a further seven to design number 20, which was externally identical but fitted with a division. All but three were fitted with a sunshine roof over the front seats. John Bull's masterful wash drawing makes the subject appear quite attractive, which it can be 'in the metal', despite being normally regarded as a rather plain style.*

Above *From January 1948 deliveries, Park Ward's saloon styling abandoned the out-swept doors and razor-edged wings of design numbers 13 and 20 in favour of design number 45, with traditional exposed running boards, but unchanged from the waistline up. Still rather staid and upright, yet somehow not unattractive, this coachwork would not have looked out of place on a pre-war Wraith. In a period of post-war austerity, even the wealthy clientele of Rolls-Royce appreciated the not inconsiderable cost saving that this design represented over the more elaborate offerings of other coachbuilders and 62 were built, plus a further four to design number 46, which had a division but was otherwise the same. Some later examples had a chromium waist moulding. Park Ward records show that all but six were fitted with a sunshine roof.*

Bottom right *The earliest post-war work of James Young Ltd had strong links with the last of their pre-war designs, both in silhouette and styling details. The front wing sweeping across the door panels to conceal the running boards was, however, a new styling feature for the post-war period. Note the very slim windscreen pillars of this design number WR17 saloon. The bonnet was supplied by Crewe with the chassis and this bonnet type, with divided side panel and single latching handle on each side, was of steel and was fitted to the very early cars only. An aluminium bonnet, with opening side panels extending right down to the wings and twin handles, was phased in from chassis WVA16.*

Above *Having got off to a slightly later start than the other coachbuilders with close-coupled saloon coachwork for the Silver Wraith chassis, it is fair to say that H. J. Mulliner got it absolutely right first time. There is an obvious link with the best of their pre-war work, while nonetheless being all new. Unlike the Park Ward versions, most of these design number 7062 cars were touring limousines, only a small number being built as saloons without a division. For some reason not readily apparent, the design number was changed to 7118 for the final dozen of these cars, the appearance remaining unchanged. About 90 in total were built. Note the slim, chromium-plated brass door window frames.*

Above & below *H. J. Mulliner & Co. excelled in interior decor, too, selecting the most beautiful of timber veneers and applying them to fascias, distinctive tapered door cappings and fine cabinetwork. This is the rear compartment of a design number 7062 touring limousine. The design of the upholstery, carried over unchanged from the last of their pre-war cars, was called RENILLUM, after their name spelt backwards. This consisted of plain cushions with piped edges and pleated-and-bolstered squabs. Most other coachbuilders copied this seating style at one time or another.*

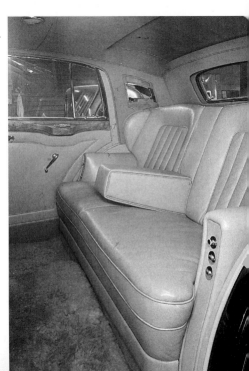

Above *This is James Young's design number WR18 introduced late in 1948. It has a great deal in common with H. J. Mulliner's design number 7062, the main differences being the absence of chrome mouldings to the waistline and sill and no razor edge to the wing crowns. This is the 1948 Earls Court Motor Show car, chassis WCB20, the first example of the design. This photograph also shows the revised wheel cover disc design that was phased in from late 1948 – in this instance with the painted portion two-toned by the coachbuilder.*

John Bull 84

Above *Freestone & Webb's early post-war bodies featured angular section wings with exposed running boards and all doors hinged on their rear edges, a basic concept unchanged from their pre-war razor-edge coachwork on the Wraith and Phantom III chassis. This is design number 3004, of which there were many variants.*

Right *Later versions of James Young design number WR18 were enhanced by a longer luggage boot with lift-up lid. This example, on chassis WME18, was owned for many years by opera singer Miss (later Dame) Joan Hammond and is now the pride and joy of Matt Smith (RROCA).*

Below *WME18's interior, showing the highly figured veneers and zebrawood crossbanding favoured by James Young Ltd, and the bench type rear seat. Interesting to compare these photographs with those of the interior of H. J. Mulliner's design number 7062 on the previous page.*

Top two pictures *Hooper introduced a distinctive cut to the rear quarter-light of their post-war cars. This is design number 8098 (with division) and 8122 (without), both known as the 'Teviot' and derived from their earlier design number 8034. Above is chassis WFC67, owned by Michael Zwar (RROCA) while below is the Teviot as it appeared in the 1948 Silver Wraith catalogue.*

Below left *This rear view, showing the distinctive double-lidded luggage compartment, is actually design number 8034, Hooper's earliest post-war design, which preceded the 'Teviot'. It was closer-coupled and the outsweep of the doors concealed the running boards. The first experimental Silver Wraith chassis, 34GVIII (later renumbered 1-SW-I), was fitted with the first of this body design, of which 66 were built.*

Below *Park Ward's design number 45 and 46 saloons were superseded in August 1949 by design number 113. The changes largely consisted of the elimination of the knife edges to the roof, rear quarters and boot to present a more rounded appearance and a larger rear window. The chrome waist moulding was now standard. It could scarcely be argued that these changes taken as a whole constituted an improvement – indeed it could be said that the best features of the earlier designs had been eliminated. 21 were built, one with division and all but one with sunshine roof.*

Right *Hooper's Teviot became 'Teviot II', design number 8235, for the 1950 season. This was distinguished by a higher front wingline with concealed running boards and front-hinged doors to the front compartment. Only twelve examples were built before being replaced by 'Teviot III', design number 8283, from early 1951.*

Middle & below *Following its first introduction, Freestone & Webb's design number 3004 changed markedly, with new wings and a six-light configuration, though the design number remained, qualified by the addition of one or more suffixes. This is design number 3004/A2/F on chassis WCB11, their 1948 Earls Court Motor Show exhibit. The James Young banner which appears to be over this stand actually refers to the neighbouring stand of the rival coachbuilder. Right is John Bull's rendering of this design, which was further changed for the 1949 Show with front-hinged doors to the front compartment.*

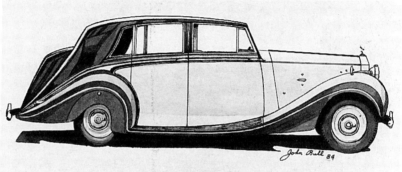

Top & left *After Hooper designer Osmond Rivers' first visit to the U.S.A. in 1950, he decided to abandon the 'composite' method of construction in favour of all metal, using only aluminium alloy and no steel. Design number 8283, 'Teviot III', was the first to use this mode of construction. Note the slim chrome-plated frames around the side windows, which were merely superimposed on the painted integral window surrounds to give the visual impression of 'half-frame' doors while retaining greater structural integrity. The heavy export-type bumpers and overriders seen on these cars began to appear on the Silver Wraith for the home market from late 1949 and were standard by mid-1950. They better suited the more massive appearance of the Silver Wraith than had the earlier, less substantial early Wilmott-Breeden type, which were retained for home-market Bentleys. 46 Teviot IIIs were built, including one on the final short wheelbase Silver Wraith chassis, LWVH116.*

Left *These interior views of design number 8283 show that Hooper did not apply crossbanding to the edges of their timber veneers and their rather slab-like door cappings were very unlike those of H. J. Mulliner and James Young, both of whom favoured a more delicate approach. This is WOF12, which was exhibited on the Rolls-Royce Ltd stand at the 1951 Earls Court Motor Show.*

This page *H. J. Mulliner's design number 7249 first appeared in late 1950 and was the replacement for their earlier design numbers 7062 and 7118. It was a six-light touring limousine design with a higher front wingline, top-hinged bootlid and push-button door handles in which H. J. Mulliner's mastery of this style of coachwork was very much in evidence. The car at bottom left is believed to be WHD89, the 1950 Earls Court Show car and the first of the design to be completed. Note how well this outstandingly well-balanced design lends itself to the two-tone treatment, with the colours divided along the waistline or (bottom right) with the lighter shade confined to the side panels between the waistline and the wings. This car, on left-hand drive chassis LWME21, has the optional Silver Dawn-pattern built-in headlights with paired grilles below them, and twin foglights which by 1949 were standard for export. At middle right is yet another variation on the two-tone theme, with the upper, lighter shade extended to the side panels with only the wings and waist moulding finished in the darker colour. This is the 1951 Festival of Britain exhibition car, WME49.*

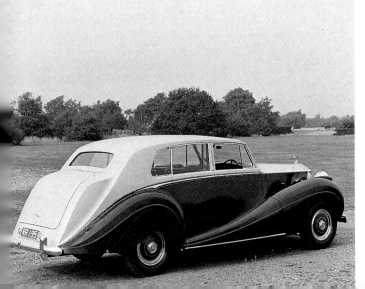

Top, left & right *Another variant of H. J. Mulliner's design number 7249, on chassis WSG26, featured smaller rear quarter-lights which allowed the mirrored companions to the interior quarters to be retained. These had otherwise been dropped in the transition from the four-light design number 7118 to the six-light 7249. This car was delivered new to Sir Horace Evans, physician to H.M. The Queen, and is owned now by Gail Cooke (RROCA).*

Below *Chassis WLE12 was the second H. J. Mulliner design number 7249 touring limousine to be delivered. This superb design featured a self-supporting lift-up lid to the luggage compartment. The tools were fitted in a tray beneath the carpet on the right-hand side and the spare wheel was stowed within the boot rather than in a separate compartment below as had been the case with earlier designs.*

Above *Another car to design number 7249, on chassis WOF30, built for exhibition on the H. J. Mulliner stand at the 1951 Earls Court Motor Show. The first owner was singer James Melton of Park Avenue, New York City, who no doubt preferred the right-hand drive with floor-mounted gear change to the column-shift arrangement then being offered on left-hand drive cars. In 1952 it was awarded first prize in the International Motor Sports Show in New York and was shown in colour in Gulf Oil advertising of the period with Mr Melton and the six foot tall trophy alongside. Inset is a scale model of the car built in 1957 by Saul Santos for Mr Melton. Both WOF30 and the model are owned now by Kansas collector Roger Morrison (RROC Inc).*

Below *Vincents of Reading, still motor dealers in that Berkshire town to this day, built seven bodies on Silver Wraith chassis – six saloons and a hearse. This was their second from last, chassis WOF1, on their stand at the 1951 Earls Court Motor Show.*

Above *One of the author's favourites. Traditional razor-edge styling yet with plenty of flowing curves. Few cars had external running boards this late. This is Freestone & Webb's 1951 Earls Court Show car, design number 3091/A, a 'Saloon Limousine', on chassis no. WOF3.*

Below left *Interior detail, by John Bull, of WOF3. The view of the rear quarter shows the sliding panel with transparent insert in the roof, with its inner sliding shutter, and dark ruby glass panels which slide across the quarter-lights.* **Below right** *The division cabinetwork includes a cocktail cabinet with a vanity case above the cocktail vessels and picnic tables with mirrors that fold out behind them when they are pulled out. Motor Show cars were frequently used to demonstrate the range of fittings and luxury extras offered by the coachbuilders, and extra care was lavished on their finish and presentation.*

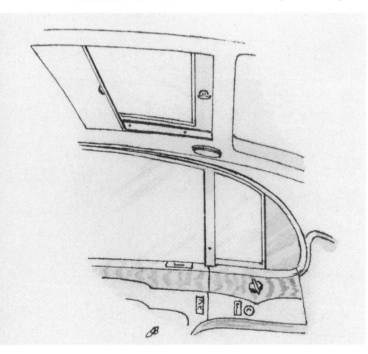

Above *Park Ward records, in their list of prototype bodies, show the first of this design, on chassis WGC28, as design number 114. However, it is listed elsewhere in the same records as design number 144, which was the number adopted for all subsequent cars of* *this design except for one with a division, which was design number 314. WGC28 was Park Ward's 1949 Earls Court Show exhibit and introduced this rather avant-garde styling to the public. 121 of these six-light saloons were built. Early examples had a smaller backlight* *and there were several variations of chrome sill and rear spat mouldings. The headlamps were the built-in Silver Dawn type. The photograph shows WOF11, the 1951 Earls Court exhibit.*

Above *Rear seat, Park Ward design number 144. The large quarter-light made for excellent vision and helped make these saloons ideal for touring.*

Above left *Normally the centre section of the fascia, housing the instruments, was raised above the surrounding areas. However, in this example of Park Ward's design number 144 saloon it is recessed. Other than that, the layout is standard Silver Wraith. The woodwork is the rather plain style, without crossbanded edges, favoured by Park Ward before 1952.*

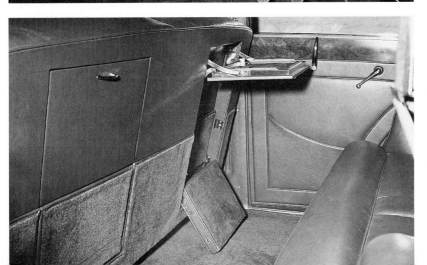

Left *The front seating of design number 144 was, in nearly all cases, of the bench type with folding centre armrest. The picnic tables behind the front seat were leather covered on their outer surfaces and there was a pair of folding footrests below them.*

Left *A total of six cars of Park Ward design number 144 styling were built to a four-light configuration. Two were early cars and retained the same design number. A further three were to design number 262 while one, a prototype, was design number 259. John Bull's drawing shows that this configuration was an attractive variation on the more usual six-light car, albeit with more restricted vision from the rear compartment.*

Left & below *Other coachbuilders imitated this styling concept after Park Ward initiated it. This is James Young's interpretation, displayed at the 1950 Earls Court Show. Note the special bumpers with built-in number plate housing and reverse lights. Design number WR25, of which 27 examples were built.*

Right *Freestone & Webb soon followed suit with this styling concept, offering both four-light and six-light designs. This is their four-light saloon, design number 3070.*

Right *The old firm of Rippon Bros, of Huddersfield, built five bodies for Silver Wraiths. This is their third, on chassis WHD87, which they exhibited at the 1950 Earls Court Show. Similar cars were exhibited by them at the '51 and '52 Shows.* **Above** *John Bull's interior drawing shows detail in the rear compartment of the '52 Show car, on chassis WVH4.*

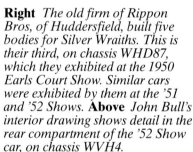

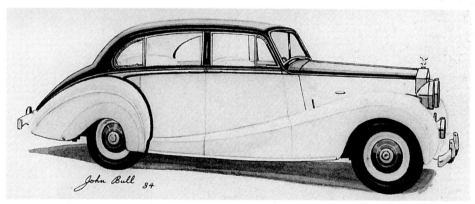

Bottom right *Hooper's designer Osmond Rivers wrote that in 1948 he 'sat down in cold blood to produce a "New Look" to get away from the "classic" designs which had continued after World War II'. The front wings tapered back to the rear extremities of the car, with no rear wings as such. The first of these, design number 8181, was exhibited at the 1948 Earls Court Show and is believed to have been the first Silver Wraith to be fitted with built-in headlamps in lieu of the standard R.100s. The subject of this photograph, one of six later duplicates, was built for the Maharajah of Mysore on chassis WGC31. Mr. Rivers said that he made this design 'rotund' in the belief that there would be a reaction against 'razor-edge'. In this he later admitted to have been partly wrong and adapted the 'new look' to meet the continuing demand for razor-edge styling.*

Above & left *The first of Osmond Rivers' 'new look' designs with razor-edge styling was this car on chassis WGC16, to design number 8234. It was exhibited on the Rolls-Royce Ltd stand at the 1949 Earls Court Motor Show and was the forerunner of many similarly styled cars on the Silver Wraith long wheelbase, Silver Dawn and Bentley chassis. The built-in headlamps of the then recently introduced Silver Dawn were specified. Note also that the standard Silver Wraith centre pass lamp was not fitted and that small foglamps replaced the standard horn grilles for this one-off design. Owner: Matthew Sysak (RROC Inc).*

Above, left *Interior views of WGC16, showing the flame-pattern veneers and contrasting piping to the upholstery, the latter a feature frequently seen on Motor Show cars.*

Top right *Roberto Rossellini, the Italian film producer, commissioned Ghia to build this limousine body on Silver Wraith chassis LWOF48. Note that the radiator shell is mounted considerably further forward than standard, to give a long bonnet look. The styling concept was repeated, rather more successfully, on Silver Dawn chassis LSHD22 (see Chapter Three).*

Right *Drophead coupé bodies were only built in small numbers on the Silver Wraith chassis. Freestone & Webb only built one, but obviously put much thought and effort into its appearance, which was very successful aesthetically, unlike the designs of some other coachbuilders, who tended to treat a drophead as merely a saloon with the top cut off. Design number 3056 on chassis WFC69.*

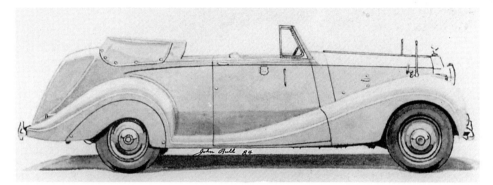

Right & bottom right *An example of the phenomenon alluded to above was Gurney Nutting's design number WR20, which was obviously a drophead version of the James Young saloon design number WR18. Twelve of these dropheads were built by Gurney Nutting who were then, like James Young Ltd, part of the Jack Barclay group. John Bull's drawing (above right) shows WCB40, built for the Maharajah of Mysore, while right is WCB22, the 1948 Gurney Nutting Earls Court Show exhibit. Later cars of this design had a longer more rounded boot which improved matters considerably.*

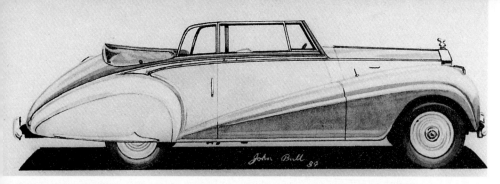

Top left *Unusually, Park Ward's saloon styling adapted very well to drophead coupé form. Five were built on short wheelbase chassis, to three different design numbers – 201, 225 and 291 – all similar. John Bull's drawing shows the genre.*

Left *In designing a drophead coupé the boot seems often to have presented problems. This was the case with Hooper's early design for the Silver Wraith which had a rather bulbous boot not matched to the otherwise razor-edged and attractive lines of the car. Two of these were built, to design number 8090, of which this is the second, on chassis WDC31.*

Left *Inskip of New York were the main importers of Rolls-Royce cars between the Wars, often building bodies on the imported chassis. This activity was somewhat curtailed post-war but they did build a brace of roadsters on early Silver Wraith chassis, with lots of chrome and a distinctive cut to the tops of the doors. The flat bumpers and large overriders seen on this car were fitted to certain export cars prior to the introduction of the heavy export pattern. This is WZB36, owned by Andrew Darling (RROC Inc).*

Bottom left *This drophead coupé on chassis WOF50 is one of only two post-war Rolls-Royce cars bodied by E. D. Abbott of Farnham – the other being a Silver Wraith fixed head coupé. Note the massive, solid appearance. Owner: Gil Frederick (RROC Inc.)*

Above & right *This fixed head coupé by the French coachbuilder Saoutchik, on chassis WTA45, was originally built as a sedanca coupé, but the de ville extension was subsequently welded up and a sunroof fitted. It is in this later guise that the car is seen in our two photographs. Note the extended gear lever seen in the three-quarter front view, which was taken in Kensington Gardens in the 1950s. Owner: W. Magalow.*

Below *Freestone & Webb built this razor-edge fixed head coupé, design number 3014, on chassis WVA74.*

Above *Owner A. R. Illingworth (RREC) was kind enough to send this photograph of his fixed head coupé by Rippon on chassis WFC29, a 1949 Earls Court Show exhibit. It has been in Mr Illingworth's family since new, having been originally delivered to his father-in-law, W. H. Smith.*

Left *The two-door saloon, or 'Saloon Coupé' to use the coachbuilder's term, was a pre-war speciality of James Young Ltd. They did it very well. Their early post-war designs of this body type were similar in silhouette to the pre-war cars, but the more rearward mounted front axle of the Silver Wraith mitigated against the superb proportions of their efforts on the Phantom III and Wraith chassis being repeated. This is believed to be WTA18, the first of three saloon coupés to design number WR16.*

Right *If the early Park Ward Silver Wraith saloons were somewhat lacking in panache, their seven-seater limousines were doubly so. The first eight (design number 17) had flat running boards and short front wings that finished rather abruptly at the scuttle. From deliveries commencing early in 1948 this particularly pedestrian looking design had evolved into design number 51, seen here, which shared the wings, running boards and some other panels with the contemporary design number 45 saloon. This design represents by far the majority of Park Ward 7-passenger limousines, or 'Enclosed Limousines' as their makers called them, on short wheelbase Silver Wraith chassis, with 37 built. A later redesign saw the rather heavy-looking tail treatment improved as design number 146, but only eleven examples were built before construction of seven-seater bodies was concentrated on the more suitable Long Wheelbase chassis.*

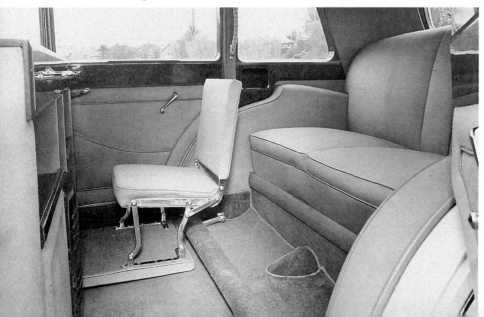

Left *Plain, but exceedingly comfortable, the Park Ward enclosed limousines were the roomiest in the rear compartment of all the short wheelbase Silver Wraiths. This was achieved, as was always the case with spacious seven-seaters within this wheelbase constraint, at the expense of driver's compartment legroom and boot space. The upholstery material was West of England cloth, while the front compartment was usually upholstered in leather. Note the occasional seats, one shown stowed and the other folded out for use. Though the photograph shows design number 51, designs 17 and 146 were similar inside.*

Top right *HRH Princess Marina, the Duchess of Kent, ordered this 7-passenger limousine from H. J. Mulliner, who built it to design number 7171 on chassis no. WFC25. Again, it is very clear that the short wheelbase Silver Wraith chassis was not long enough to take spacious seven-seater coachwork without the boot appearing stunted. Note the blue 'police light' above the windscreen – a standard fitment on cars for British royalty. The registration number YR11 was transferred from the Duke of Kent's pre-war Wraith WHC2, a Hooper limousine, and subsequently went onto Phantom IV 4AF12, then Phantom V 5VA23.*

Above *Rear interior, WFC25.*

Right *Of identical exterior appearance to their design number 7171, were H. J. Mulliner's design numbers 7278 and 7280 seven-seaters. This car, with the roof-mounted luggage rack fitted by the coachbuilder to several of these limousines to counter the lack of boot space, is chassis LWOF35, design number 7280.*

Bottom right *An early post-war speciality of H. J. Mulliner on the Silver Wraith chassis was the sedanca de ville, of which they offered several designs from 1946 to 1953. This is the first production Silver Wraith, chassis WTA1, fitted with design number 7019 sedanca de ville for the County Borough of Derby. Note the square section bumpers that were fitted to a handful of the very earliest cars.*

Above *Design number 7019 was short-lived (13 built), but the following design number 7055 which replaced it in mid-1947 was more numerous, with around 60 being built. As the photograph of an early example on chassis WYA65 shows, there was little, if any, external difference between these two H. J. Mulliner designs,* **see previous page**.

Above & right *The interior of the design number 7055 sedanca de ville was extremely luxurious, with characteristic H. J. Mulliner furnishings including RENILLUM style upholstery in the customer's choice of leather or West of England cloth, both of which are shown in these photographs. Note the sideways facing occasional seats.*

Above *Later H. J. Mulliner sedanca de ville designs featured forward-hinged front doors and concealed running boards. This is design number 7042, of which only four were built, commencing with this one on chassis WZB3 for Princess Mdivani. It is a closer-coupled design than 7055, with no occasional seats.*

Right & below *A later seven-seater sedanca de ville than design number 7055 is this one, with forward-hinged front doors, concealed running boards and rear quarter-lights of a shape more usually associated with Hooper coachwork. The H. J. Mulliner design number is not known, and the only example known to the author is on chassis WFC99.*

To conclude the section on short wheelbase Silver Wraith coachwork, four fine photographs by Tom Solley of chassis LWME58, with sedanca de ville coachwork by Franay of Paris, owned by Joseph Williamson (RROC Inc). It was built new for Greek shipping magnate Aristotle Onassis. Note the stainless steel cladding to the door jambs – a characteristic feature of Franay coachwork.

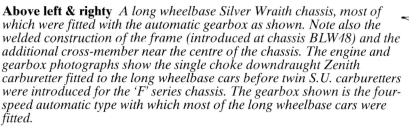

Above left & righty *A long wheelbase Silver Wraith chassis, most of which were fitted with the automatic gearbox as shown. Note also the welded construction of the frame (introduced at chassis BLW48) and the additional cross-member near the centre of the chassis. The engine and gearbox photographs show the single choke downdraught Zenith carburetter fitted to the long wheelbase cars before twin S.U. carburetters were introduced for the 'F' series chassis. The gearbox shown is the four-speed automatic type with which most of the long wheelbase cars were fitted.*

Right & bottom right

H. J. Mulliner's design number 7249 touring limousine was retained until the short wheelbase Silver Wraith chassis was discontinued at the end of 1953. It was then 'stretched' to suit the long wheelbase chassis, to become design number 7356. Note that there is no removable spat to the rear wing. The bumpers/overriders, standing radiator mascot and all front and rear lighting were all of the Silver Cloud type from the 'E' series (chassis deliveries to coachbuilders commencing February 1955), though R.100 headlamps, as shown in the photograph, could still be specified. 76 were built, including one on the final Silver Wraith chassis, LHLW52.

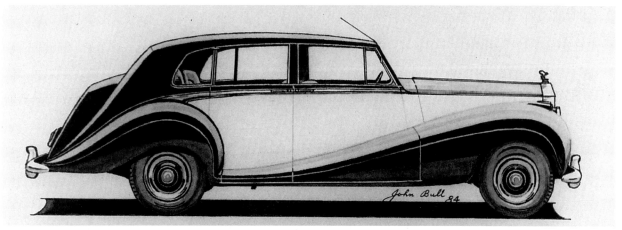

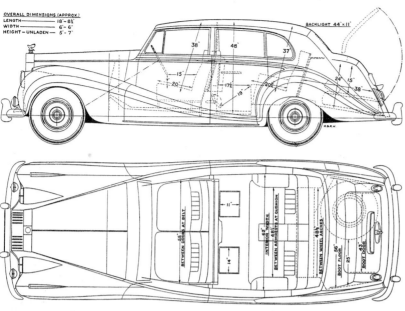

OVERALL DIMENSIONS (APPROX)
LENGTH — 18'- 8¼"
WIDTH — 6'- 6"
HEIGHT — UNLADEN — 5'- 7"

BACKLIGHT 44" × 11"

ROLLS-ROYCE SILVER WRAITH TOURING LIMOUSINE   DESIGN 7356

On this page *The interior of design number 7356 changed little from that of the short wheelbase 7249, except that it was noticeably more roomy in the rear compartment. Note the very typical Mulliner woodwork, with flame-pattern veneers and extensive use of cross-banding. Even the boot was luxuriously carpeted.*

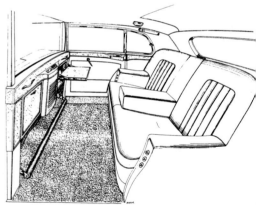

Top right *Very similar to H. J. Mulliner's long wheelbase touring limousine was Freestone & Webb's offering on the same chassis type. This is design number 3131/A/L 'Saloon Limousine' on chassis CLW31. Being a pre-'E' series chassis the bumper hardware and lighting are of the Silver Dawn pattern and the radiator mascot is the kneeling type.*

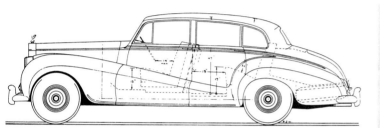

Above & right *Park Ward offered this touring saloon styling for the long wheelbase Silver Wraith chassis. The designer's wash drawing **(above right)** shows the early version, design number 550, while the two photographs and the line drawing show the later design number 702, with 'E' series and later modifications. Both these designs were fitted with what Park Ward termed a 'half division' – i.e. there was a fixed bulkhead between the front and rear compartments below the waistline, with elaborate cabinetwork, but no glass partition above. The same designs with a 'full division' were 598 and 703. A total of 66 of these four designs was built.*

Left *The rear interior of a Park Ward long wheelbase Silver Wraith touring saloon. In this photo it is not possible to determine whether this is an early or later car, but the buttons in the ends of the side armrests indicate a 'full division' car.*

The two coachbuilder's drawings **(below)** *show the rear compartment and boot details of design number 702. The earlier 550 was similar, while 598 and 703 were also similar but with an electrically operated glass partition above what was otherwise the 'half division'.*

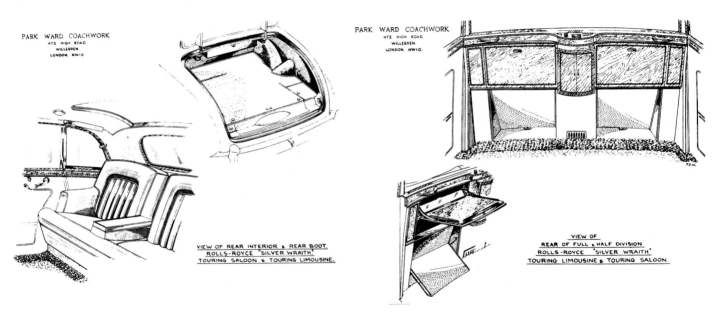

PARK WARD COACHWORK
473 HIGH ROAD
WILLESDEN
LONDON. NW10.

VIEW OF REAR INTERIOR & REAR BOOT.
ROLLS-ROYCE "SILVER WRAITH."
TOURING SALOON & TOURING LIMOUSINE.

PARK WARD COACHWORK
473 HIGH ROAD
WILLESDEN
LONDON. NW10.

VIEW OF
REAR OF FULL & HALF DIVISION
ROLLS-ROYCE "SILVER WRAITH"
TOURING LIMOUSINE & TOURING SALOON.

This page *James Young's design number WRM31 for the long wheelbase Silver Wraith had the high wingline that had become fashionable. Though this was a touring limousine, small, sideways-facing occasional seats, as shown in the interior drawing, could be specified.* **Previous page (bottom)** *An earlier version of this design, WRM30, had a steeper slope to the top of the rear wing, to suit the older pattern tail-light, and rather clumsy double swage lines to both front and rear wings. The long leather-covered grab handles seen in the interior photograph* **(right)** *were a distinctive feature of James Young coachwork during this period, though the artist's impression shows the shorter and more conventional chrome plated type. 28 cars were built to design number WRM30 and 47 to WRM31.*

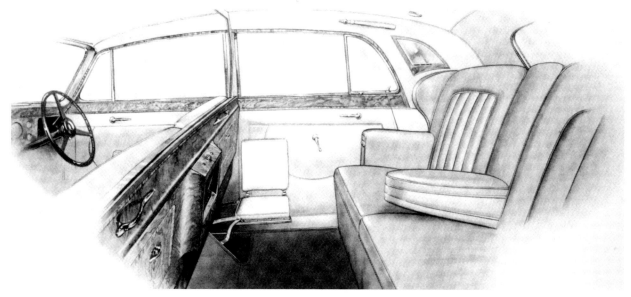

Hooper designer Osmond Rivers' 'new look', with front wings flowing right through to the tail and no separate rear wings, was developed for the long wheelbase Silver Wraith chassis, to which it was ideally suited. The first design was number 8390, a touring limousine of which many variants followed. The coachbuilder's wash drawing **(top left)**, for once closely resembling the reality **(below left)**.

Below *Another design number 8390 touring limousine, seen from an angle which shows the sweeping lines to full advantage.*

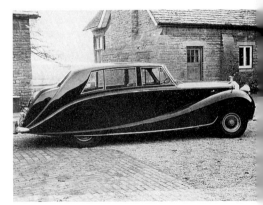

Below *One of the many variations on the 8390 theme was this version, with the front wing ending at the cutaway rear spat – somewhat spoiling the lines it is felt. This is believed to be FLW99, exhibited on the Hooper stand at the 1957 Earls Court Motor Show.*

Above *Another variant – a one-off – was this four-light version, design number 8476, built for Lady Dovercourt. No trace of this car can be found in Rolls-Royce records so the chassis number cannot be ascertained. The coachbuilder's records indicate FLW42 but that chassis was bodied by James Young according to the Rolls-Royce records. It is certainly 'E' series or later. Note the R.100 headlamps, which were unusual on a late long wheelbase car, and the very small, non-standard door handles.*

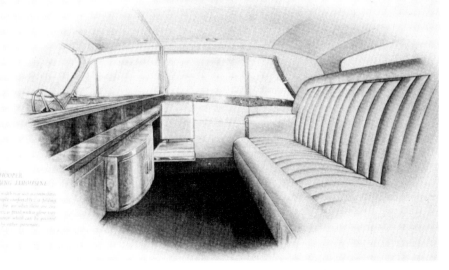

Above, left & right *Rear interiors of Hooper's design number 8390 and variants thereof – above, the artist's impression and right, the opulent reality. Note the sideways-facing occasional seats that were made possible on touring limousines by the long wheelbase chassis.*

This page *Though sharing the silhouette – and all-metal mode of construction – of the 'Lightweight' saloons on the Bentley Mk VI and R-type chassis, H. J. Mulliner's design number 7348 touring limousine was a little more sparing in the use of swaging on the wings, was much larger and had a curved, as opposed to vee, windscreen. 20 examples were built. The large treadle-type accelerator pedal with which left-hand drive cars were fitted can be clearly seen in the interior photo.*

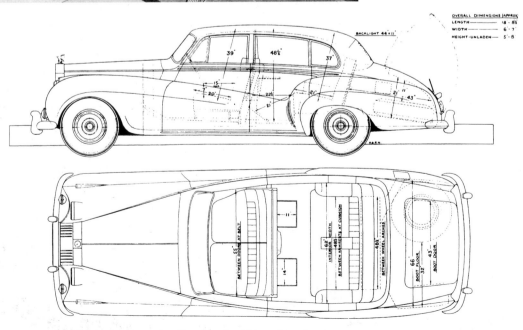

I. MULLINER & CO. LTD.
CHISWICK, LONDON W.4

ROLLS-ROYCE SILVER WRAITH SPORTS LIMOUSINE
ALL METAL CONSTRUCTION

DRG. No. 7348

Top right & below right *The long wheelbase Silver Wraith chassis was particularly well suited to seven-seater limousine coachwork. In nearly all cases the opportunity was taken to provide more spacious rear compartments rather than increase the luggage capacity. Park Ward's limousines retained the very rounded outline of their earlier designs, though with front-hinged doors to the driver's compartment, concealed running boards and a more modern wingline. The photograph shows the first design number 408, on chassis ALW5. Only nine examples were built before it was modified, becoming design number 551, to suit a change to the chassis layout introduced from chassis BLW39 in mid-1953. This involved mounting the radiator four inches further forward. The artist's impression shows design number 551 with the optional R.100 headlamps.*

Below, left & right *From the 'E' series, the design number changed to 704 to suit the Silver Cloud-style bumpers and lighting – though the Silver Cloud rear lights were not adopted for this design and, as shown by the photograph below right, taken outside the Park Ward offices in Willesden, R.100 headlamps were still sometimes fitted in lieu of the standard built-ins, seen on the car below left. At the same time, the boot and rear window were enlarged. 36 examples of design number 704 were built.*

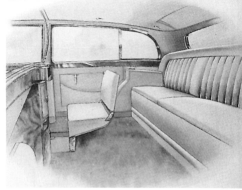

Above, below & opposite *The interior of the Park Ward design number 408, 551 and 704 limousines changed little over the seven year period in which they were built. The photo above and below and the artist's impression opposite show the standard rear compartment layout, with forward-facing occasional seats and a small central cocktail cabinet, while the photograph below shows a more elaborate cabinet incorporating an 'EKCO' television set.*

Below *H. J. Mulliner's first offering on the long wheelbase chassis – and indeed the first use of that chassis by any coachbuilder – was design number 7276, a seven-passenger limousine, the first of which appeared on chassis ALW1 in January 1952. 46 were built on 'A' and 'B' series chassis. This photograph, taken by the author in Los Angeles in 1990, shows a left-hand drive example, chassis LALW30. It is interesting to note that what I have been terming the Silver Cloud-type bumper/overrider design actually began to appear on Nth. American export Silver Wraiths (and on Bentley Continentals) some two years before the Silver Cloud's introduction! Note the Hooper-style rear quarter-light.*

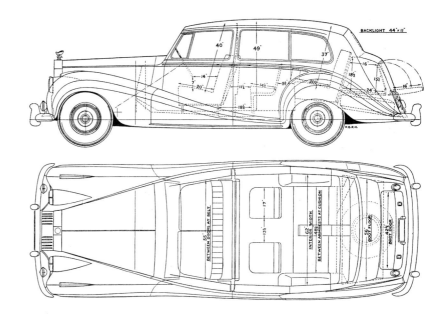

This page *Commencing with chassis LBLW53, H. J. Mulliner's seven-passenger limousine design shared the waist-down panelwork with their design number 7356 touring limousine. This was design number 7358, of which 33 were built. The interior decor was typically H. J. Mulliner. Note the forward-facing occasional seats made possible by the long wheelbase chassis.*

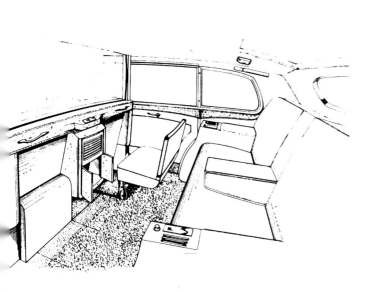

Top left & below *James Young, too, were able to adapt their touring limousine designs to offer – for the first time – a seven-passenger configuration. This was design number WRM35S, of which 15 were built on 'E' series and later long wheelbase chassis. The origins of the same firm's superb Phantom V designs which were to follow were very evident in this design while the slim, chrome-plated door window frames and low roof-line helped avoid the tall, heavy appearance with which Mulliner's design number 7358 was afflicted.*

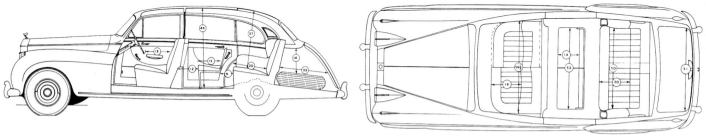

Left & bottom left *The styling of seven-passenger limousines was nearly always more formal and conservative than the same coachbuilder's touring limousines and saloons. Nowhere was this more evident than in the case of Hooper. On this and the following pages we see that firm's seven passenger limousine offerings on the Silver Wraith long wheelbase chassis, design numbers 8330, 8400 and 8469, all of which were similar. Above left is one of several early 'B' series left-hand drive cars of design number 8330 built for Her Majesty's Ambassadors abroad. Bottom left is another ambassadorial car, also design number 8330, on chassis BLW75, built as suitable London transport for H.E. The Nepalese Ambassador to the United Kingdom. The noticeably (4 inches) longer bonnet of cars from chassis BLW39 onwards is discernible when comparing these two photographs.*

Above, above left *The frontal view (above, left) of FLW97, design number 8460, shows the Silver Cloud-type 'standing' (as opposed to 'kneeling') mascot, bumper overriders, built-in headlamps and foglights fitted from the 'E' series onwards, while the more imposing R.100 headlamps with which many, if not most, of these Hooper seven-seaters were fitted, are shown in the artist's impression (above, right).*

Right *The rear compartment of ALW23, the first example built of design number 8330. Cloth upholstery was standard for these Hooper seven-seater limousines. The controls for the radio can be seen in the right-hand armrest. The interior door handle and window winder set in the rather slab-like timber door cappings is typically Hooper.*

Below *This is ELW11, Hooper design number 8400 seven-passenger limousine, built for Radio & Allied Industries and exhibited on the Rolls-Royce stand at Earls Court in 1955. Note the twin radio aerials and bulky early two-way radio equipment fitted in the boot. A far cry from today's cellular telephones!*

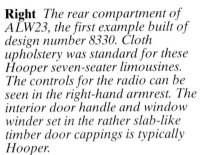

Top left & below *Two long wheelbase Silver Wraith designs by Freestone & Webb, sharing a somewhat bizarre wingline. The rather hearse-like eight-seater limousine top left is one of two built to design number 3225. The first of these, FLW25, was seen under construction in an article on Freestones in* The Autocar, *August 17th, 1956, in which it was described as 'an outsize nine-seater'. It was subsequently exhibited on the coachbuilder's stand at the 1956 Earls Court Motor Show. A further example was built on chassis HLW11. The fixed head coupé left was their design number 3183, a one-off, on chassis CLW39.*

Left *Prince Saoud of Saudi Arabia commissioned his favoured coachbuilder Franay to build this roomy sedanca de ville body on left-hand drive long wheelbase Silver Wraith chassis LELW31. It was a star exhibit at the 1952 Paris Salon des Automobiles.*

Bottom left *James Young really only started building sedanca de ville coachwork when the other coachbuilders were giving it up – and then only in very small numbers. An obvious derivative of their contemporary long wheelbase touring limousine, this is LDLW105, one of 3 built to design number WRM27. The photo was taken at the coachbuilder's photographer's favourite photographic location near the Bromley works.*

Top right & middle *Landaulette coachwork was very rare after World War II. However, Park Ward built eight examples on long wheelbase Silver Wraith chassis – two of design number 558, which was a landaulette variant of the seven-passenger limousine design number 704, and a further six of design number 727, derived from the later limousine design 704. The subject of our photograph (above) is the later design, 727, with 'E' series and later fittings. Below is BLW92, design number 8403, a landaulette on the long wheelbase chassis by Hooper. It was built for the Governor of Singapore and was subsequently owned by* Royal Rolls-Royce Motor Cars *author, the late Andrew Pastouna. Two further landaulettes were built by Hooper to design number 8445.*

Below *Any open coachwork on a Silver Wraith chassis is rare, particularly the long wheelbase chassis. This is a one-off 7-passenger cabriolet with division by H. J. Mulliner, design number 7347, on 1953 chassis LBLW37. It was built for Marshal Tito of Yugoslavia and 'presented by the people of Slovenia'. Photographed by Klaus-Josef Roßfeldt in Slovenia, July 1993.*

Top left *HLW47, one of two cars with Hooper 'Allweather' coachwork, design number 8548, which were delivered to the Commonwealth of Australia government as part of a batch of six long wheelbase Silver Wraiths with consecutive chassis numbers (HLW45 to HLW50). HLW47 and its companion Allweather, HLW49, were used by various members of the Royal Family when visiting Australia. Only one other car was built to this design, on the penultimate Silver Wraith chassis LHLW51, for H.H. The Emperor of Ethiopia.*

Left *HLW47. The front interior photo shows that the variable ride control lever on the steering wheel boss had given way to a Silver Cloud-type switch on the side of the steering column by this final Silver Wraith series.*

Below *Whilst Hooper's formal coachwork was usually very sober – to the point of being downright staid – their open coachwork was often much more flamboyant, like this cabriolet on chassis ALW11 for Nubar Gulbenkian. Note the metal cover under which the hood completely disappears and the Perspex covers over the headlights in the noses of the wings.*

Opposite page, top *Park Ward records indicate that they built eight long wheelbase drophead coupés – one design number 547, three design number 571 of which this is one on chassis DLW149, and four design number 705, which incorporated the 'E' series modifications.*

ROLLS-ROYCE
SILVER WRAITH

		Basic Price	Purchase Tax			Total Price		
CHASSIS		£2,695	£674	8	6	£3,369	8	6
TOURING SALOON	(Coachwork by Park Ward & Co. Ltd.)	£5,270	£2,636	7	0	£7,906	7	0
SEVEN PASSENGER LIMOUSINE	(Coachwork by Park Ward & Co. Ltd.)	£5,570	£2,786	7	0	£8,356	7	0
TOURING LIMOUSINE	(Coachwork by Hooper & Co. Ltd.)	£5,395	£2,698	17	0	£8,093	17	0
SEVEN PASSENGER LIMOUSINE	(Coachwork by Hooper & Co. Ltd.)	£5,570	£2,786	7	0	£8,356	7	0
TOURING LIMOUSINE	(Coachwork by H. J. Mulliner & Co. Ltd.)	£5,380	£2,691	7	0	£8,071	7	0
FOUR DOOR SALOON	(Coachwork by James Young Ltd.)	£5,445	£2,723	17	0	£8,168	17	0
Power assisted steering is available on these cars at extra cost		£110	£55	0	0	£165	0	0

ROLLS-ROYCE LTD · 14-15 CONDUIT STREET · LONDON W.I
Telephone: Mayfair 6201   Telegrams: "Rolhead Piccy, London"   Works: Crewe, Cheshire

The specification and prices are subject to alteration without notice.

May, 1957.

Chapter Three

The Standard Steel Saloon, the Coachbuilt alternative and the Continental

Bentley Mk VI & R-type, Rolls-Royce Silver Dawn

'Make a mental list of the world's fine automobiles – French, Italian, American, anything – and ask yourself this simple question: Could I, after driving 600 miles or more from home base to race venue, cruising at eighties and nineties for hours at a stretch in the process, could I willingly and zestfully set myself, the same evening, to thrash the same car around a completely unfamiliar circuit for further hours at a stretch? Yes, and enjoy it. To say that I have done this, and hope to do it again, implies no personal boast; any fit and habitually fast driver could do it, and go to bed without an ache in his body, on any saloon Bentley that had Rolls-Royce craftsmanship behind it.'

– from *My Ten Bentleys* by Raymond Mays, describing his experiences with his Mk VI Standard Steel Saloon, the tenth of a succession of Bentleys which he owned and enjoyed throughout his distinguished racing career.

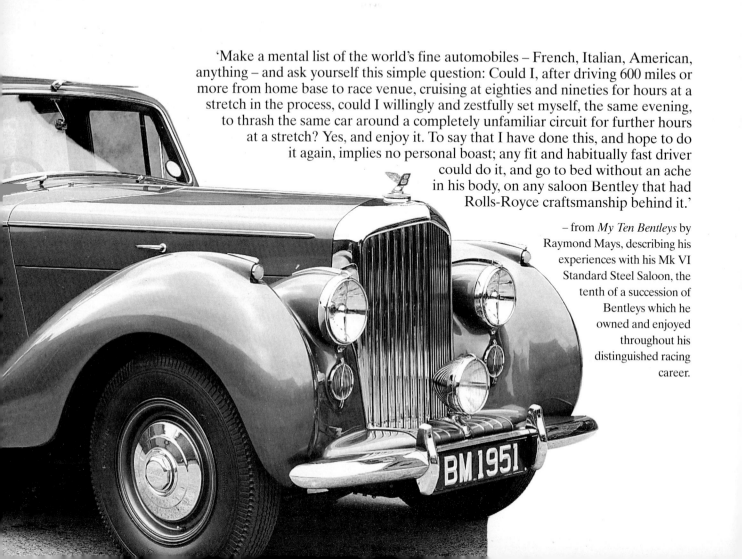

After the war, considerable doubt surrounded the capacity of the surviving coachbuilders, using their traditional, leisurely methods – applying hand-formed aluminium panels to seasoned ash, composite or all-metal body frames – to turn out bodies in sufficient numbers to fulfil the Company's intention of greatly increasing the volume of motor car output. Advanced metalworking techniques developed by Rolls-Royce Ltd's own coachbuilding subsidiary Park Ward, resulted in patent number 470698 being obtained in 1935 to cover the Park Ward all-steel body frame. However, even this construction method could do little more than slightly increase the capacity of one coachbuilder and came nowhere near offering the means to meet the volume envisaged and ultimately achieved.

This emphasis on increasing output was the keystone of post-war Rolls-Royce motor car policy and was an essential requirement if the Rolls-Royce car was to survive. An approach was made to the Pressed Steel Company of Oxford to examine the feasibility of a standardised pressed steel body. The cost of tooling alone came out at around a quarter of a million pounds, which may not sound like a large sum today, but this was 1945 and it meant that some 5,000 standardised cars would need to be built and sold to render the project economic. This appeared not only to cut across the very individuality and exclusiveness that had always characterised Rolls-Royce cars and contributed in no small measure to their appeal to the class of buyer at which they were aimed, but also to set a production target that had never been equalled by any previous model other than the Silver Ghost – which had been produced over a twenty year production run. There was some boardroom opposition including, it is said, a certain amount from Managing Director

Arthur Sidgreaves to the proposed styling, but the writing was on the wall and the bold step was taken.

The first standard steel saloon was designed by the Company's coachwork designers Bill Allen and Ivan Evernden, the latter of whom had also been responsible for a number of 1930s body styles – in fact his work in coachwork design can be traced back to the range of 'standard' bodies offered by Barker & Co. on the Twenty Horsepower chassis in the 1920s. Several subtle Park Ward features were evident in the standard steel saloon design and the resulting car was quite striking – even if it could be argued that it fell short of being beautiful. While no pre-war Rolls-Royce or Bentley, other than the experimental Vanvooren-bodied 'Corniche' Bentley, had built-in headlights, the styling mock-up presented to the board for approval boldly sported headlamps that were stylishly flared into the front wings, which were teardrop-shaped and did not follow the pre-war norm of flowing back under the doors to form running boards.

The assembly, finishing and interior trimming of the standard steel saloons were all carried out at Crewe to a very high standard, equal in all respects to the best coachbuilders' work. Upholstery was in the finest Connolly hide, the carpets were top quality Wilton edged with leather and the headlining was West of England woollen broadcloth – all traditional coachbuilders' materials. The fascia, door cappings and little luxuries like the vanity mirrors (or 'companions') in the rear quarters were all finished in beautiful figured walnut veneer in the best coachbuilding tradition. All this work was carried out by hand by highly skilled craftsmen and no effort was spared to ensure that the standard saloon would withstand the most critical comparison with ele-

gant and luxurious coachbuilt cars. As related in Chapter One, the only flaw in the entire concept lay in the indifferent and even downright poor quality of early post-war sheet steel, which if allowed to rust would do so with disconcerting speed. The protective processes by which the ravages of rust in motor car bodies may be prevented, or at least minimised, were less than fully understood in those days and though Rolls-Royce took rather more care than other manufacturers, considerable numbers of early standard steel cars succumbed.

At first, the standard steel saloon bodies were only fitted to the Bentley Mk VI chassis, the first complete car being delivered in September 1946. The Mk VI differed from the Rolls-Royce Silver Wraith in having a shorter wheelbase (10ft), smaller wheels (16in) and a higher performance engine (twin S.U. carburetters and, at first, a high-lift camshaft). The third production Mk VI chassis (B6AK) was the first to be fitted with standard steel saloon coachwork. A total of 4,188 of the 5,200 Mk VI chassis were so fitted. In addition, all but 14 of the Rolls-Royce Silver Dawns to the end of the 'D' series (280 cars) carried the same coachwork, though with a modified bonnet to match the Rolls-Royce radiator.

The Silver Dawn was originally contrived as a means by which greater market penetration could be achieved in North America, where the Bentley marque was less well known than Rolls-Royce. Although attempts had been made to sell the Silver Wraith in that market, it was not offered with left-hand drive until 1949 (nor, for that matter, was the Bentley Mk VI).

In 1947 four Silver Wraiths and three Mk VIs, one of which was a standard steel saloon, were despatched on a 20,000 mile 'show the flag' exhibition tour of the United States, but the fact that all seven cars were right-hand drive could only have detracted from the otherwise excellent impression that such magnificent cars must have created. The days when right-hand drive on the finest quality cars was accepted, even expected, were long gone. Despite this, Rolls-Royce had not offered a car with left-hand drive since the special run of AJS and AMS series Phantom II chassis between 1931 and 1934. Moreover, none of the small horsepower models nor the Bentleys had ever been available with left-hand drive, being offered instead on a seemingly 'take it or leave it' basis. This attitude would no longer do in the post-war world and Rolls-Royce could no more ignore the calls to 'export or perish' than any other British firm. Export earnings were vital and the United States was (and remains) easily the most important export market. Market research indicated that although the standard steel saloon was somewhat smaller than the cars Americans were accustomed to, it was the most acceptable form of coachwork for that market. However, if Americans were going to pay $14,000 for a car built by Rolls-Royce they wanted the name Rolls-Royce on it and not Bentley.

The answer, introduced in April 1949, was a Rolls-Royce version of the Mk VI called the Silver Dawn and built at first for export only. The Silver Wraith version of the 4,257cc engine was used – i.e. with a single Stromberg carburetter in lieu of the twin S.U.s of the Bentley. The Silver Dawn's radiator shell was a new design with, for the first time on a Rolls-Royce, fixed 'shutters' – 22 in number – with coolant temperature regulation by thermostatic by-pass arrangement as on the Bentley.

Other than the change of appearance from Bentley to Rolls-Royce the standard steel coachwork remained externally unchanged. Some consideration was given to altering the scuttle shape to suit the Rolls-Royce bonnet and a prototype was built to evaluate the proposal, but baulking at the £100,000 quoted by Pressed Steel to tool up for this, the Company opted instead for the expedient of a bonnet top which changed in profile from front to rear to accommodate the transition from Rolls-Royce radiator to Bentley scuttle. Twin fog lamps as on export Bentleys, and export-type bumpers were standard on all Silver Dawns.

The interior of the Silver Dawn standard steel saloon was similar to that of the Bentley except that the fascia was laid out in the Silver Wraith fashion, with the instruments and switches grouped around a centrally mounted speedometer and with the classic 'switchbox' adjacent to the steering column. With left-hand steering came Rolls-Royce's interpretation of steering column gearchange – a feature to which most American motorists were by that time accustomed. This was beautifully engineered in an effort to ensure that no lost movement developed in the somewhat complicated linkages over long periods of use. At the same time, left-hand drive was also made available on the Silver Wraith and Bentley. Curiously, left-hand drive versions of the Bentley Mk VI conformed to Rolls-Royce engine specification – i.e. with Stromberg carburetter – possibly in order to rationalise spare parts stocks in the U.S.A. and Canada. It is worth pointing out that not all Silver Dawns were built with left-hand drive, even before the model became generally available on the home market – a considerable number had right-hand drive for such valuable export markets as Australia.

From the 'C' series of 1951 ('M' series in the case of the Bentley) the 3⅝ inch bore, 4,566cc engine was introduced. Right-hand drive Bentleys with this engine had a more efficient dual exhaust system with tailpipes emerging at each rear corner of the car. In 1952 the Silver Dawn and Bentley chassis were extended rearwards to accommodate new 'long boot' standard steel saloon coachwork. This change took effect from the 'E' series Silver Dawn (chassis SKE2) and 'R' series Bentley (chassis B2RT) – hence the retrospectively adopted model designation Bentley R-type, although it was initially described in the motoring press by the factory designation 'B7'. With this change came the option, for export only at first, of the automatic gearbox – a development of which, more anon. Other chassis changes included modifications to the rear suspension to take account of the longer overhang and increased luggage carrying capacity. The rear springs were longer and wider, with a reduced number of leaves, and the rear shackle bracket position was altered to bring the shackle eyes above the chassis rail. A new aluminium fuel tank of revised shape allowed the spare wheel to be stowed as low and as far forward as possible. All R-type Bentleys, including those with left-hand drive, had twin S.U. carburetters, but now with an automatic cold starting device consisting of a butterfly strangler between the air intake silencer and the carburetters operated by a temperature sensitive bi-metallic strip located in the water heated induction manifold, and a fast idle cam to provide for a suitably fast idle when the engine was cold. This enabled both the mixture and hand throttle controls to be eliminated from the steering wheel centre – leaving only the ride control lever. The Silver Dawn, together with other models fitted with the Stromberg (and later Zenith) carburetter, had an automatic cold starting device from its inception.

The new 'long boot' standard steel coachwork remained unchanged up to a point just behind the centre pillar, but was largely new aft of that point. The task of redesigning the tail fell to John Blatchley, who had been Gurney Nutting's chief designer from 1936 until 1939, when he joined Rolls-Royce Ltd. The swage line at the waist, instead of turning sharply forwards and downwards to follow the leading edge of the rear wing as on the 'short boot' body, was carried right through to the tail. The rear wings were extended rearwards and given a new swage line and a lower wheel arch without the detachable spat. The new luggage boot lid was of aluminium alloy and was hinged on its upper edge with torsion bars to make the lid self-supporting. Luggage capacity, with the lid fully closed, was increased to a useful 17.4 cubic feet, which sounds rather less useful when translated to 0.49 cubic metres! The result, both from an aesthetic and a practical point of view was most satisfactory. Only 50 'E' series and later Silver Dawns and 283 R-type Bentleys had coachbuilt bodies, the remainder being 'long boot' standard steel saloons.

The automatic gearbox, at first available for export only, was introduced concurrently with the long boot coachwork and was derived from the contemporary General Motors 'Hydra-Matic', which was chosen by Rolls-Royce as the best then available. The first 100 gearboxes were bought in from Detroit and carried plates bearing the words 'G. M. Detroit Transmission Division – Built for Rolls-Royce Ltd.' Later, production of the automatic gearbox commenced at Crewe and it was then offered as an option on the home market. An extension on the rear of the gearbox carried the friction disc brake servo and the ride control pump.

The combination of General Motors-type automatic gearbox and Rolls-Royce range selector was a considerable improvement over other automatic transmission systems of the time, firstly in having four forward speeds and secondly in giving the driver the facility to make manual changes when desired – and particularly in enabling second gear to be held for engine braking on steep descents. In those days of the fluid coupling, as opposed to the more efficient torque converter, an adequate number of forward speeds was important. It is noteworthy that the 1992 Rolls-Royce and Bentley cars again have a four-speed transmission, though for entirely different reasons and with an overdrive fourth gear. The selector lever, mounted on the steering column, had five positions marked N, 4, 3, 2 and R. With '4' selected, the gearbox worked automatically through all four forward gears, while '3' allowed it to change only up to third (unless a speed of approximately 60mph was exceeded, in which case top gear came in as a safety measure to prevent over-revving). In position '2', first and second gears only were available (second only in later versions), with no safety up-change override.

The automatic gearbox was, of course, available on the Silver Wraith as well as on the Silver Dawn and Bentley R-type.

A very special coachbuilt model was the Bentley Continental – nowadays known as the R-type Continental to distinguish it from the later S-type versions and indeed from the current cars with the Continental appellation. The Continental chassis differed from the standard in having higher gearing, higher compression ratio, more efficient large bore exhaust system, lower scuttle and steering column, a different shaped fuel tank and modified suspension. The coachwork, too,

was very special indeed. H. J. Mulliner & Co. were commissioned to build the sleek two-door sports saloon bodies to the requirements of Rolls-Royce's Belper styling team, led by John Blatchley.

Some of the features of the body design resulted from extensive wind-tunnel testing at the Company's Hucknall Flight Establishment. The rear wings, for example, were designed to achieve the maximum degree of lateral stability at high speed while the windscreen was exceptionally heavily curved, the tests having shown that it was desirable to have a slip angle at the windscreen pillars as near to 45 degrees as possible. This was difficult to achieve at the time in safety glass and the prototype had a two-piece windscreen for that reason.

The model designation Continental was applied to variants of two Rolls-Royce models before the War but has been reserved exclusively for Bentleys post-war. The concept of a Bentley sports saloon with higher than standard performance is also a pre-war one. The Bentley Corniche was an experimental Mk V with a streamlined four-door body by Vanvooren of Paris and displayed styling traits that would have been regarded with less than universal approval had they been repeated after the War, particularly the absence of a traditional Bentley radiator. On the other hand, it was essential that the Continental be sleek and sporting in appearance. Significantly, the early drawings and works memoranda dealing with the Continental referred to it as 'Corniche II'. The principal features of the Mulliner Continental coachwork were wind-cheating shape and light weight, with the latter attribute progressively sacrificed in favour of heavy bumpers, larger seats and other creature comforts and, later on, automatic transmission. On the earliest examples even the seat frames and bumpers were of aluminium. The 4,887cc engine introduced for the 'D' series was intended to compensate for the weight gains.

As a high performance car the Continental could scarcely have been a greater success. It was, in fact, the fastest genuine four-seater car in the world at the time. Maximum speed, at around 120 mph, was higher than the tyres available at the time could reasonably have been expected to cope with and rapid tyre wear was a problem. Acceleration, with the high gearing used, was much the same as that of the standard Bentley to around 60mph, but once the Continental got into its stride most other performance cars of the period were out-classed. Speeds in excess of 50, 80 and 100 mph were possible on the indirects which means that it was possible to comfortably exceed today's motorway speed limit in second gear!

Put simply, the Bentley R-type Continental is one of the great classic motor cars of all time and certainly one of the most sought after of the post-war period. Today they are highly prized collectors' items, particularly the early, lighter examples with the delightful synchromesh gearbox.

TECHNICAL SPECIFICATION

Bentley Mk VI/R-type & Rolls-Royce Silver Dawn

Engine

Dimensions
Six cylinders in line.
Bentley A to L series and Silver Dawn A and B series: Bore 3.5 inches (89mm), stroke 4.5 inches (114mm), cubic capacity 260 cu. in. (4,257cc)

Bentley M series onwards, Silver Dawn C series onwards and Bentley Continental A to C series: Bore 3.625 inches (92mm), stroke 4.5 inches (114mm), cubic capacity 278.6 cu. in.(4,566cc)
Bentley Continental D series onwards: Bore 3.75 inches (95.25mm), stroke 4.5 inches (114mm), cubic capacity 298.2 cu. in. (4,887cc)
Compression ratio 6.4:1 (from Bentley R-type chassis B93TO and Silver Dawn chassis SMF62 onwards 6.75:1, Bentley Continental to chassis BC18A 7.27:1, BC19A to BC3C 7.1:1, BC4C onwards 7.2:1).

Cylinder block/Crankcase
Iron monobloc casting. 1948: 30% chrome iron liners at tops of bores.

Crankshaft
1% chrome molybdenum steel (EN.19) nitrided. Bolt-on balance weights. Seven main bearings of copper-lead-indium.

Pistons
Aluminium alloy (RR.53) tin plated. Granodised piston rings, one compression, one L-section and one slotted oil control ring.

Cylinder head
Aluminium alloy (RR.50) with inserted valve seats.

Valve gear
Overhead inlet, side exhaust valves. Exhaust valves in KE.965. Stellite coated seats and tips. Camshaft driven by helical gears.

Carburetter
Right-hand drive Bentley to chassis B81HP twin S.U. type H.4 (1½" bore).
Right-hand drive Bentley from chassis B83HP onwards: twin S.U. type H.6 (1¾" bore).
Left-hand drive Bentley A to P series and Silver Dawn to chassis SFC100: Stromberg dual downdraught carburetter with accelerator pump and automatic choke.

Silver Dawn from chassis SFC102 onwards: single Zenith downdraught carburetter with accelerator pump and automatic choke.
Bentley from R series onwards: twin S.U. type H.6 (1¾" bore) with automatic choke.
Bentley Continental A to C series: twin S.U. type H.6 (1¾" bore), all but the first few cars with automatic choke.
Bentley Continental D and E series: twin S.U. type HD.8 (2" bore) with automatic choke.
Water heated hot spot. Bentley Mk VI, very early Bentley Continental and Silver Dawn A to D series had a hand throttle control on steering wheel boss. Air intake silencer incorporating mesh air filter element (oil bath type air cleaner on cars for use in dusty conditions.)

Ignition system
Ignition by high tension coil and Delco-Remy distributor with twin contact breaker points. Early cars were fitted with a spare coil for emergency use. Firing order 1,4,2,6,3,5

Lubrication system
Helical gear oil pump in crankcase driven by skew gear from camshaft. Floating oil intake in sump incorporating gauze strainer. By-pass filter on side of cylinder block. Pressure relief valve incorporating high and low pressure feeds. High pressure to the main and big-end bearings, camshaft bearings and skew gear drive to oil pump and distributor, low pressure to valve gear and timing gears. Sump capacity 16 pints (2.4 U.S. gallons, 9 litres). Bentley M series onwards, Silver Dawn C series onwards and all Bentley Continentals, full-flow oil filter.

Cooling system
Fixed radiator shutters. Thermostat on front of engine with radiator by-pass to give quickest possible warm-up from cold. Belt driven centrifugal coolant pump and fan.

Chassis

Dimensions

Overall length, Bentley Mk VI, Wilmot Breeden bumpers 15' 11½" (4,864mm)
Overall length, Bentley Mk VI and Silver Dawn A to D series, Pyrene bumpers 16' 4½" (4,991mm)
Overall length, Bentley R-type, Wilmot Breeden bumpers 16' 7½" (5,067mm)
Overall length, Bentley R-type and Silver Dawn E series onwards, Pyrene bumpers 16' 11½" (5,169mm)
Overall length, Bentley R-type and Silver dawn E series onwards, heavy export bumpers 17' 6" (5,334mm)
Overall length, Bentley Continental, early type bumpers 17' 2½" (5,245mm)
Overall length, Bentley Continental, heavy export bumpers 17' 7½" (5,372mm)
Wheelbase 10' (3,048mm)
Front track 4' 8½" (1,435mm)
Rear track 4' 10½" (1,486mm)

Frame

Channel section frame of riveted (from Bentley R-type chassis B349TO onwards and Silver Dawn F series onwards, welded) construction with cruciform centre bracing. Box section pan to support front suspension components.

Suspension

Front: independent by coil springs and rubber bushed wishbones, double acting hydraulic dampers and anti-roll bar.
Rear: semi-elliptic leaf springs protected by leather gaiters. Controllable hydraulic dampers by an oil pump mounted on the gearbox and an overriding control on the steering wheel boss.

Steering

Marles type cam and roller. Fore and aft side steering tube (drag link) to centre steering lever pivoted on front chassis cross member and two-piece cross steering tube (track rod). Turns lock to lock, 3½.

Transmission

Four forward speeds and reverse. Right-hand change (column change on left-hand drive cars). Synchromesh on second, third and top gears.
Ratios: Top 1:1, Third 1.34:1, Second 2.02:1, First 2.98:1, Reverse 3.15:1.
Single dry-plate, centrifugally assisted clutch.
Optional from left-hand drive Bentley chassis B2RT, right-hand drive Bentley chassis B2SR, Silver Dawn SKE2 and Bentley Continental chassis BC1D onwards and standard from left-hand drive Bentley chassis B1TO, right-hand drive Bentley chassis B2WH and Silver Dawn chassis SMF2: Rolls-Royce 4-speed automatic gearbox and fluid coupling, with selector mounted on the right of the steering column.
Ratios: Top 1:1, Third 1.45:1, Second 2.63:1, First 3.82:1, Reverse 4.3:1.
Two-piece propeller shaft with needle roller bearing universal joints and centre bearing.
Rear axle: semi-floating type with hypoid gears. Ratio, Bentley A to X series and 3.727:1, optional from Bentley chassis B445SP and standard from Y series and Silver Dawn chassis SRH2 onwards 3.416:1, Bentley Continental 3.077:1.

Brakes

Hydraulic front, mechanical rear. Operation by means of friction disc servo on the offside of the gearbox, which applies the front brakes through a Lockheed master cylinder and assists the application of the rear brakes. Handbrake on rear wheels by pull-out handle under right side of fascia through a cable and mechanical linkage.

Exhaust system

Bentley A to L series, Silver Dawn A to G series, left-hand drive M to P series and Bentley Continental single pipe system with two lagged expansion boxes. Right-hand drive Bentley M series onwards, all Bentleys from R series and Silver Dawn H series onwards twin system with four lagged expansion boxes.

Centralised lubrication system

All bearings in the steering and suspension systems, including the rear spring main leaf and shackles, fed with oil from a reservoir and pump mounted on the bulkhead in the engine compartment. Pump

Firts

	Chassis	Year
Bentley Mk VI chassis	B2AK	1946
Bentley Mk VI standard steel saloon	B6AK	1946
Silver Dawn	SBA2	1949
Left-hand drive Bentley Mk VI	B485CD	1949
4,566cc litre Bentley Mk VI	B2MD	1951
4,566cc litre Bentley Mk VI standard steel saloon	B62MD	1951
4,566cc litre Silver Dawn	SFC2	1951
Silver Dawn with Zenith carburetter	LSFC102	1952
Bentley R-type	B2RT	1952
Bentley R-type standard steel saloon	B20RT	1952
'Long Boot' Silver Dawn	SKE2	1952
Availability of automatic gearbox (export)	B16RT, SKE2	1952
Bentley Continental	BC1A	1952
Welded chassis frame	B349TO, SNF1	1953
Availability of automatic gearbox (home)	B134TN	1953
Silver Dawn with twin exhaust system	SRH2	1954
Bentley Continental with 3¾" bore (4,887cc) engine	BC1D	1954

operated by a pedal under the fascia, to be operated once every 100 miles (160 km).

Fuel system
Rear mounted petrol tank, capacity 18 gallons (21.6 U.S. gallons, 81.8 litres). S.U. dual fuel pump mounted in the frame. Filter between tank and pump.

Electrical system
12 volt positive earth system with 55 amp/hour battery. Lucas special equipment dynamo and starter motor with reduction gearing and gentle-engagement pinion. Lucas built-in headlamps. Lucas centre lamp (twin Lucas fog lamps began to appear on export cars from 1948 and were standard on Silver Dawns and Bentley Continentals). Medium wave/Long wave Radiomobile radio with push-button tuning and two speakers. Direction indicator switch on the fascia capping rail. Hot water type interior heater under the front passenger's seat with electric blower. Heated rear window fitted from Bentley chassis B311NY and Silver Dawn chassis SFC94.

Other accessories
Trico vacuum operated windscreen washer.

Road wheels and tyres
16 inch steel disc well-base wheels, on five studs, carrying 6.50 x 16 India tyres. Tyre pressures, Bentley Mk VI and Silver Dawn A to D series, front 25 lb/sq. in., rear 30 lb/sq. in., Bentley R-type and Silver Dawn E series onwards, front 24 lb/sq. in., rear 33 lb/sq. in.

Coachwork

Standard steel four-door factory saloon bodies fitted to 4,188 Bentley Mk VI, 2,037 Bentley R-type and 697 Silver Dawn chassis. All steel construction (aluminium boot lid on 'long boot' cars, i.e. Bentley R-type and Silver Dawn from E series onwards). The remainder were built by the following coachbuilders:

Coachbuilder	Bentley Mk VI	Bentley R-type	Silver Dawn A to D	Silver Dawn E to J	Bentley Continental
H. J. Mulliner	301	67	1	2	193
James Young	209	69	–	11	–
Park Ward	167	50	11	17	6
Freestone & Webb	103	29	–	6	–
Hooper	61	41	–	12	–
Abbott	19	16	–	–	–
Graber	18	7	–	–	3
Vanden Plas	21	–	–	–	–
Gurney Nutting	19	–	–	–	–
Harold Radford*	17	–	–	–	–
Facel Metallon	17	–	–	–	–
Franay	8	2	–	–	5
Pininfarina	5	–	1	–	1
Rippon	5	–	–	–	–
David Joel	5	–	–	–	–
Windovers	4	–	–	–	–
Ramseier†	4	–	–	–	–
Simpson & Slater	2	–	–	–	–
Seary & McReady*	2	–	–	–	–
Kong	2	–	–	–	–
Ghia	1	–	1	–	–
Figoni	1	–	–	–	–
Eadon	1	–	–	–	–
J. A. Holland	1	–	–	–	–
Duncan	1	–	–	–	–
Ronald Kent	1	–	–	–	–
Westminster	1	–	–	–	–
Vincents	1	–	–	–	–
Baker	1	–	–	–	–
Alburnsons	1	–	–	–	–
Saoutchik	1	–	–	–	–
Cooper	1	–	–	–	–
Vanvooren	1	–	–	–	–
Denby	1	–	–	–	–
Mulliner (Birmingham)	1	–	–	–	–
Beutler	1	–	–	–	–
Chapron	–	–	–	1	–
Others	7	2	–	1	–
Totals	1,012	283	14	50	208‡

* Harold Radford fully coachbuilt 'Countryman' saloons were built to order by Seary & McReady, a firm in which Harold Radford had a financial interest. Figures for Harold Radford do not include their well known adaptations of standard steel saloons nor the two cars which bore Seary & McReady sill-plates and which are listed separately.
† The name of the firm Fritz Ramseier & Co. of Berne was later changed to Carrosserie Worblaufen.
‡ Including experimental car 9BVI, later renumbered BC26A.

Chassis and engine numbers

Bentley Mk VI
Chassis series and sub-series starting with 1 use odd number only, those starting with 2 use even numbers only. Engines are numbered consecutively. The number 13 was omitted from chassis numbering.

Series	Chassis numbers	Engine numbers
A	B2AK-B254AK*, B1AJ-B247A	B1A-B250A
B	B2BH-B400BH, B1BG-B401BG	B1B-B400B
C	B2CF-B500CF, B1CD-B501CD	B1C-B500C
D	B2DA-B500DA, B1DZ-B501DZ	B1D-B500D
E	B2EY-B500EY, B1EW-B501EW	B1E-B500E
F	B2FV-B500FV, B1FU-B601FU	B1F-B550F
G	B1GT-B401GT	B1G-B200G
H	B2HR-B250HR, B1HP-B251HP	B1H-B250H
J	B2JO-B250JO, B1JN-B251JN	B1J-B250J
K	B2KM-B200KM, B1KL-B201KL	B1K-B200K
L	B2LJ-B400LJ, B1LH-B401LH	B1L-B400L
M	B2MD-B400MD, B1MB-B401MB*	B1M-B400M
N	B2NZ-B500NZ, B1NY-B501NY	B1N-B500N
P	B2PV-B300PV, B1PU-B301PU	B1P-B300P

Total: 5,202 cars.

* Plus experimental cars 1BVI and 4BVI, later renumbered B256AK and B403MB respectively.

Bentley R-type
Chassis series and sub-series starting with 1 use odd number only, those starting with 2 use even numbers only. Engines are numbered consecutively. The number 13 was omitted from chassis numbering.

Series	Chassis numbers	Engine numbers
R	B2RT-B120RT*, B1RS-B121RS	B1R-B120R
S	B2SR-B500SR, B1SP-B501SP	B1S-B500S
T	B1TO-B401TO, B2TN-B600TN	B1T-B500T
U	B1UL-B251UL, B2UM-B250UM	B1U-B250U
W	B2WH-B300WH, B1WG-B301WG	B1W-B300W
X	B2XF-B140XF	B1X-B70X
Y	B1YA-B331YA, B2YD-B330YD	B1Y-B330Y
Z	B1ZX-B251ZX, B2ZY-B250ZY	B1Z-B250Z

Total: 2,322 cars.

* Plus experimental cars 12BVII and 14BVII, later renumbered B124XRT and B122XRT respectively.

Bentley R-type Continental
Chassis and engines are numbered consecutively, omitting 13 from chassis numbering.

Series	Chassis numbers	Engine numbers
A	BC1A-BC25A*	BCA1-24
B	BC1B-BC25B	BCB1-24
C	BC1C-BC78C	BCC1-77
D	BC1D-BC74D	BCD1-73
E	BC1E-BC9E	BCE1-9

Total: 208 cars.

* Plus experimental car 9BVI, later renumbered BC26A.

Silver Dawn
Chassis series and sub-series starting with 1 use odd number only, those starting with 2 use even numbers only. Engines are numbered consecutively. The number 13 was omitted from chassis numbering.

Series	Chassis numbers	Engine numbers
A	SBA2-138, SCA1-63	S1A-S100A
B	SDB2-140	S1B-S70B
C	SFC2-160	S1C-S80C
D	SHD2-60	S1D-S30D
E	SKE2-50, SLE1-51	S1E-S50E
F	SMF2-76, SNF1-125	S1F-S100F
G	SOG2-100, SPG1-101	S1G-S100G
H	SRH2-100, STH1-101	S1H-S100H
J	SUJ2-130, SVJ1-133	S1J-S131J

Total: 761 cars.

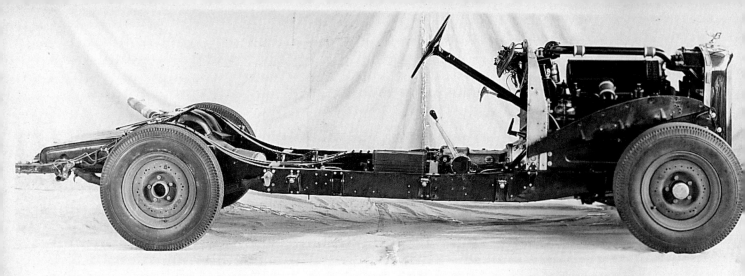

Above *The chassis of the Bentley Mk VI, complete and ready for coachwork to be mounted, either standard steel saloon or coachbuilt. This is a quite late 4,257cc chassis. The engine has the 1¾ inch carburetters fitted from chassis B83HP. The radiator-warmed windscreen demisting system, the ducting for which can be seen above the engine, was fitted from chassis B193DZ.*

Below *The earliest standard steel saloons were relatively plain, with no chrome strip on the waistline. This is B146BH, owned by Tony Davidson (RROCA).*

Left inset *Likewise, the interior of the earliest cars were trimmed in a restrained, almost austere style, with unpleated leather upholstery and no picnic tables behind the front seats. However, only the finest materials were used and the overall effect rivalled the best of the coachbuilders' work.*

Top right *The chromium plated strip at the waistline and rear wheel spats appeared in late 1947. The driver's side front window is shown open and it can be seen that the chrome edge strip between the quarter-light and the actual drop window went down with the glass on these early cars.*

Right *Another 1948 car. This three-quarter rear view shows the razor-edged lines to the wing crowns, rear quarters and boot. The chrome embellisher below the boot handle was introduced at the same time as the waist strip, as were the chrome strips atop the headlight and sidelight fairings. The boot could be secured in the open position and used as a platform for extra luggage, a weather-proof roller shutter protecting the boot contents. The separate compartment below the main lid housed the spare wheel, jack and other road tools.*

Bottom right *The final form of the 4,257cc Mk VI with the later pattern wheel trim discs introduced in 1949. Around the same time a different specification began to emerge for export cars. The heavy export-type bumpers and overriders and the paired foglamps seen here indicate an export car, and left-hand drive became available for the applicable markets. The most likely destination of this car was Australia – easily the biggest export market for right-hand drive Mk VIs and Silver Dawns.*

Left *This view of the rear compartment of a standard steel Mk VI shows that the standard of finish and luxury appointments was comparable to that of most coachbuilt cars. The combination of pleated upholstery with square-section rear side armrests and raised centre panels to the front seats identifies this as a late 1947 to 1948 car. The folding picnic tables and rear footrests were also introduced at this time. The contrasting piping to the upholstery, often seen on motor show cars of the period (of which this was probably one), has enjoyed a revival in popularity in recent years. The mirrors in the rear quarters could be illuminated for night use. Note that the floor is free of all but the merest suggestion of a transmission hump.*

Left & above far left *The Mk VI standard steel saloon front compartment and fascia in close-up. Note the adjustable door armrests, quick-lift driver's window operating handle, the knob above the windscreen for folding the radio aerial parallel to the screen and the handle for opening the sunshine roof – all standard features of these luxurious cars. The sliding control over the driver's side window operated the silk rear window blind while the two knobs on the windscreen capping rail were for manually parking the wipers. These were eliminated with the advent of self-parking wipers in 1952. The lockable tray below the glove compartment housed a selection of small tools and spare bulbs. On the steering wheel boss were controls for the hand throttle (open/closed), mixture (start/run) and ride control (normal/hard).*

Left & far left *A bench seat with folding centre armrest could be fitted in lieu of the standard front bucket seats. This usually came with a single, large folding picnic table for the rear compartment passengers, but occasionally a division was specified, as shown here, for chauffeur driven cars. Normally though, the Mk VI was regarded as very much an owner-driver car.*

Above *The Silver Dawn was contrived as a means to extend the application of standard steel saloon coachwork to the market sector that required a Rolls-Royce car as opposed to a Bentley. The opening vents ahead of the front doors, which replaced a more leak-prone single vent on the scuttle top, identify this example as a 4,566cc car of 1951 or early '52. The Silver Dawn, at least in its earlier short boot form shown here, was sold primarily in export markets, notably the United States, Canada and, with right-hand drive, Australia. All Silver Dawns, regardless of destination country, had twin foglamps and export-type bumpers.* **Inset** *Inside, the Silver Dawn differed from the Bentley Mk VI only in its fascia layout, which conformed to that of the Silver Wraith, with separate gauges grouped around a central speedometer and the ignition/lighting 'switchbox' in front of the driver beside the steering column. Note the column-mounted gearchange lever on the left-hand drive cars. The controls on the steering wheel boss are for the hand throttle and ride control, no mixture control being fitted to Silver Dawns (or left-hand drive Mk VIs) due to the use of a fully automatic Stromberg carburetter on those models.*

Above left & right *The 1951 'M' series Mk VIs saw a ⅛ inch increase in engine bore, giving 4,566cc. These 4½ litre 'big bore' Bentleys, in right-hand drive guise only, could be identified by their twin exhaust system with tail-pipes emerging at the rear corners of the car.*

Left *On the 'M' series Bentleys, 'C' series Silver Dawns and later cars, generous leather upholstered side headrests were provided for rear seat passengers. The shape of the mirrored companions was altered to suit.*

93

Top left *The early post-war work of James Young Ltd resembled, both in silhouette and details, their last pre-war coachwork, except that the front wings swept across the doors, rather than under them, with concealed running boards. This is their design number C-11 saloon. The slim chromium plated door window frames and razor-edge styling with crisp swage lines are among the features that set this coachbuilt car apart from the standard steel saloon.*

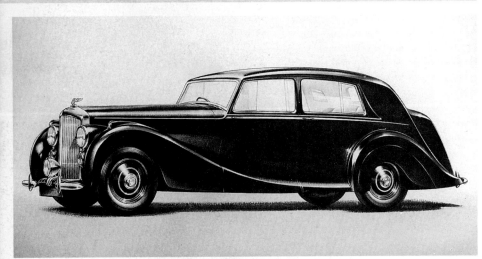

Left *All five major surviving coachbuilders offered coachwork for Bentley Mk VI chassis, as did several smaller firms, both in Britain and on the continent. The saloons offered as alternatives to the standard steel body were not always as satisfactory in terms of structural strength, but being largely of aluminium were less rust-prone. The designer's ink and wash drawing shows H. J. Mulliner's earliest post-war design for the Mk VI. It is believed that only one car was built to this design, on the first experimental chassis 1BVI, illustrated in Chapter One.*

Bottom left & opposite page *Four early Hooper designs on the Mk VI chassis. This four-light saloon with its large R.100 headlights, exposed trumpet-type horns and external running boards must have appeared rather old-fashioned when new but to the 1990s collector it would be a real gem!*

THE STANDARD SALOON, THE COACHBUILT ALTERNATIVE & THE CONTINENTAL

Top right *Also with R.100 headlights, but this time a saloon of six-light configuration, another early Hooper design.*

Right *Another four-light saloon, this time with standard headlights and graced with an attractive and eye-catching two-tone paint scheme.*

Below *A similar car, built for the Maharajah of Mysore, has twin 'pass-lamps' in lieu of the usual single lamp normally mounted on the centre apron and flag masts on the front wings. The two-tone paint treatment is rather different from that of the car above. Note the Maharajah's crest on the doors.*

Above & below *Freestone & Webb's designs for the early Mk VI chassis were also rather dated looking for the period, but had lots of character. The four-light saloon is reminiscent of their pre-war 'top hat' saloons, while the six-light saloon is slightly later and has more elaborate swaging on the wings and scalloping on the waistline. Both have exposed external running boards.*

Left *John Bull's drawing shows a typical Freestone & Webb saloon interior of the early post-war era. The semi-circular glove compartment door is characteristic of this coachbuilder during this period.*

Above & top right *The earliest 'production' design from H. J. Mulliner was this six-light saloon, design number 7122. The front doors are hinged on their leading edge and the door window frames are the slim chromium-plated type pioneered by Mulliners for their pre-war 'High Vision' designs. This two-tone car with brocade upholstery was built for the Maharajah of Baroda on 1946 chassis B30AK. It was not only the first of this design but also the first post-war production car bodied by H. J. Mulliner. The perspex panel in the rear compartment roof is another 'High Vision' feature. The bonnet, boot and spare wheel compartment lids were standard steel saloon panels supplied by Crewe.*

Right & below *Possibly a 1950 motor show exhibit, H. J. Mulliner's very pretty design number 7122 has remained unchanged. The combination of later type wheel discs and single exhaust pipe identify this as a late 4,257cc car.*

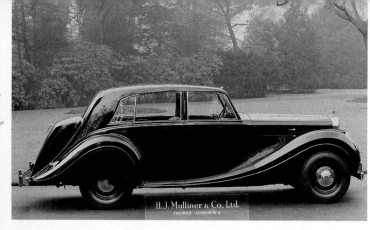

Above top left *Under the influence of designer Herbert Nye, who had worked under Osmond Rivers at Hooper before joining H. J. Mulliner in late 1947, a few examples of design number 7122 sported rear quarter-lights of a shape more usually associated with Hooper coachwork.*

Above top right *Upholstered in the highest quality top grain hide, the interiors of these H. J. Mulliner saloons were the very model of the English coachbuilder's art. The keen eyed will notice that the timber garnish rail for the driver's door had not been fitted when the photograph was taken. Note the completely flat floor.*

Above left *This photograph of another late 4,257cc design number 7122 car not only shows one of the alternative two-tone schemes available but also provides a glimpse of the luxurious interior with supremely comfortable seating for four persons. Note the conventional sunshine roof as compared to that of the Maharajah of Baroda car.*

Above & below *John Bull's drawing shows how the front wingline of H. J. Mulliner's saloon (below) was raised to sweep over the door skins at a higher point for 1951. This was their design number 7220. The above drawing shows how Freestone & Webb's saloon was similarly modernised around the same time.*

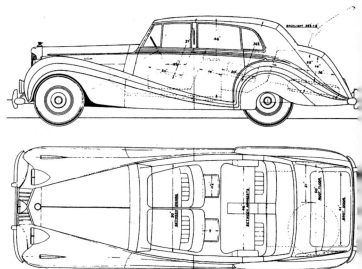

This page *Around 1950 several coachbuilders began to evolve designs that with their flowing winglines and long, shapely boots made the standard steel saloon appear decidedly dated. On this page are three interpretations by different coachbuilders on what is essentially a common theme. The top two pictures show Park Ward's six-light saloon of a design more usually associated with their Silver Wraiths. Only two Park Ward saloons were built on Mk VI chassis and both are shown here. Above is design number 230, on 1950 chassis B93GT, photographed outside the coachbuilder's Willesden offices, while below is design number 238 on chassis B235HP, missing its rear spats, outside London's Royal Albert Hall. The difference between these two designs is far from obvious. Perhaps the best looking of the three coachbuilders' work is H. J. Mulliner's 'Lightweight' saloon (below right). Not only was the shape entirely new but so was the method of construction, using extruded 'Reynolds Metal' framing with aluminium panels. Note the divided vee windscreen. The James Young version (bottom right) has more in common with the Park Ward cars but with unspatted rear wings, a slightly curved windscreen and the distinctive door handles with square push-buttons that first appeared at this time. These handles are integral with the chrome waist moulding. John Bull's drawing shows the luxurious interior. All these cars have their own distinctive bumper and overrider designs, except B235HP which has standard Wilmott-Breeden home market overriders.*

Above *Two pages devoted to H. J. Mulliner's 'Lightweight' saloon, design number 7243, in this instance the first example built, on chassis B355GT of 1950. The side view shows to advantage the masterful styling, which has more in common with the later S Series cars than with the Mk VI standard saloon. For the premium price of £5,105 (the standard steel saloon cost £3,674 in late 1950) one had a much more imposing and modern looking motor car.*

Left *The unpleated cloth upholstery of this car is non-standard for this design. There are folding armrests on both sides of each front seat.*

Bottom left *By any standards the luggage capacity was huge, in marked contrast to the standard steel saloon which had yet to acquire the longer (R-type) boot. The set of fitted suitcases shown, available at extra cost, could all be accommodated in the boot despite the presence therein of the spare wheel. Note the self-supporting boot lid.*

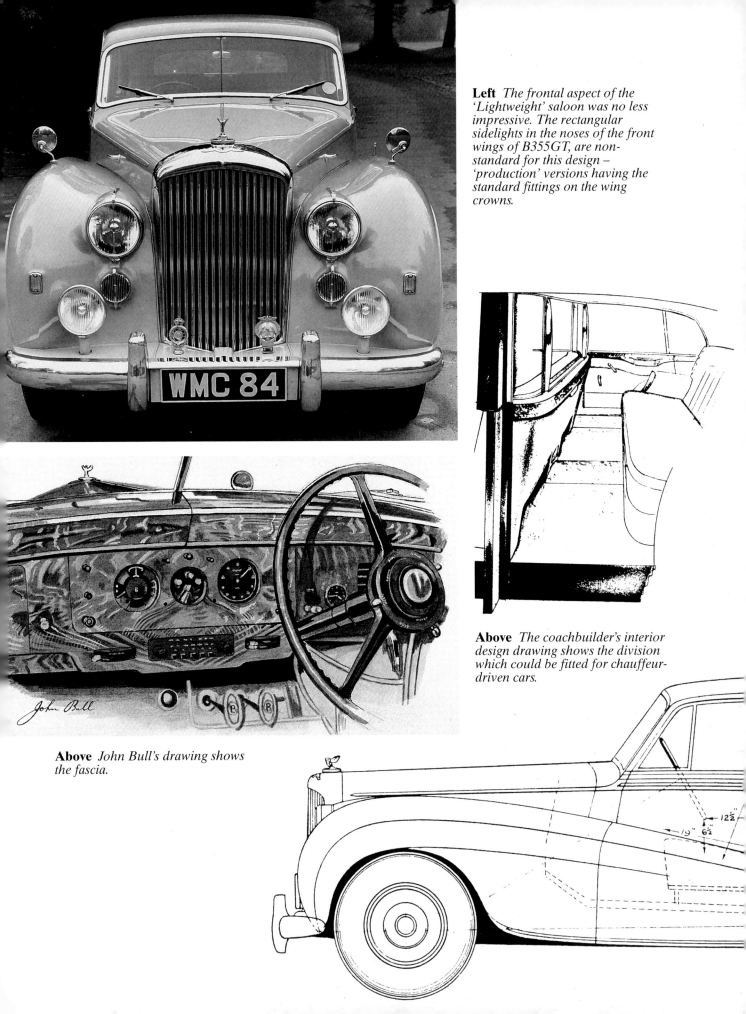

Left *The frontal aspect of the 'Lightweight' saloon was no less impressive. The rectangular sidelights in the noses of the front wings of B355GT, are non-standard for this design – 'production' versions having the standard fittings on the wing crowns.*

Above *The coachbuilder's interior design drawing shows the division which could be fitted for chauffeur-driven cars.*

Above *John Bull's drawing shows the fascia.*

Left & below *Two saloons bodied by the old-established Yorkshire coachbuilder Rippon Bros. of Huddersfield. The upper car is a distinctive sports saloon which was exhibited at the 1949 Earls Court Motor Show. The interior view, by John Bull, shows the fine walnut veneers and leather furnishings and the pair of buttons in the door capping rail for the electric window lifts. The lower car is Rippon's later design, having perhaps something of a Park Ward flavour.*

Left *Hooper's Chief Designer, Osmond Rivers, was the creator of this bold and innovative styling. The front wings flowed gently down in a concave line to the base of the tail. The absence of separate rear wings enabled the interior, particularly the rear compartment, to have greater effective width. This photograph of the saloon design number 8294 clearly shows these features as well as the heavily curved windscreen of laminated glass, another novel feature of the design which interestingly blends well with the razor-edge styling. Note that the bonnet latching handle is fitted, unusually, on the chrome waistline strip, though the door handles are not. The 2½ litre Daimler Empress had similar Hooper coachwork and this has given rise to the practice of erroneously referring to Rolls-Royce and Bentley cars with this styling as 'Empress Line'. Osmond Rivers only ever referred to it as his 'new look' – though 'Empress Line' is probably here to stay.*

Above *Special coachwork on the Silver Dawn chassis is in any case unusual, but this saloon, photographed by Thomas T. Solley (RREC) while in his ownership, is particularly so. It is chassis LSTH22, bodied by the Italian coachbuilder Ghia and exhibited by them at the 1952 Turin Motor Show. It also won the Grand Prix d'Honeur at the Villa Borghese, Rome, in the same year. The radiator shell was reduced in height by 3¼ inches by the coachbuilder and mounted 6 inches forward of its normal position in order to blend with the lines of the coachwork. Note the front bumper with its special mounting for the small Italian number plate.*

Above *The alligator-type bonnet – extremely unusual on a Rolls-Royce – when opened reveals a much wider than standard engine bay with ducts each side carrying air to outlets beneath the fascia.*

Left *The fascia is painted imitation woodgrain on steel. There is no wood in the coachwork other than the front face of the under-fascia tool tray.*

Above *A specialist line of James Young Ltd before the war was the two-door saloon, to which they applied the term 'Saloon Coupé'. Their early post-war products, though quite different below the waistline, with more modern winglines and no running boards, were distinctly similar in outline. This designer's illustration shows the first James Young post-war design, their two-door sports saloon, design number C-10. 62 were built, of which the final 13 had detail differences and were designated C-10N.*

Above left *This is the very first production Bentley Mk VI, chassis B2AK, which was bodied by James Young with the first of their design number C-10 two-door sports saloons.*

Left *Freestone & Webb's early two-door styling for the Mk VI. Note the exposed running boards favoured by this coachbuilder until well into the 1950s.*

Right & below *Amongst the more avant-garde of their designs, Freestone & Webb built a brace of these rakish coupés and also offered a drophead coupé with similar styling below the waistline. This is chassis B281BG, built for Prince Veranund of Siam (now Thailand). The Prince served as a fighter pilot in the RAF and kept the car at Weybridge Automobiles – the original suppliers and the scene of the upper photograph – while on tours of duty. The radiator mascot is a chrome Spitfire. Note the second-hand pre-war Wraith and new early Silver Wraith in the showroom. Right is a three-quarter rear view showing the rounded boot but otherwise crisp razor-edge lines. Its twin, on chassis B288BH, was delivered to actor Stewart Granger.*

Right *The first H. J. Mulliner body to use their newly developed all-metal 'Lightweight' mode of construction, using extruded 'Reynold's Metal' framing, was this coupé of rather advanced styling on Bentley Mk VI chassis B9EW. This car was exhibited at the 1949 Earls Court Motor Show. Note the shallower (measured front to rear) radiator shell, alligator type bonnet and headlights built into the front wing noses.*

Left *The styling of Park Ward's fixed head coupés was similar to that of their saloons. However, it is difficult to escape the conclusion that it presented a heavier, aesthetically less satisfactory appearance in two-door configuration.*

Below *Four interior views of similar cars, one of which is a left-hand drive car showing the steering column gearchange, treadle-type accelerator pedal and twist-to-release handbrake adopted for these left-hand drive export cars.*

Above *For the 1949 Earls Court Show James Young forsook their basically pre-war appearance in favour of this much more rounded look. This was their design number C-10AM saloon coupé.*

Right *This is the 1949 Show car, James Young stand, on chassis B185EW. The luxuriously carpeted boot was much more capacious than that of the early design and the fitted luggage shown could be supplied at extra cost. Also shown is the special James Young bumper which was usually fitted to Show cars and was available at an additional £50 (plus purchase tax). In order to support the boot area of this and subsequent designs, which were considerably longer than the standard steel saloon, the chassis rails were extended rearwards by the coachbuilder. After the B.7, later to become known as the R-type, was introduced, this was no longer necessary.*

Above & left *Although beauty is in the eye of the beholder, it is difficult to escape the feeling that if James Young had persisted with designs such as these the demise of the firm as a coachbuilder could well have been hastened! The upper car, design number C-10M, has its radiator shell painted in the body colour and despite today's Bentley Turbo models being similarly treated it is doubted that Rolls-Royce would have really approved at the time. The radiator shell was moved forward slightly to lengthen the bonnet. This is chassis B495CD which was exhibited on the James Young stand at the 1948 Earls Court Motor Show. Three other examples were built, though not all with the painted radiator. The lower car, on which the Bentley radiator shell was dispensed with entirely, was specially built for Mr Jack Barclay and was designed by a Frenchman in conjunction with James Young's own Chief Designer, the brilliant A. F. McNeil. It looks as though the French designer prevailed and one wonders whether Mr McNeil lent whole-hearted support to the resulting styling concept! It was known at the works as '3000', its own specially created body number.*

Left *For 1950 the James Young saloon coupé design was improved with swaging to the wings, front wings now in a continuous convex curve to better match the rear wing shape and chrome waist moulding incorporating distinctive new door handles with square push-buttons. Design number C-10BM, of which 35 were built.*

*James Young design number
C-10BM interior details.* **Right**
*The sumptuous front seats with
folding centre armrests.*

Below *Picnic tables behind the
front seats and the leather-covered
grab rails which are a distinctive
feature of James Young
coachwork.*

Below *In the door – a bottle storage compartment
with lockable sliding door...*

Left *...a swing-out holder for glasses – and a
bottle opener! This was not standard and was
probably a Show car feature.*

Right *For the 1952 season, James
Young's two-door coachwork
acquired a higher wingline and
unusual louvered grilles below the
headlights. The sidelights were
mounted in the noses of the front
wings and were rectangular, as
were the rear lights. This is the
1951 Earls Court Motor Show
exhibit, James Young stand, on
chassis B48MD. Design number
C-17, of which 12 were built.*

Left & below left *Two views of a rare offering from H. J. Mulliner, the two-door saloon variant of their 'lightweight' saloon. Less practical than the four-door car, perhaps, but very stylish.*

Above & inset *Even more rare was this variant – a coupé which was more close-coupled and had an even longer boot than the two-door saloon above. Though the longer boot is not obvious in this three-quarter front view, the considerably shorter rear quarter-light gives the game away. These H. J. Mulliner designs came well after the 1949 introduction of a left-hand drive version of the Mk VI chassis, so the reason for the unusual combination of right-hand drive and km/h speedometer on this car is open to speculation. There is a quick-lift window handle on the driver's door, so the pair of buttons on the capping rail are probably for an electric window on the near side. The country of delivery was Switzerland.*

THE STANDARD SALOON, THE COACHBUILT ALTERNATIVE & THE CONTINENTAL

Below & this page *Hooper's 'new look' in two-door guise, together with two views of the interior of a similar car. The white switches in the door cappings are for the electric window lifts, the winders below being for the swivelling quarter-panes. The top of the right-hand gear lever can be seen with first gear selected (first being the only gear in which the lever would be so far forward.)*

This page *Three examples of Pininfarina designs. Opposite are John Bull's renderings of two Mk VIs which, like the James Young car on page 108, have forsaken the Bentley radiator shell. These cars were marketed under the name 'Cresta' – a concept initiated before the war for presentation at the 1939 Paris Salon. Events obliged postponement of the project until 1948 when it was revived using the Mk VI chassis. The design work was carried out by Pininfarina and the first car was built by them on chassis B323CD at the instigation of Franco-Britannic Autos, French special retailers for Rolls-Royce and Bentley cars. After this prototype, 16 further examples were constructed by Facel Metallon ('Forge et Ateliers de Construction d'Eure-et-Loire' – FACEL) of Paris. Approval was forthcoming from Rolls-Royce Ltd, who supplied special Mk VI chassis with shortened and lowered steering column, 3.42:1 final drive ratio and km/h speedometers. The upper car with the broad grille is the original 1948 design while the 1950 car (in left-hand drive) has the more recognisably Bentley grille. The Silver Dawn (top) was built by Pininfarina on chassis SCA43 and exhibited at the 1951 Turin Motor Show. The 'fastback' two-door saloon styling exhibits some elements of the then yet to be introduced R-type Bentley Continental.*

Right *The coupé at right in this photograph was built in 1951 by the Swiss coachbuilder Graber on 1947 Mk VI chassis B190BH, which was originally a standard steel saloon. The drophead coupé (or 'cabriolet' in continental European parlance) to the left of the photo shares similar styling features, having been built by the same coachbuilder on 1951 chassis B74NZ.*

Right *Pininfarina built five bodies on Bentley Mk VI chassis, all coupés – four fixed head and a drophead. This fixed head coupé is believed to be the last of the five, on chassis B332MD.*

Left *Vanvooren built only one body on a post-war Rolls-Royce or Bentley chassis – the two-door saloon seen here in California, on Bentley Mk VI chassis B332LEY.*

Left *Drophead coupé coachwork had enjoyed considerable popularity on the pre-war Bentley chassis and after the war Rolls-Royce realised that there would continue to be a demand for such cars. A prototype drophead coupé, on experimental chassis 5BVI, was on the road by 1947. This was bodied by Park Ward using as many standard steel saloon body parts as possible to minimise cost. This was a less than complete success aesthetically and the much more satisfactory design in this photograph was developed for production. Still using the standard steel panelwork forward of the scuttle, it was otherwise all new. Unfortunately the hood envelope, which considerably neatens the appearance with the hood down, had not been fitted when the photograph was taken. Note the scimitar motif on the rear wing of this example.*

Below *The more rearward mounting of the front axle on the post-war cars meant that, with the notable exception of the Phantom IV, there was insufficient room between the front wheels and the scuttle to fit a sidemount spare without its being too high to be completely satisfactory visually. Nevertheless, this is an impressive feature of this Mk VI Park Ward drophead coupé, chassis B182CF, owned by John Berrys (RROC Inc).*

Top right *H. J. Mulliner, for the earliest of their Bentley Mk VI drophead coupés, used their pre-war device of a fully disappearing hood. When stowed the hood was completely out of sight beneath the metal panel clearly visible in this photograph. This made for neatness but interrupted the lines of the car somewhat, though the remainder of the coachwork, particularly the wings, is characteristic of this coachbuilder for the period.*

Right *Windovers built coachwork on Rolls-Royce and Bentley chassis in considerable numbers before World War II, but survived after the war only long enough to build eight bodies, equally divided between the Silver Wraith and the Bentley Mk VI, their drophead coupé design for the latter being the subject of John Bull's drawing. Like the early Park Ward dropheads, the panelwork forward of the scuttle is that of the standard steel saloon.*

Right *James Young built three of these very pretty three-position drophead coupés, shown in John Bull's drawing in the coupé de ville position, to their design number C-23.*

Bottom *H. J. Mulliner also turned their hand to the three-position drophead style, on a one-off basis, on 1948 Mk VI chassis B382CF, owned by J. Bidwell-Topham (RREC). Very elegant, but the rather ungainly height of the rare post-war sidemount spare wheel is again in evidence.*

This page *For 1950 Park Ward stopped using the standard steel front wings and bonnet for their drophead coupés in favour of their own by then standard long front wings, with the doors hinged at the front. This very satisfactory design is shown with the power-operated hood in the lowered and raised positions. Left is the interior – which was designed for maximum comfort for four people, hence the coachbuilder's term 'foursome drophead coupé'.*

Above & left *H. J. Mulliner, like Park Ward, changed their drophead coupé designs to match their later saloon styles. Their 'lightweight' saloons were quickly followed by this stylish drophead. John Bull's drawing shows the four-light design on the Bentley Mk VI chassis while the photograph shows Silver Dawn chassis SHD50, which is uniquely of two-light configuration, design number 7296.*

Right *On this and the following pages are several examples of European open coachwork on Bentley Mk VI chassis. This one is by Pininfarina and appears to the artist's eye to be 'rather American-looking', but to the writer it is more reminiscent of the large Morris and Wolseley saloons of the same era. It was built on Bentley Mk VI chassis B435CD and was, in fact, Pininfarina's only drophead coupé body on a Rolls-Royce or Bentley chassis.*

Right *This smart three-position drophead coupé, shown in John Bull's drawing in the elegant coupé de ville position, was bodied by Swiss coachbuilder Fritz Ramseier & Co. of Berne (the name of which company was subsequently changed to Carrosserie Worblaufen), who built three bodies on Mk VI chassis. This is believed to be chassis B237AJ of 1947, but the firm built another three-position drophead on a 1950 chassis, B88FV. The other car built by this firm was a drophead coupé on 1947 chassis B181AJ, which was attributed to Franay on p.41 (centre) of* Bentley: the Cars from Crewe, *by Rodney Steel.*

117

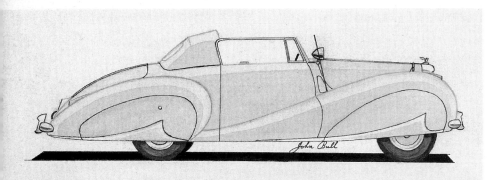

Top left *The French coachbuilder Franay built eight bodies on Bentley Mk VI chassis. This drophead coupé, with spats all round and large slabs of chrome plate, exhibits all the flourish and exuberance often associated with this coachbuilder. This is believed to be the second of two cars to this design (the first being illustrated below) and has been attributed to another French coachbuilder, Saoutchik, in at least two other books. However, it has been positively established that in fact that firm built only one Mk VI body which you will see on the opposite page.*

Above *At the 1947 Paris Salon de l'Auto, Franay exhibited this spectacular drophead coupé, built for F. Gadol of Bolougne on chassis B20BH. The photograph was taken at one of the extravagant concours d'elegance so beloved of the French of the period, probably Engheim in June, 1948 where it was awarded the Grand Prix. It spent much of its early life similarly ravaging the competition on the European concours circuit only to fall on hard times later. In fact, by 1980 it had deteriorated into an almost hopeless 'basket case.' It was then acquired by Californian collector and restorer Gary Wales who carried out a spectacular restoration of this amazing car between 1988 and 1991.*

Above *B20BH after restoration, carried out by owner Gary Wales (RROC Inc), who in the process put his own interpretation on, and further embellished, the already flamboyant shapes in chrome on the spats and used hundreds of Philippine frog-skins for the upholstery! It will also be noticed that the original one-piece windscreen has been changed to an opening vee type. Many prestigious concours wins followed this remarkable restoration.*

Left *Less flamboyant, but nevertheless displaying a certain French flavour, is this rather pretty Franay drophead coupé. Note the absence of outside door handles on this and the previous two Franay cars. In each case the chrome button on the scuttle side releases the door. This is chassis B26BH, owned by Samuel Ornstein (RROC Inc).*

Right *The cutaway doors, absence of side windows and fold-flat windscreen probably call for the use of the term tourer to describe this car, the only post-war Bentley bodied by the French coachbuilder Saoutchik. Note the louvered bonnet top and opening panel below which the hood disappears. Chassis B440CF, built in 1948 for Curt E. Forstmann.*

Above *The Swiss coachbuilder Graber built this drophead coupé on 1948 Mk VI chassis B190CF, photographed in Switzerland in September, 1986 by Thomas T. Solley (RREC) when in his ownership.*

Left *There is no woodwork in the coachwork. The fascia and door cappings are metal panels painted in the body colour and the instrument panel is 'snailed' aluminium.*

Above *Handsome Marchal headlamps are fitted in lieu of the usual Lucas fittings.*

119

Left *Another Swiss firm, Gebruder Beutler of Thun, built this smart drophead coupé, the modern lines of which belie the age of the chassis, B139BG of 1947. It is owned nowadays by Swiss collector O. Keller.*

Below, left & right *This drophead coupé with disappearing hood was built by Freestone & Webb in 1951 on Bentley Mk VI chassis B101NY. Owner: Roy Woollett (RREC).*

Left & above *Abbott of Farnham built nineteen bodies on Bentley Mk VI chassis, all two-door saloons and drophead coupés. Left is their drophead coupé on 1949 chassis B495EW, which was owned when Tom Clarke took the photograph by John Donner (RREC). Above is a similar car, though with two-light window configuration, chassis B177KL of 1951.*

Above & below left *Designer A. F. McNeil's wash drawing depicts a specialist line of J. Gurney Nutting & Co. – the two-light sedanca coupé. It has not been possible to determine whether this strikingly rakish design was ever actually built, but it seems probable that it was not. However, the design (C-15) represented by John Bull's and the coachbuilder's drawings (below, left), sharing the fake hood irons but otherwise of different design throughout, was built – one for the 1947 'Show the Flag' tour of America and three further examples. Gurney Nutting belonged to the Jack Barclay group at that time and were soon merged with James Young Ltd.*

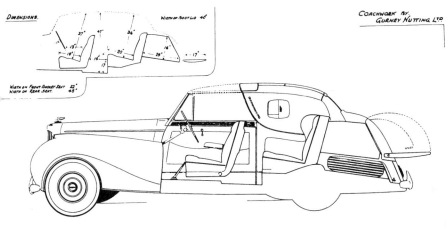

DIMENSIONS.

COACHWORK BY.
GURNEY NUTTING LTD.

DESIGN. C-15
TWO DOOR SEDANCA COUPÉ

SHEWING INTERIOR LAYOUT.

Below *Both Gurney Nutting and then James Young built these unusual sedanca coupés, which had a teardrop-shaped window in lieu of completely blind rear quarters but was otherwise unchanged from design number C-15 opposite. The de ville extension is shown open and closed.*

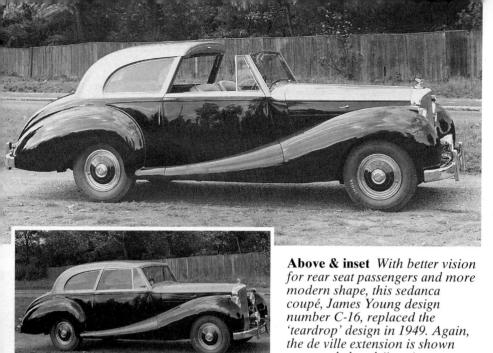

Above & inset With better vision for rear seat passengers and more modern shape, this sedanca coupé, James Young design number C-16, replaced the 'teardrop' design in 1949. Again, the de ville extension is shown open and closed (inset).

Above The sumptuous interior of the C-16 sedanca coupé. James Young woodwork, with its tightly figured walnut veneer and bold zebra-wood crossbanding, was a distinctive feature. Note the solution adopted to the problem of sun visors in these open-fronted cars.

Below Another sedanca coupé, this time by Franay, on left-hand drive Mk VI chassis B182LLJ, displayed on the coachbuilder's stand at the 1951 Paris Salon de l'Auto. Note the coachlamps on the scuttle and the purely decorative 'hood irons'.

Right & below right *These two similar sedanca coupés were built by Hooper for (above) the Maharajah of Mysore and (below) the Prince Regent (later Crown Prince) of Iraq. The R.100 headlamps were only fitted to a very small number of Bentley Mk VIs.*

Bottom *A Harold Radford 'Countryman' estate car. The timber panelling below the waist was walnut or mahogany veneer on aluminium. John Bull's drawing depicts the 'Mk I' version, of which 8 were built by the small coachbuilding firm Seary & McReady of Southgate to Radford's specifications, the first on 1947 chassis B397BG which was completed in July, 1948 and exhibited at the Earls Court Motor Show of that year. Harold Radford is said to have conceived the design in the bath! The car was described as having 'unusually commodious luggage accommodation' – which was undeniable given that there was no rear seat! One benefit of this was that it qualified as a commercial vehicle and was therefore purchase tax exempt. With the rate at 66⅔% at that time this was a significant saving, which needed to be balanced against the fact that commercial vehicles were subject to a speed limit of 30mph! The price in 1948 was £3,530.*

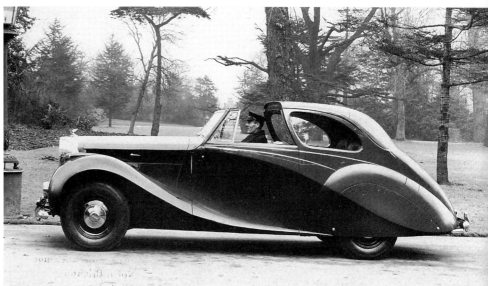

Right *Rippon Bros. of Huddersfield also used timber panelling, in the best 'shooting brake' tradition, calling their version a 'Continental Touring Saloon'. Standard steel front wings were employed but modified with a sidemount spare wheel well.*

Right *By 1951 Harold Radford had a controlling financial interest in Seary & McReady, who built the 'Countryman' bodies to his design, so the firm's name was changed to Harold Radford (Coachbuilders) and it became a subsidiary of Harold Radford Ltd. The 'Mk II' Countryman, seen here as drawn by John Bull was, at a glance, relatively ordinary looking, despite the unusual bodyside swaging. However, the tail and interior treatment made for a highly practical estate car. Like all but the first of the 'Mk I' model, these cars had a rear seat, each half of which could be folded flat as in so many of today's estate cars.*

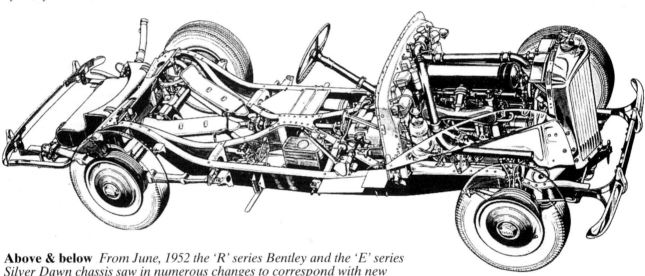

Above & below *From June, 1952 the 'R' series Bentley and the 'E' series Silver Dawn chassis saw in numerous changes to correspond with new standard steel coachwork with longer boot. The chassis above is the B.7, or Bentley R-type as it became known, with original riveted frame and synchromesh gearbox. The automatic gearbox was available only on export cars at first, but later on home market cars, too. Below is the later chassis with welded frame, introduced at chassis B349TO (Bentley) and SNF1 (Silver Dawn), and automatic gearbox.*

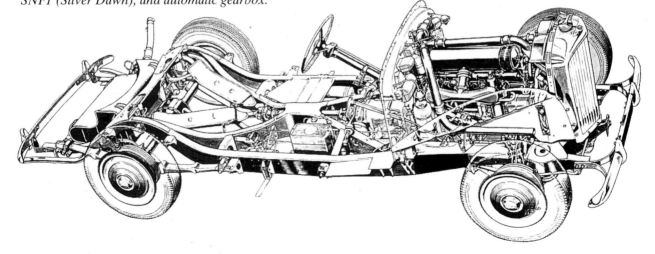

Above *1954 Silver Dawn chassis SRH66 after completion of a superb restoration by Gary Wales (RROC Inc). The dual exhaust system was standard on the Bentley R-type and first appeared on the Silver Dawn from the start of the 'H' series. The flat bumpers seen on this chassis are non-standard for this model and would have been fitted by the coachbuilder – in this instance Hooper.*

Right *SRH66. This photograph shows the altered rear spring shackles, which brought the rear of the spring above the frame to modify the handling of the car with the longer overhang of the long boot standard steel body which most of the 'E' series and later Silver Dawn (and Bentley R-type) chassis carried. Note also the altered fuel tank shape, with recess for the spare wheel. The quality of Gary Wales's restoration is very much in evidence here.*

Bottom right *The Rolls-Royce four-speed automatic gearbox used for the 'E' series and later Silver Dawn, the Bentley R-type and also the Silver Wraith from the same time (mid-1952) was a development of the General Motors 'Hydra-Matic' used in Oldsmobiles and other G.M. cars. The first batch of export automatic cars actually had G.M. gearboxes, fitted before production commenced at Crewe. The extension bolted to the back of the gearbox carried the pump for the ride control, the control linkage for which can be seen here, the speedometer drive and the friction disc brake servo.*

Below *The steering column-mounted gear range selector lever for the automatic gearbox. This remained essentially unchanged until replaced by an electric selector on the Silver Shadow range of cars introduced in 1965 and beyond that in limited numbers until the three-speed transmission was adopted for the Phantom VI for 1979.*

Above & inset *An exhibition cut-away view of the automatic gearbox and the complex componentry displayed.*

Left *The maker's plate showing that the automatic gearbox was made under licence to General Motors. The first batch of gearboxes came in complete from Detroit and carried G.M. builder's plates endorsed 'for Rolls-Royce Ltd.'*

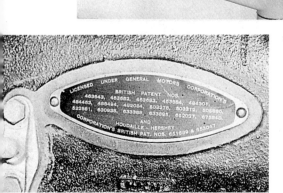

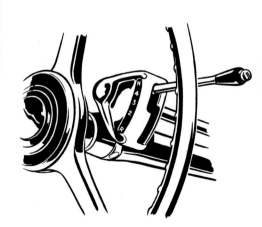

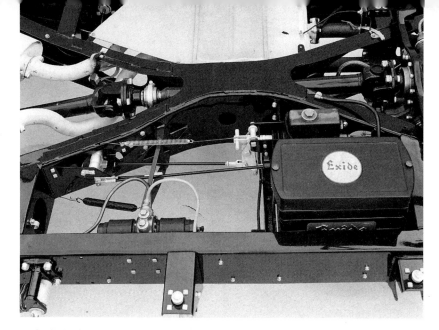

The following series of photographs show detail of SRH66, the Silver Dawn restored by Gary Wales. **Right** Here we see the welded frame with the twin S.U. fuel pump mounted on the chassis rail nearest the camera, aft of the battery. Note the divided propeller shaft with its centre support bearing.

Below right The offside of the engine showing the single Zenith carburetter fitted to Silver Dawns from chassis LSFC102 as a replacement for the Stromberg originally used. The choke was automatic on both types.

Bottom right Engine bay bulkhead detail, offside. The emergency lead-light, which plugs into the charging socket on the fascia, can be seen in its clips atop the bulkhead. Below that is the fuse-box and the vacuum-operated windscreen washer. The windscreen demister was supplied with cold air (via the vent below the offside headlamp) or hot air (through the radiator matrix). A flap valve at the junction of the hot and cold ducts was operated via a cable by a control below the fascia from chassis SNF1 (Silver Dawn) and B2TN (Bentley R-type). Before this the bonnet needed to be opened to reach the hot/cold valve.

Below Front suspension detail showing the flexible line to the hydraulic front brakes and the centralised chassis lubrication line to the kingpins.

Left *The steel bar running from the radiator to the bulkhead is a temporary fitment pending refitting of the body, which in this instance was a Hooper saloon.*

Right *The frontal aspect and offside of the engine bay.*

Left *Earlier Silver Dawns had the instruments laid out Silver Wraith-style, but from chassis SNF1 the layout was rationalised with that of the Bentley, as seen here on SRH66.*

Above *John Blatchley's contribution to the styling of the Mk VI standard steel saloon had been confined to detail, Ivan Evernden and Bill Allen having done the spade-work. However, the task of re-designing the tail for the R-type Bentley and its Silver Dawn counterpart fell to Blatchley, who by that time had become Chief Styling Engineer. The small bumpers and overriders of this R-type identify it as a home market car.*

Right *The extended rear wing and long boot made for a sleeker looking car than its short boot predecessor, a fact that is particularly apparent when viewed from three-quarters rear. Unlike that of the short boot car the bootlid was hinged at the top and all the luggage shown could be accommodated. A leather strap provided in the tool kit enabled the self-supporting bootlid to be secured down when it could not be fully closed due to being loaded beyond its normal capacity, the number plate bracket being adjustable to suit. The bootlid was of aluminium alloy.*

Below, right & left *The long boot standard steel saloon in Silver Dawn guise. The design lent itself to two-tone paint schemes, which differed from the two-toning of the short boot cars due to the waistline continuing in an unbroken line right through to the tail, whereas on the short boot car the waist swage line reversed direction aft of the rear door window and followed the leading edge of the rear wing right to the sill, hence the rear wing being finished in the upper colour in two-tone schemes on short boot cars, but in the lower colour on long boot cars. Any departure from this in either case, as sometimes seen on 'restored' cars, is incorrect. Left is a two-tone long boot Silver Dawn with the darker colour on top while right the different effect of having the lighter colour on top is seen.*

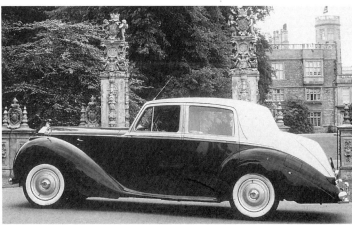

Left *The gear range selector as fitted to automatic R-type Bentleys and Silver Dawns – in this instance the latter in left-hand drive guise. The button in the end of the lever has to be depressed to enable the selector to be moved in or out of 'N' (neutral) or 'R' (reverse). Both the Bentley R-type and the 'E' series and later Silver Dawn had only one control on the steering wheel boss – for the ride control. The twist-to-release handbrake and large accelerator pedal seen here were fitted to left-hand drive cars only.*

Left & below *The interior furnishings of the Bentley R-type and long boot Silver Dawn remained much as the late short boot cars. The fascia layout shown, with the radio built into the underside of a pull-out picnic tray and speaker behind a grille above the instrument panel, is that of the Bentley from chassis B2TN and Silver Dawn from SNF1.*

Right *Bentley R-type chassis B217TO, again showing how well suited the design was to two-tone colour schemes. This car was a Conduit Street demonstrator and was the subject of 1953 road tests in The Motor (14th October) and The Autocar (6th November).*

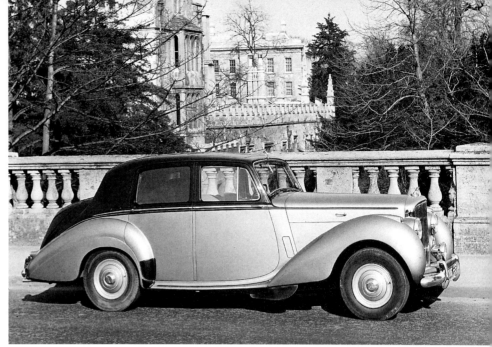

Right *The R-type chassis, with its rearward extended frame and modified spring shackles, was better suited to H. J. Mulliner's 'lightweight' saloon, obviating the need for the coachbuilder to extend the chassis rails to support the long rear overhang.*

Below *The final Silver Dawn chassis, LSVJ133, was fitted with a 'lightweight' saloon body by H. J. Mulliner and was the only Silver Dawn so fitted.*

Above *James Young built eleven four-light saloon bodies for Silver Dawns, all on the 'F' series and later chassis. Nine of these were to this C-20SD design.*

Right *a Bentley R-type with James Young design number C-20 four-light saloon coachwork and (below) the solitary example of design number C-20SDB on Silver Dawn chassis SOG42. At a glance they appear almost identical, but detail differences serve to illustrate the almost infinite variety that was still inherent in Rolls-Royce and Bentley coachwork well into the 1950s. The Bentley's rear quarter-light extends further rearward. The Bentley's sill panels open with the doors whereas those of the Silver Dawn form fixed steps below the doors. The Bentley waist swage line turns forward to follow the leading edge of the rear wing while that of the Silver Dawn continues towards the tail. The Silver Dawn has aprons built into the front wings behind the front bumpers. The headlamps of the Bentley are thrust up higher. The bonnet shut-line of the Silver Dawn is at the waist, but lower on the Bentley. The noses of the front wings are squarer on the Silver Dawn.*

Above *This open boot has the higher, squarer lines of the Silver Dawn design number C-20SD, but the bumper badge reveals that it is actually a Bentley, design number C-22. The luggage accommodation is truly huge and luxuriously carpeted.*

Top right *Hooper's distinctive 'new look' saloons had been introduced towards the end of the Mk VI Bentley's run and was continued unchanged for the R-type. Design number 8294.*

Above right *The same design appeared, in much smaller numbers, on the 'E' series and later Silver Dawn chassis, as design number 8401. This is chassis SRH46, which was taken to Australia by Bob McCulloch (RROCA) and is now in France.*

Right *Hooper's Chief Designer Osmond Rivers with one of his creations on Silver Dawn chassis STH99, photographed in Denmark in 1980 when Mr Rivers was 85. Hoopers built this car for the Earl of Derby who bequeathed it to his god-son who lives in Denmark.*

Bottom right *For the 1952 Earls Court Motor Show Freestone & Webb copied the Hooper look, putting their own interpretation on it. Despite its obvious derivation, Freestone's design was never quite as crisp, but nevertheless had a sleek appearance and a character quite distinct from Hooper's. Note the large, flat bumpers with built-in number plate housing.*

Above *For the Bentley R-type and 'E' series and later Silver Dawn Park Ward's efforts were concentrated almost entirely on two-door saloon and drophead coupé designs. The later cars had a new wingline that had metamorphosised from their rather uncompromising convex line into the compound curves seen on this fixed head body on chassis STH93 (below) which was photographed when in the ownership of Harold Spiller (RROCA).*

Above *For 1953 James Young's design C-17, which was designed for the Mk VI chassis, was modified to become C-18, with grilles below the headlamps like those of the S-type cars which followed in 1955, and sidelights reverting to the conventional type and position. There are numerous other subtle changes. The chrome windscreen surround has disappeared, the wheel arches have developed a distinct flare and the leading edge of the rear wing is more sharply defined, all of which points to the bespoke nature of James Young coachwork of the period. Such variations were rarely seen on Park Ward coachwork, for example, which was much more standardised. The car illustrated, on a very early R-type chassis, B30RT, was exhibited on the James Young stand at the 1952 Earls Court Motor Show. 10 examples were built.*

Left *More James Young variety. This design has departed from the conventional in having its headlights built into the ends of the front wings and built-in foglights. The radiator shell is noticeably lower than standard and is probably the Continental type, though the car is not, of course, a Continental. This gives the bonnet a markedly increased slope.*

Top right *This car, for the 1954 season, reverted to conventional frontal appearance, though still with the lower radiator shell. Note that the front wings of this design 'fade out' before reaching the rear wings. Design number C-21.*

Right *This interior view of a James Young two-door R-type shows the extensive use of bold and beautifully figured burr walnut veneer for which the firm was famous. Note the speedometer of this car which the coachbuilder moved from its standard position and placed directly in front of the driver. Just visible are the tinted Perspex sun visor extensions which slide out for use. The ring-pull on the cantrail over the driver's door is for the rear window blind which is operated by pulling the ring forward and hooking it over the stud just aft of the sun visor. The seat cushions are unpleated while the squabs are in pleated and bolstered style – a popular combination with all coachbuilders from the late 1930s to the 1950s.*

Below *Abbott of Farnham produced sixteen bodies on Bentley R-type chassis, mainly to the sleek two-door sports saloon design which is often confused with, and sometimes even offered for sale as, a Continental. In fact, no Continental chassis were bodied by this firm, though the chassis for these cars were specially fitted with certain Continental features and the coachwork appears equally aerodynamically efficient as most Continentals. The very long luggage boot seems to have been gained largely at the expense of rear seat legroom.*

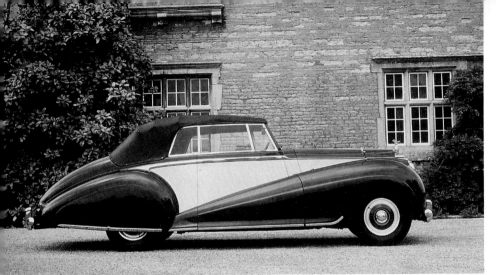

Left & below *Fifteen 'E' series and later Silver Dawns were fitted with drophead coupé coachwork by Park Ward. Some of these were built to the same design number 322 as most of the eleven built on the earlier 'A' to 'D' series chassis, as seen above on 1953 chassis LSMF10. Others had a higher wingline and came in a two-light style, design number 465, an example of which is shown (below) after completion outside the office building at the coachbuilder's Willesden works.*

Below *The interior of Park Ward's design number 465 was very 'blind' for rear seat passengers. A four-light version with the higher wingline of the 465 was also offered. This was design number 555.*

Below *We have already seen SHD50, H. J. Mulliner's Silver Dawn drophead coupé. Only two of these bodies were built on Silver Dawn chassis. This is the other one, on chassis LSLE31 – this time with the more usual four-light configuration, design number 7297. The Bentley R-type chassis saw this design in greater numbers.*

Right *Easily mistaken for a Mulliner drophead is this one-off edition built on 1954 Silver Dawn chassis LSTH79 by Henri Chapron of Paris. Photographed by Tom Solley when in the ownership of John Harwood (RROC Inc).*

Right & below *This is the prototype R-type Bentley Continental, built in 1951 as experimental chassis 9BVI. Although the sleek H. J. Mulliner coachwork set the style for production Continentals, this prototype differed in a number of details, including a different fascia, one inch higher roofline, divided windscreen and no winged-'B' mascot or dummy filler cap on the radiator shell. The bumpers were of aluminium alloy as a contribution to weight minimisation. After being fitted with a standard Continental radiator shell and allocated production chassis number BC26A, she was owned for many years by Bentley Drivers Club stalwart and erstwhile President Stanley Sedgwick and has more recently been the subject of a comprehensive body-off restoration for present owner Victor Gauntlett. Her registration number OLG-490 led to her being affectionately known as 'Olga'.*

Above *The seating, in early Continentals at least, was built with weight minimisation in mind without sacrificing comfort. Later, customers seemed to rather miss the point and demanded heavier, thicker seats which somewhat compromised the original concept. Headroom in the back seat was only slightly less than that of the standard steel saloon, which given the Continental's sleek body shape is quite remarkable.*

Top left *The heart of the R-type Continental. The combination of higher performance engine, more efficient exhaust system, high gearing, light weight and wind-tunnel proven aerodynamic efficiency enabled the Continental to achieve a speed of 100 mph in third gear. The prototype car 9BVI was tested to a top gear maximum of 124 mph in France. It was easily the fastest genuine four-seater car in the world at the time.*

Top right *The flat, one-piece fascia was a feature of all Mulliner Continentals from the first production R-types to the S3. There was a revolution counter and even an oil temperature gauge (between the speedometer and the rev counter) and the usual comprehensive Bentley instrumentation took the form of individual gauges rather than the four-in-one instrument of the standard chassis. The controls on the steering wheel indicate that this is an early synchromesh gearbox car without the automatic cold-start device.*

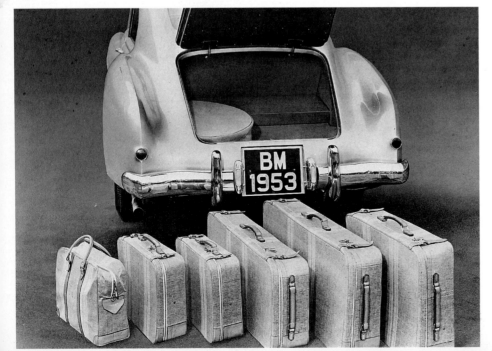

Left *A view of the tail of a Mulliner Continental showing the distinctive finned rear wings which acted as stabilisers at speed. Despite the apparent shallowness and awkward shape of the boot, all the fitted luggage shown could be accommodated.*

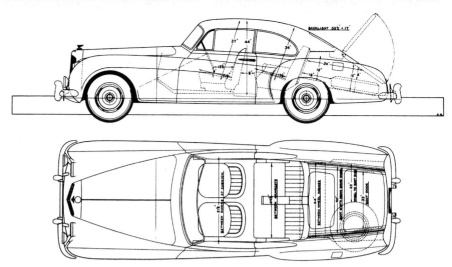

H.J. MULLINER & CO. LTD.
CHISWICK · LONDON, W.4.

BENTLEY CONTINENTAL SPORTS SALOON

DRG. No. 7277
REVISED DRAWING 22.7.54.

Above *Production Bentley Continentals, like this one with Windsor Castle as a back-drop, employed the same lightweight method of construction as the prototype, with aluminium panels over a 'Reynolds Metal' light alloy framework. However, they quickly acquired features like the heavy export bumpers and so put on weight. From the 'D' series of 1954 the engine capacity was increased to 4,887cc to counter the effects of the extra weight. H. J. Mulliner carried out the design work, with input from Rolls-Royce Chief Styling Engineer John Blatchley.*

PARK WARD COACHWORK
473, HIGH ROAD,
WILLESDEN
LONDON, NW10

Right & below right *Only fifteen of the 208 R-type Continentals wore bodies by coachbuilders other than H. J. Mulliner. Six of these were by Park Ward, to two designs – a pair of two-door saloons, design number 648 (drawing) and four drophead coupés, design number 647 (photograph). These cars were designed by Rolls-Royce Chief Styling Engineer John Blatchley, who had taken over the external styling of Park Ward coachwork in 1952 in order to introduce a degree of 'family resemblance' between the factory product and the special bodies. The Park Ward designs for the S-type Continentals which followed were slight enlargements of these R-type designs.*

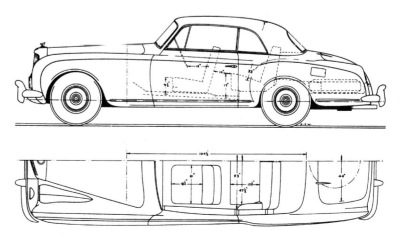

BENTLEY CONTINENTAL SALOON

DESIGN NO. 648

SCALE IN FEET

Chapter Four

A Phantom for Royalty

The Phantom IV

'…it is possible to hope that Rolls-Royce may now be encouraged to embark on the production of further examples of this superb chassis. It must be said, however, that at present no other orders are being accepted.'

The Autocar July 7th 1950

As related in Chapter One, the Rationalised Range proposed for introduction after 1940 included a straight-eight replacement for the Phantom III. The overhead inlet, side exhaust valve eight cylinder engine had already been tried and tested with complete success in four experimental cars. One of these, the Silver Phantom, chassis no. 30GVII, was fitted with a large Park Ward seven-seater limousine body and became known as 'Big Bertha'. This was the forerunner of the Phantom IV.

Another straight-eight powered experimental car was a special Bentley Mk V, chassis no. 11BV. Although the official Experimental Department name for this car was 'Comet', its scorching performance earned it the fond epithet 'Scalded Cat'. While the Chassis Division's Chief Engineer W. A. Robotham (Rm) was using Scalded Cat after the War, it attracted the attention of the Duke of Edinburgh, who borrowed it. While there is a world of difference between a Bentley Mk V with a straight-eight shoehorned into it and the huge limousine that eventually emerged as the Phantom IV, some writers have put two and two together and linked the Duke's obvious enjoyment of Scalded Cat with the Royal order that followed. Regardless of whether or not there was an element of truth to this, the fact remains that during 1949 Rolls-Royce Ltd received an order from HRH Princess Elizabeth and the Duke of Edinburgh for a large limousine.

At that time, the Royal cars for State use were supplied by Daimler – a role that Rolls-Royce considered was rightfully theirs. The Company's management would no doubt have been very keen to ensure that the car to be supplied was the best there had ever been. The largest car in the range was the 10ft 7in wheelbase Silver Wraith, a chassis best suited to owner-driver coachwork and not big enough for a limousine of the proportions envisaged. The proposed Phantom III replacement was not intended to be proceeded with in the difficult post-war economic climate, but the decision was taken to make an exception for this very special order.

The Phantom IV chassis, with its huge 12ft 1in wheelbase, represented the ultimate 'stretch' of the Rationalised frame design. It differed from the shorter Silver Wraith and Bentley Mk VI chassis in having an additional cross-member at the centre of the cruciform bracing and 10-stud road wheel mounting. The 5,675cc eight cylinder engine was supplied with fuel by a twin S.U. pump from a 23 gallon tank, with filler necks on each side of the car, and a separate twin pump for a four gallon reserve supply. It was assumed at that time that this first Phantom IV chassis, 4AF2, would be the only one, and it was handbuilt at Clan Foundry, Belper, near the Derby works rather than at Crewe. 4AF2 was fitted with characteristically handsome H. J. Mulliner Enclosed Limousine coachwork and supplied to the Royal couple through Car Mart Ltd in July 1950. It was built under the code-name 'Nabha'. The delivery was accompanied by an announcement that the Phantom IV had been 'Designed to the special order of their Royal Highnesses, the Princess Elizabeth and the Duke of Edinburgh.' The Rolls-Royce ousting of Daimlers from the Royal Mews had begun.

A second Phantom IV chassis quickly followed. This was 4AF4 which was bodied by Park Ward as a works lorry and used by the Experimental Department, then still located at Belper, and as a works delivery vehicle.

Three cars ordered at the end of 1948 by General Franco of Spain, two heavily armour-plated limousines and a large cabriolet, were built as Phantom IVs rather than over-burden the Silver Wraith chassis and eventually eighteen cars were built in all. Orders were not accepted from any customers other than Royalty and Heads of State. Even two of the three cars supplied by Rolls-Royce Ltd to themselves ultimately came into the ownership of members of the British Royal family. With the exception of the aforementioned works lorry and a solitary car for Prince Talal al Saoud bodied by Franay, the French coachbuilder then favoured by the Saudi Royal Family, Phantom IV coachwork was the exclusive domain of two coachbuilders, H. J. Mulliner (nine) and Hooper (seven).

TECHNICAL SPECIFICATION

Rolls-Royce Phantom IV

Engine

Dimensions
Eight cylinders in line.
A & B series: Bore 3.5 inches (89mm), stroke 4.5 inches (114mm), cubic capacity 346 cu. in. (5,675cc)
C series: Bore 3.75 inches (95.25mm), stroke 4.5 inches (114mm), cubic capacity 397.5 cu. in. (6,515cc)
Compression ratio 6.4:1.

Cylinder block/Crankcase
Iron monobloc casting with 30% chrome iron liners at tops of bores.

Crankshaft
1% chrome molybdenum steel (EN.19) nitrided. Bolt-on balance weights. Nine main bearings of copper-lead-indium.

Pistons
Aluminium alloy (RR.53) tin plated. Granodised piston rings, one compression, one L-section and one slotted oil control ring.

Cylinder head
Aluminium alloy (RR.50) with inserted valve seats.

Valve gear
Overhead inlet, side exhaust valves. Exhaust valves in KE.965. Stellite coated seats and tips. Camshaft driven by helical gears, six bearings.

Carburetter
Stromberg dual downdraught carburetter with accelerator pump and automatic choke. Water heated hot spot. Hand throttle on steering wheel boss (synchromesh gearbox cars only). Air intake silencer incorporating mesh air filter element (oil bath type air cleaner on cars for use in dusty conditions).

Ignition system
Ignition by high tension coil and Delco-Remy distributor with twin contact breaker points. Spare coil fitted for emergency use. Firing order 1,6,2,5,8,3,7,4.

Lubrication system
Helical gear oil pump in crankcase driven by skew gear from camshaft. Floating oil intake in sump incorporating gauze strainer. By-pass filter on side of cylinder block. Pressure relief valve incorporating high and low pressure feeds. High pressure to the main and big-end bearings, camshaft bearings and skew gear drive to oil pump and distributor, low pressure to valve gear and timing gears. Sump capacity 18 pints (2.7 U.S. gallons, 10 litres). From chassis 4BP5, full-flow oil filter.

Cooling system
Radiator shutters controlled by thermostat in header tank. Auxiliary thermostat in cylinder head to give quickest possible warm-up from cold. Belt driven centrifugal coolant pump and fan. 4AF2 and 4BP5 fitted with auxiliary cooling system for processional use, consisting of a second radiator mounted in the rear of the chassis with electric fans and an electric coolant pump mounted on the outside of the offside chassis

rail, brought into use by means of a tap operated by the driver.

Chassis

Dimensions
Overall length 19' 1½" (5,829mm)
Wheelbase 12' 1" (3,683mm)
Front track 4' 10½" (1,486mm)
Rear track 5' 3" (1,600mm)
Chassis weight 3,304 lb (1,499 kg).

Frame
Channel section frame of riveted (later welded) construction with cruciform centre bracing and crossmembers. Box section pan to support front suspension components. Two sidemount spare wheel carriers. Heavy export type bumpers and overriders fitted as standard.

Suspension
Front: independent by coil springs and rubber bushed wishbones, double acting hydraulic dampers and anti-roll bar.
Rear: semi-elliptic leaf springs protected by leather gaiters. Controllable hydraulic dampers by an oil pump mounted on the gearbox and an overriding control on the steering wheel boss.

Steering
Marles type cam and roller. Fore and aft side steering tube (drag link) to centre steering lever pivoted on front chassis cross member and two-piece cross steering tube (track rod). Turns lock to lock, 3½. Right-hand steering, all cars.

Transmission
Four forward speeds and reverse. Right-hand change. Synchromesh on second, third and top gears. Ratios: Top 1:1, Third 1.343:1, Second 2.02:1, First 2.985:1, Reverse 3.15:1.
Single dry-plate clutch.
From chassis 4BP5: Rolls-Royce 4-speed automatic gearbox and fluid coupling, with selector mounted on the right of the steering column. The following chassis were retrospectively fitted with this

feature: 4AF2 (1956), 4AF4 (1952), 4AF12 (1954).
Two-piece propeller shaft with needle roller bearing universal joints and centre bearing.
Rear axle: semi-floating type with hypoid gears. Ratio, 4.25:1.

Brakes
Hydraulic front, mechanical rear. Operation by means of friction disc servo on the offside of the gearbox, which applies the front brakes through a Lockheed master cylinder and assists the application of the rear brakes. Handbrake on rear wheels by pull-out handle under right side of fascia through a cable and mechanical linkage.

Exhaust system
Twin pipe system with four lagged expansion boxes and single tail pipe.

Centralised lubrication system
All bearings in the steering and suspension systems, including the rear spring main leaf and shackles, fed with oil from a reservoir and pump mounted on the bulkhead in the engine compartment. Pump operated by a pedal under the fascia, to be operated once every 100 miles (160 km).

Fuel system
Rear mounted petrol tank with filler necks on both sides of the car, capacity 23 gallons (27.6 U.S. gallons, 104.5 litres). Two S.U. dual fuel pump sets mounted in the frame, one pair to operate the main system and the other the reserve system, capacity 4 gallons (4.8 U.S. gallons, 18.1 litres). Filters between tank and pumps on both systems.

Electrical system
12 volt positive earth system with 78 amp/hour battery. Lucas special equipment dynamo and starter motor with reduction gearing and gentle-engagement pinion. Lucas R.100 headlamps. Twin Lucas fog lamps. Medium wave/Long wave Radiomobile radio with push-button tuning and two speakers. An hydraulically operated scuttle

mounted aerial was specified as standard but other types were fitted to some cars. Direction indicator switch mounted on an extension arm to the right of the steering column on 4AF2, but on the fascia or fascia capping rail on all other cars. Three interior heaters were normally fitted –

one under the fascia, one under the front passenger's seat and one under the offside of the rear seat, each with its own blower.

Other accessories
Trico vacuum operated windscreen washer.

Road wheels and tyres
17 inch steel disc wheels with semi-drop centre rims, on ten studs, carrying 7.00 x 17 Dunlop Fort 'C' tyres. Tyre pressures (not applicable to armour protected cars) 28 lb/sq. in. front, 39 lb/sq. in. rear. 'B' and 'C' series cars had 8.00 x 17 tyres.

Coachwork

All bodies built by outside coachbuilders to owners' specifications, as follows:

H. J. Mulliner	9
Hooper	7
Park Ward (works delivery wagon)	1
Franay	1
Total	18

Chassis and engine numbers, coachwork and original owners

Due to the very special nature of this very limited run of cars, a different format has been used to list them, with their coachbuilders, body types, original owners and delivery dates included.

Chassis	Engine	Coachwork	Design number	Built for	Delivery date
4AF2	P1A	H. J. Mulliner Special Limousine	7162	H.R.H. Princess Elizabeth	July 1950
4AF4	P2A	Park Ward open delivery wagon*	–	Rolls-Royce Ltd	
4AF6	P3A	H. J. Mulliner drophead coupé	7205	Shah of Persia	Dec. 1951
4AF8	P4A	H. J. Mulliner 6-light saloon	7206	Sultan of Kuwait	July 1951
4AF10	P5A	Hooper 7-passenger limousine	8292	Duke of Gloucester	Sept. 1951
4AF12	P6A	Hooper 7-passenger limousine	8307	Rolls-Royce Ltd†	July 1951
4AF14	P7A	H. J. Mulliner enclosed limousine	7181	General Franco	June 1952
4AF16	P8A	H. J. Mulliner enclosed limousine	7181	General Franco	July 1952
4AF18	P9A	H. J. Mulliner cabriolet	7183	General Franco	March 1952
4AF20	P10A	Hooper special sedanca de ville	8293	H. H. Aga Khan	April 1952
4AF22	P11A	Franay cabriolet	–	Prince Talal al Saoud Ryal	June 1952
4BP1	P1B	Hooper touring limousine	8361	King Feisal II	March 1952
4BP3	P2B	Hooper touring limousine	8370	Prince Regent of Iraq	March 1953
4BP5	P3B	Hooper landaulette	8399	Rolls-Royce Ltd‡	May 1954
4BP7	P4B	H. J. Mulliner 7-passenger limousine	7368	H.R.H. Princess Margaret	July 1954
4CS2	P1C	H. J. Mulliner 6-light saloon	7376	Sultan of Kuwait	Nov. 1955
4CS4	P2C	H. J. Mulliner 6-light saloon	7376	Sultan of Kuwait	Aug. 1955
4CS6	P3C	Hooper 7-passenger limousine	8425	Shah of Persia	Oct. 1956

* Dismantled January 1964 after a period of use by the Experimental Department and as a works lorry.
† Built for the use of Lord Hives and subsequently acquired by H.R.H. The Duchess of Kent.
‡ Subsequently acquired by the Royal Household, for whose use it was built, after Experimental use.

Above, top *The Phantom IV, at 12ft 1in, was the longest of the Rationalised Range of chassis. This is 4AF2, the first Phantom IV and originally intended to be the only one. It was built to the order of the then Princess Elizabeth and the Duke of Edinburgh. The small home-market bumpers shown here always looked rather inadequate on the Silver Wraith and were not in fact fitted to any of the eighteen Phantom IVs as delivered.*

Above & left *These three-quarter rear views of the same chassis clearly show the very long riveted plate in the centre of the cruciform member and the additional cross-member at this point. Other points of difference from the other early post-war chassis included a 23 gallon petrol tank with fillers both sides and ten stud mounting for the road wheels.*

Top right & below right *Two views of the 5,675cc straight-eight engine, again chassis 4AF2. The offside view is perhaps the more interesting of the two, showing the fusebox, regulator, chassis lubrication pump/reservoir, windscreen washing equipment and demister blower. In this view it can also be seen that the coolant from the radiator header tank enters the water pump via a rather different route from that of the six cylinder engines. The dual choke Stromberg carburetter was the same as that fitted to early Silver Wraiths and Silver Dawns.*

Bottom right & below
H. J. Mulliner & Co. were entrusted with the design and construction of the coachwork for 4AF2, as indeed they were for just over half of the Phantom IVs. A youthful Queen Elizabeth II is seen in the rear compartment before an enthusiastic crowd. Note that the royal car carries no registration plates and is fitted with a blue police light or 'theatre light' above the windscreen. The radiator mascot depicts St George slaying the dragon. When delivered new in July 1950 this car was painted Valentine green, but this was short-lived as the Phantom IV quickly replaced straight-eight Daimlers for use on State occasions and was repainted in 1952 in the royal colours of claret and black. The rear compartment features a seat that can be wound forward by means of the handle above the heel-board and a transparent panel in the roof with an electrically operated sliding cover. The rear window blind and division are also electrically operated.

Left *4AF4 was the second Phantom IV and served as a works delivery truck and test vehicle. The 'coachwork' was by Park Ward – the front portion at least being recognisably so! In 1952 it was fitted with the larger (6,515cc) B81 engine and automatic gearbox, in which guise it was undoubtedly the highest performance lorry in Britain, which several drivers found to their cost. With the blanket 30mph speed limit then in force for commercial vehicles the constabulary would have taken a dim view of the 90 of which this vehicle showed itself to be capable on numerous occasions! 4AF4 was dismantled at the end of 1963.*

Left *The third PIV built, and the second delivered to a customer, was 4AF6 for the Shah of Persia. The coachwork was again by H. J. Mulliner, but the design of the huge drophead coupé body was by no means characteristic of that coachbuilder. The colour scheme was light metallic blue with white leather upholstery. This is the only Phantom IV of those delivered to customers that is thought to have been scrapped (in 1959) though the body survives on a Phantom III chassis.*

Below *4AF8 was a saloon, without division, by H. J. Mulliner for the Emir of Kuwait. The two-tone paint scheme – an unusual combination of Orange Biscuit over Royal Blue – does little to disguise the fact that the lines are very similar to those of 4AF2, though without the sidemount spare wheels or swivelling vents to the rear compartment and with the addition of side scuttle ventilators.*

Top right *The first Phantom IV built for a customer by a coachbuilder other than H. J. Mulliner was 4AF10, for HRH The Duke of Gloucester who favoured Hooper & Co. The swivelling vents in the rear quarterlights are similar to those of 4AF2. The Duke's penchant for the unusual is evident in the ventilating panes above the side windows, the external sidelights, additional lights on the scuttle and an all black paint scheme with matt finish to the side panels between the waistline and the wings. John Bull's drawing shows most of these features clearly.*

Right & below *Perhaps one of the prettiest Phantom IVs was 4AF12, originally delivered to Rolls-Royce Ltd Managing Director Ernest Hives, upon being elevated to the peerage as Baron Hives. The 7-passenger limousine coachwork is by Hooper and displays their distinctive rear quarter-light shape. 'Hs' is said to have used the car only infrequently, apparently preferring his Bentley R-type. In 1954 4AF12 was sold to HRH Princess Marina, Duchess of Kent, after being fitted with an automatic gearbox. The front compartment interior view was taken at the Hooper works after this change and shows the flame pattern veneers widely used by coachbuilders at that time.*

This page *Late in 1948 Rolls-Royce Ltd received an order from General Franco of Spain for three Rolls-Royce cars, two limousines and a cabriolet, to be fitted with elaborate armour plating. While the Phantom IV chassis was not specified, or even known outside the Company at that time, it was decided that the best way to cope with the huge additional weight would be to build the three cars as Phantom IVs. The limousine in the photograph above, taken at the coachbuilder's popular photography location in Gunnersbury Park, West London, is 4AF16. Again, the lines are similar to those of 4AF2 – very elegant and distinctively H. J. Mulliner. The other Franco limousine, on chassis 4AF14, was to the same design number, 7181, while the cabriolet, on chassis 4AF18, sharing a similar wingline and panelwork below the waistline, was design number 7183. The photograph of 4AF18 shows the hood raised, while John Bull's drawing shows the hood down mode.*

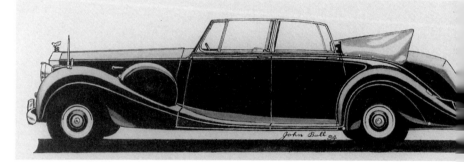

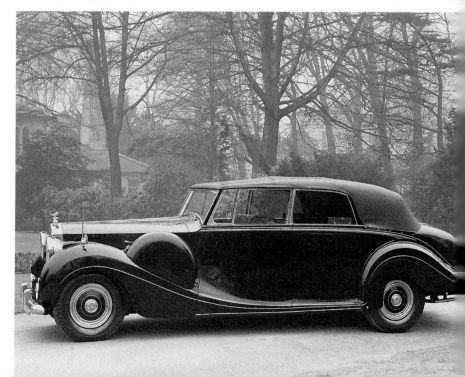

Top right *4AF20 is a very elegant sedanca de ville, the only body of that type on a Phantom IV chassis, shown here with the de ville extension closed. HH Prince Aga Khan was the customer and Hooper the coachbuilder. The paintwork was dark green with a lighter green band at the waistline. Interior upholstery was in red Connolly hide. It was shipped to France on April 6th 1952 and delivered by Franco-Britannic Autos of Paris.*

Right *4AF22 was the only PIV bodied by a foreign coachbuilder, Franay of Paris. It was built for HRH Prince Talal al Saoud for use in France. With front wings ending somewhat abruptly at the front of the flat external running boards, the design of this cabriolet could perhaps be regarded as a little awkward.*

Right *The first 'B' series Phantom IV was 4BP1, delivered to HM King Feisal II of Iraq and fitted with Hooper touring limousine coachwork of similar lines to the Aga Khan's sedanca de ville, 4AF20. John Bull's drawing shows the elegant profile.*

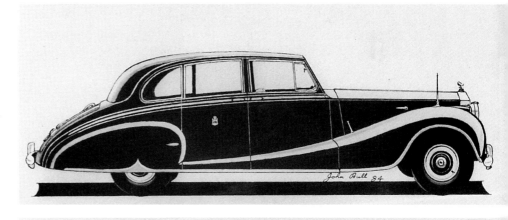

Bottom right *4BP3 is another Hooper touring limousine, this time built to Osmond Rivers' famous razor-edged 'new look' without separate rear wings, for the Prince Regent of Iraq. Again, John Bull's drawing shows the very elegant profile.*

Above *The two Iraqi Phantom IVs outside Hooper's Western Avenue, Acton works before being driven to Marseilles for shipping to Baghdad for the King's coronation in May 1953.*

Below *4BP5 is a Hooper landaulette built for Rolls-Royce Ltd and used for testing by the Experimental Department, who specially stiffened the chassis. It left the coachbuilder's in April 1954 and was intended for the use of HM The Queen. Code-named 'Jubilee', 4BP5 was the first PIV fitted with the automatic gearbox. John Bull's drawing shows the profile.*

Above *4BP5. This view of the driver's compartment shows the boldly figured walnut veneer used. The switch marked 'POLICE' to the right of the steering column operates the blue light above the windscreen – a feature of all Royal cars.*

Right *4BP7 is a 7-passenger limousine by H. J. Mulliner, delivered to HRH Princess Margaret in July 1954. The metamorphosis of Mulliner coachwork in the early 'fifties is readily apparent when comparing this car with earlier H. J. Mulliner PIVs. The front wingline is higher, sweeping down across the doors much less steeply. The winged horse Pegasus takes the place of the Spirit of Ecstasy on this elegant Rolls-Royce car, which was finished in black.*

Above *The rear seat of 4BP7 shown in its fully-forward position. The controls for the division, rear window blind and various interior lights can be seen, as can the shutter over the radio controls in the offside armrest and the handle for winding the seat forward in the base of the seat cushion.*

Above *The first two 'C' series Phantom IVs were 4CS2 and 4CS4, for which H. J. Mulliner built saloon bodies with external lines similar to those of 4BP7, for the Emir of Kuwait, HH Shaikh Sir Abdulla al Salim al Sabah. These became stablemates for his earlier PIV, 4AF8. The subject of the photograph is 4CS2, which was finished in light green over Opaline green.*

Right *John Bull's drawing shows the handsome profile of 4CS6, the final Phantom IV, a Hooper limousine similar to 4BP1. The customer was HRH The Shah of Persia. This car was at the Hythe Road Service Station for servicing when the Shah was deposed and Iran became an Islamic Republic. It was subsequently the subject of a dispute between Rolls-Royce Motors Ltd and the Iranian government.*

Chapter Five

The Meeting of the Marques

The Rolls-Royce Silver Cloud and Bentley S-type

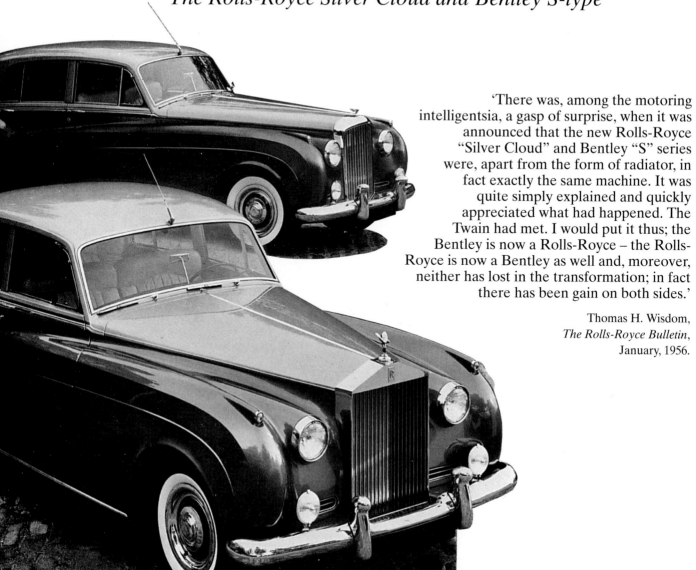

'There was, among the motoring intelligentsia, a gasp of surprise, when it was announced that the new Rolls-Royce "Silver Cloud" and Bentley "S" series were, apart from the form of radiator, in fact exactly the same machine. It was quite simply explained and quickly appreciated what had happened. The Twain had met. I would put it thus; the Bentley is now a Rolls-Royce – the Rolls-Royce is now a Bentley as well and, moreover, neither has lost in the transformation; in fact there has been gain on both sides.'

Thomas H. Wisdom,
The Rolls-Royce Bulletin,
January, 1956.

By 1952 the Silver Dawn and Bentley R-type Standard Saloons were beginning to look decidedly dated. The chassis was basically pre-war in concept and the lengthening of the body to provide a longer luggage boot did little to disguise the otherwise 1946 styling. The end for these models came in the spring of 1955, the last deliveries being made in May of that year. Deliveries of the all-new Silver Cloud and Bentley S-type had commenced the previous month. These new models represented a further advance on the road to range rationalisation in that for the first time the Rolls-Royce and Bentley versions shared the same twin S.U. carburetter power unit. The following year the Silver Wraith, which remained in production until the end of 1958, received the same engine.

The United States market responded quickly to the new models, with sales more than doubling virtually immediately. This was no accident. In fact it is certain that the Silver Cloud and S-type were designed with the potentially more lucrative North American market firmly in view and that their large size, together with their light, low-geared steering and soft suspension were intended to appeal to the trans-Atlantic buyer. It should be pointed out, however, that none of these attributes were taken to anything like the absurd extremes seen on contemporary American cars!

Essentially, the new chassis design followed previous post-war practice fairly closely, though with a host of detail improvements. The welded box-section frame brought an improvement in torsional rigidity of no less than 50% over its channel-section predecessor, for a trifling weight penalty of 14lb.

Other changes to the chassis layout included the repositioning of the rear semi-elliptic springs inboard of the frame side members and the addition of a substantial 'Z' type axle control rod, one end of which was attached to the right-hand frame side member and the other to the top of the axle casing. Each rear spring consisted of nine, instead of seven, leaves with those on the right-hand side being slightly thicker than their counterparts on the left, partly because the car was heavier on that side and partly to resist propeller shaft torque. Although they were still enclosed in leather gaiters, the rear springs were no longer fed with oil from the centralised chassis lubrication system, being packed with grease instead. The centralised lubrication system was only retained in a greatly abbreviated form, being confined to a few points on the front suspension and, on early cars, the steering ball-joints.

The braking system, while still based on the traditional friction-disc servo, was the subject of considerable improvement. Girling 'Autostatic' brakes were fitted, in which the shoes were in constant contact with the drums. The front brakes were of the two trailing shoe type, to avoid the 'self-servo' action of leading shoes often relied upon by other makers to provide a light pedal but notorious for causing fade under severe conditions of use. At the rear, leading and trailing shoes were used, actuated by a combined hydraulic and mechanical expander. For the first time, both front and rear brakes were hydraulically actuated, though the direct mechanical linkage between the pedal and the rear brakes was retained, mainly to impart 'feel' to the pedal. There was an increase in friction area amounting to almost 30% despite the reduced drum diameter dictated by the stylists' requirement for fifteen inch instead of sixteen inch wheels. In response to criticisms of 'servo lag', the servo was geared to revolve at 0.179 of the propeller shaft speed instead of 0.095. The whole scheme provided smooth, powerful, fade-free braking from the high speeds of which the car was so effortlessly capable, with pedal pressures so light that road-testers invariably expressed amazement. From May 1956 the master cylinder and fluid reservoir were duplicated, with an extra set of expanders for the front shoes. The system was split so that one circuit activated one shoe in each front drum while the other worked the rear brakes and the remaining shoes at the front. Thus, with the pedal still mechanically linked to the rear brakes, there were effectively three braking systems, each capable of stopping the car in the unlikely event of servo, hydraulic or mechanical failure. A twist-to-release handbrake, as fitted to earlier left-hand drive cars, was standard on the Silver Cloud and S-type cars.

With the introduction of the Silver Cloud series, Rolls-Royce Ltd abandoned use of their own distinctive terminology for the main steering linkage components. Thus their 'cross steering tube' and 'side steering tube' became more mundanely the track rod and drag link respectively – the former being a three-piece linkage and the latter a transverse mounted affair connected to an extension on one of two idler levers pivoted between the chassis and the centre member of the track linkage. The steering was lower geared than previously but this only partially accounted for the $4\frac{1}{2}$ turns of the steering wheel lock-to-lock compared to $3\frac{3}{4}$ of the earlier models, the remainder being due to greater front wheel movement made possible by revisions to the front suspension design. This gave the new models a slightly smaller turning circle than their shorter predecessors. The new front suspension layout comprised long lower and short upper wishbones with the upper pairs pivoted on the shafts of the horizontal piston-type shock dampers.

Early in 1956 power-assisted steering was offered as an option, at first for export only. American motorists had by that time become accustomed to having power steering on large luxury cars and an expensive car without it would undoubtedly have been less saleable in that market. On cars fitted with power-assisted steering the steering ratio was raised from 20.6:1 to 18.7:1, which brought a modest reduction in the turns of the wheel lock-to-lock to 4¼. No doubt, with the benefit of power-assistance, the ratio could have been raised further, but Rolls-Royce were committed to combating the now discredited 'sneeze factor' – i.e., the possibility of the car being thrown off line by slight inadvertent movements of the steering wheel with very light but high-geared steering. It is on record that a number of chassis being fitted with coachbuilt bodies at the time the p.a.s. option was announced were retrospectively fitted in response to demands from customers that their cars be of the latest specification – at considerable expense to the Company.

The steering wheel hub was, for the first time, completely unencumbered by control levers, the last of these (the 'ride control') having given way to a two-position switch on the side of the steering column. This switch, marked 'N' (normal) and 'H' (hard) operated solenoids in the rear dampers which altered the 'slow leak', doubling the degree of damping while the switch was in the 'H' position, thus eliminating the need for the gearbox-driven oil pump and associated piping of earlier ride control schemes.

The engine of the new cars was basically the 4,887cc unit used for the 'D' series R-type Continental, with full-length high chromium content cylinder liners and a new six-port cylinder head to improve breathing. The new head was attached by means of set bolts rather than on studs as hitherto. The twin S.U. carburetters were

of a new diaphragm type (HD.6) and were mounted on a revised induction manifold, one half of which was integral with the head while the other half, carrying the carburetters, was bolted to it. This arrangement allowed the internal shape of the induction gallery to be more accurately controlled, while simplifying casting and facilitating future maintenance.

Between 1955 and 1959 the 4.9 litre six cylinder power unit underwent a continuous programme of modification and improvement, not the least of which was the fitting of 2-inch (HD.8) carburetters together with increased diameter (2 inch) inlet valves and raised compression ratio (from 6.6:1 for the standard car and 7.25:1 for the Continental – of which more anon – to 8:1 for both versions.) The result was a silky smooth engine of great refinement and considerable power output, the latter certainly more than 'adequate', as the Company rather modestly described it!

If the chassis design and mechanical features of the Silver Cloud and S-type went largely unnoticed, it was because the magnificent new Standard Saloon coachwork stole the limelight. The new cars were as modern and sleek in appearance as their predecessors had been outdated and upright. Above all, they were considerably larger, and looked it. The aesthetic appeal of the styling was utterly beyond criticism. Chief Styling Engineer John Blatchley and his team had carried out their task to perfection. The only negative aspect was that the standard saloon was now so impressive that it was responsible for driving one of the final nails into the coffin of the traditional British coachbuilding trade. The few remaining coachbuilders were hard pressed to improve upon such superb lines and high quality interior furnishings.

The main body structure was produced in 20-gauge steel, with

18- and 16-gauge 'Birmabrite' aluminium alloy for the doors, boot lid and bonnet lids to minimise weight. To combat corrosion, zinc plated steel was used for the sills and certain other vulnerable areas. As had already become common practice in the coachbuilding trade since the late 'thirties, slim (stainless steel) door window frames were used for a larger glass area and lighter appearance. As before, the body shells were supplied by the Pressed Steel Company, with all finishing and trimming work carried out at Crewe.

The increased overall size made for a noticeably more spacious interior than had been possible with the Silver Dawn and R-type standard saloons. Somewhat surprisingly, the front seating was of the bench type, though with individual squabs each adjustable for rake. A road-test report in *The Autocar* for 7th October 1955 described the seating as 'supremely comfortable', but suggested that central armrests for the front seat 'would be a useful addition'. The people at Rolls-Royce agreed, as generously proportioned folding armrests were provided in each front squab from early 1956. The rear seating was even better, being quite the most luxurious imaginable, contoured for maximum comfort for two occupants without being uncomfortable for three, and provided with a large folding centre armrest, side elbow rests and generous corner padding. As before, the standard upholstery material was Connolly 'Vaumol' hide, with West of England cloth for the headlining and deep-pile Wilton carpet edged with leather to match the upholstery. Other creature comforts included the usual folding picnic tables in the backs of the front seats, a sliding picnic tray below the fascia, vanity mirrors (incorporating night-lights) in the rear quarters, two spring-loaded leather hand grips designed to swing up above the window line when not in use, cigar lighters and ashtrays front and rear, a Radiomobile push-button radio, a rather complex heating, ventilation and demisting system and a Triplex heated rear window. The fuel filler door was opened by means of a switch on the fascia, with an emergency pull-wire in the boot. Full refrigerated air conditioning and electric windows were offered as options on the later cars.

As the engine bay bulkhead and side panels were integral with the body of the Standard Saloon it was necessary to make available a special chassis incorporating these features for coachbuilt bodies. Although several coachbuilt designs were offered, it was so difficult to improve upon the standard saloon, both in respect to exterior styling and interior furnishings, that there was an increasing tendency for the coachbuilders' efforts to be concentrated on the Bentley Continental and, to a lesser extent, the Long Wheelbase chassis introduced in 1957.

Even today, in this era of highly sophisticated motor cars, a good Silver Cloud or Bentley S is an extremely impressive car in which to ride or drive. The only noticeable noise comes from the very large tyres on rough road surfaces, but even this is never more than subdued. The lofty driving position, luxurious seating, silent performance and sure-footed handling make for exceptionally fatigue-free motoring. They are cars that certainly had no serious competitors in their day. Petrol economy, as is to be expected with so large and heavy a car, is not the Silver Cloud's best feature, though despite the 13-16mpg range quoted by *The Autocar* after a fast and punishing road-test, 20mpg is possible when touring and some owners have bettered this figure with the benefit of such modern aids as transistorised ignition. The lower octane and modern unleaded fuels are suitable.

From the earliest Rolls-Royce cars it had been customary to offer a choice of wheelbases. During 1957 a long wheelbase version of the Silver Cloud and Bentley S-type became available, the first deliveries commencing in November of that year. The frame manufacturer, John Thompson Motor Pressings, supplied a chassis frame four inches longer than that of the standard car. A standard saloon body similarly lengthened, usually with a division between front and rear compartments, was available on this chassis, as well as a number of coachbuilt editions. The lengthening of the standard saloon bodies was ingeniously carried out by Park Ward at their Willesden works. The rear doors were longer and did not carry quarter-lights, these being let into the rear quarters of the body, thus transforming a four-light saloon into a six-light limousine. So expert was the conversion that it is impossible to detect where the extra length was added. The lengthened bodies were returned to Crewe for mounting on the chassis, painting and trimming.

The Bentley Continental had been such a successful concept that any question of its continuation into the S Series era was a foregone conclusion. The Bentley Continental S-type differed from the early standard chassis in having a higher (7.25:1) compression ratio, higher (2.92:1) final drive ratio and 7.60 x 15 tyres instead of 8.20 x 15. These differences, together with the lower, more streamlined bodies fitted, sufficed to give the Continental a maximum speed of around 120mph and faster acceleration in the upper speed range than that of the standard cars. Like that of the later standard chassis, the later Continental engines had 8:1 compression ratio, accompanied by an enlargement of the inlet valves to 2 inch diameter and larger S.U. type HD.8 carburetters, for still better performance.

Somewhat incongruously perhaps, automatic transmission was standard on the Continental S-type, though a few cars were fitted with synchromesh gearbox at the customers' request. By 1957 this option was no longer available.

Although all but a handful of the previous R-type Continental chassis were fitted with H. J. Mulliner two-door sports saloon bodies, such was not the case with the Continental S-type, which saw a far greater variety of coachwork styles, including four-door saloons. H. J. Mulliner's four-door Continental was called the 'Flying Spur' and was available in four- and six-light configurations, of which the latter was the more usual. British coachbuilders between them offered no fewer than seven distinct body styles on the S1* Continental chassis.

The six-cylinder S Type cars were retrospectively called S1 after the introduction of the V-8 engined S2 in July/August 1959. The same applied to the six-cylinder Silver Cloud, which became the Silver Cloud I.

TECHNICAL SPECIFICATION

Rolls-Royce Silver Cloud & Bentley S Type

Engine

Dimensions
Six cylinders in line.
Bore 3.75 inches (95.25mm), stroke 4.5 inches (114mm), cubic capacity 298.2 cu. in. (4,887cc)
Compression ratio 6.6:1.
Bentley Continental 7.25:1.
From Silver Cloud chassis SDD136 and Bentley chassis B120EG onwards for Nth America only, 8:1.
From Silver Cloud chassis SFE9, Bentley chassis B257EK, Bentley Continental from chassis BC21BG onwards and all long wheelbase cars, 8:1.

Cylinder block/Crankcase
Iron monobloc casting with 30% chrome iron liners.

Crankshaft
Nitrided molybdenum steel, fully machined and balanced. Integral balance weights. Seven main bearings of lead-indium lined steel.

Pistons
Light alloy slit skirt.

Cylinder head
Aluminium alloy with inserted valve seats.

Valve gear
Overhead inlet, side exhaust valves. Case hardened nickel steel camshaft driven by helical gears.

Carburetters
Twin S.U. type HD.6 (1³/₄" bore). compression engines, twin S.U. type HD.8 (2" bore).

Automatic choke.
Air intake silencer incorporating mesh air filter element (oil bath type air cleaner on cars for use in dusty conditions).

Ignition system
Ignition by high tension coil and Delco-Remy distributor with twin contact breaker points. Firing order 1,4,2,6,3,5.

Lubrication system
Helical gear oil pump in crankcase driven by skew gear from camshaft. Floating oil intake in sump incorporating gauze strainer. Full-flow filter on side of cylinder block. Pressure relief valve incorporating high and low pressure feeds. High pressure to the main and big-end bearings, camshaft bearings and skew gear drive to oil pump and distributor, low pressure to valve gear and timing gears. Sump capacity 16 pints (2.4 U.S. gallons, 9 litres).

Cooling system
Fixed radiator shutters. Thermostat on front of engine with radiator by-pass to give quickest possible warm-up from cold. Belt driven centrifugal coolant pump and fan.

Chassis

Dimensions
Overall length, standard and Continental, 17' 8" (5,385mm)
Overall length, long wheelbase, 17' 11³/₄" (5,480mm)
Wheelbase, standard and Continental, 10' 3" (3,124mm)
Wheelbase, long, 10' 7" (3,226mm)
Front track 4' 10" (1,473mm)
Rear track 5' (1,524mm)

Frame
Welded box-section frame with cruciform centre bracing.

Suspension
Front: independent by coil springs, opposed piston hydraulic dampers and anti-roll bar.
Rear: semi-elliptic leaf springs protected by leather gaiters. Electrically controllable hydraulic dampers by a switch on the left of the steering column to give 'normal' or 'hard' setting.

Steering
Marles type cam and roller connected by a transverse link to a three-piece track linkage. Power assisted steering optional, at first for export only, from Silver Cloud mid-C series, Bentley late B series, Bentley Continental early B series and all long wheelbase cars. Turns lock to lock, 4¹/₄.

Transmission
Rolls-Royce 4-speed automatic gearbox and fluid coupling, with selector mounted on the right of the steering column.
Ratios: Top 1:1, Third 1.45:1, Second 2.63:1, First 3.82:1, Reverse 4.3:1.
Manual gearbox, with right-hand change lever, available on early Bentley Continental S-type.
Two-piece propeller shaft with needle roller bearing universal joints and centre bearing.

Rear axle: hypoid bevel final drive with four-star differential and semi-floating half-shafts. Ratio 3.42:1. Bentley Continental ratio 2.92:1.

Brakes
Rolls-Royce/Girling drum brakes. Hydraulic front, hydraulic/mechanical rear. Operation by means of friction disc servo on the offside of the gearbox, which applies the brakes hydraulically. Handbrake on rear wheels by pull-out, twist-to-release handle under fascia through a cable and mechanical linkage.
From Silver Cloud chassis SYB50, Bentley chassis B245BC, Bentley Continental chassis BC16BG onwards and all long wheelbase cars, twin master cylinders and duplicated front hydraulic circuits.

Exhaust system
Single large bore system with three expansion boxes, each tuned to absorb a different range of frequencies.

Centralised lubrication system
Limited centralised system supplying the bearings in the steering and front suspension, with oil from a reservoir and pump mounted on the bulkhead in the engine compartment. Pump operated by a pedal under the fascia, to be operated once every 100 miles (160 km.) Rear springs packed with grease for life.

Fuel system
Rear mounted petrol tank, capacity 18 gallons (21.6 U.S. gallons, 81.8 litres.) S.U. dual fuel pump mounted in the frame. Filter between tank and pump.

Electrical system
12 volt negative earth system with 55 amp/hour battery. Lucas special equipment dynamo and starter motor with planetary reduction gear and gentle-engagement pinion. Lucas built-in headlamps. Twin Lucas fog lamps twin filament bulbs for flashing direction indicators. Direction indicator switch on the fascia

capping rail. Medium wave/Long wave Radiomobile radio with push-button tuning and two speakers. Comprehensive interior heating/ventilation/demisting system. Refrigerated air conditioning available if required. Heated rear window. Trico electric windscreen washer system.

Road wheels and tyres
15 inch steel disc wheels, on five studs, carrying 8.20 x 15 broad base tyres. Bentley Continentals had either 7.60 x 15 or 8.00 x 15 tyres depending on body type. Tyre pressures, front 22 lb/sq. in., rear 27 lb/sq. in.

Firsts

	Chassis	Year
Silver Cloud	SWA2	1955
Bentley S Type	B2AN	1955
Bentley Continental S Type	BC1AF	1955
Centre armrests in front seat, standard saloon	SXA137, B210BA	1956
Twin brake master cylinders	SYB50, B245BC, BC16BG	1956
Revised chassis frame with splayed front end	SZB139, B27CM	1956
HD.8 (2" bore) carburetters, 8:1 compression ratio (Nth. America)	SDD136, B120EG	1957
HD.8 (2" bore) carburetters, 8:1 compression ratio (home)	SFE9, B257EK, BC21BG	1957
Silver Cloud long wheelbase	ALC1	1957
Bentley S Type long wheelbase	ALB1	1957

Coachwork

Standard four-door factory saloon body of steel construction with aluminium doors, boot and bonnet lids. Special coachwork fitted to all Bentley Continentals and some standard and long wheelbase chassis as follows:

Coachbuilder	Silver Cloud	Silver Cloud lwb	Bentley	Bentley lwb	Continental
H. J. Mulliner	45*	2†	43*	–	218
Park Ward	1*	–	1*	–	185
James Young	33	17	31	5	20
Hooper	26	13	45	7	6
Freestone & Webb	15	2	23	–	–
Chapron	–	1	–	–	–
Graber	1	–	2	–	1
Franay	–	–	–	–	1
Totals	121	35	145	12	431

* including drophead coupé adaptations of the standard saloon.
† 'Countryman' estate cars adapted from standard saloons for Harold Radford.

Note: long wheelbase adaptations of the standard saloon are not included as coachbuilt cars.

Chassis and engine numbers

Silver Cloud I
Chassis sub-series starting with 1 use odd number only, those starting with 2 use even numbers only. Engines are numbered consecutively. The number 13 was omitted from chassis numbering.

Series	Chassis numbers	Engine numbers
A	SWA2-250, SXA1-252	SA1-250
B	SYB2-250, SZB1-251	SB1-250
C	SBC2-150, SCC1-151	SC1-150
D	SDD2-450, SED1-451	SD1-450
E	SGE2-500, SFE1-501	SE1-500
F	SHF1-249, SJF2-250	SF1-250
G	SKG1-125, SLG2-126	SG1-125
H	SMH1-265, SNH2-262	SH1-263

Total: 2,238 cars.

Bentley S1
Chassis sub-series starting with 1 use odd number only, those starting with 2 use even numbers only. Engines are numbered consecutively. The number 13 was omitted from chassis numbering.

Series	Chassis numbers	Engine numbers
A	B2AN-B500AN, B1AP-B501AP	BA1-500
B	2BA-B250BA, B1BC-B251BC	BB1-250
C	B2CK-B500CK, B1CM-B500CM	BC1-500
D	B2DB-B350DB, B1DE-B351DE	BD1-350
E	B2EG-B650EG, B1EK-B651EK	BE1-650
F	B2FA-B650FA, B1FD-B651FD	BF1-650
G	B1GD-B125GD, B2GC-B126GC	BG1-125
H	B1HB-B45HB, B2HA-B50HA	BH1-47

Total: 3,072 cars.

Silver Cloud I long wheelbase
Chassis and engines are numbered consecutively, omitting 13 from chassis numbering.

Series	Chassis numbers	Engine numbers
A	ALC1-26*	C1A-C25A
B	BLC1-51	C1B-C50B
C	CLC1-47	C1C-C46C

Total: 122 cars.

* Plus experimental car 28B, later renumbered ALC1X.

Bentley S1 long wheelbase
Chassis and engines are numbered consecutively, omitting 13 from chassis numbering.

Series	Chassis numbers	Engine numbers
A	ALB1-36	B1A-B35A

Total: 35 cars.

Bentley Continental S1
Chassis and engines are numbered consecutively, omitting 13 from chassis numbering.

Series	Chassis numbers	Engine numbers
A	BC1AF-BC101AF*	BC1A-BC100A
B	BC1BG-BC101BG	BC1B-BC100B
C	BC1CH-BC51CH	BC1C-BC50C
D	BC1DJ-BC51DJ	BC1D-BC50D
E	BC1EL-BC51EL	BC1E-BC50E
F	BC1FM-BC51FM	BC1F-BC50F
G	BC1GN-BC31GN	BC1G-BC30G

Total: 431 cars.

* Plus experimental car 27B, later renumbered BC102AF.

Right *'The twain have met.' The Rolls-Royce Silver Cloud and Bentley S Series standard saloons appeared to be identical cars except for radiator shells and badges. In fact, the bonnets were also different and the Silver Cloud's front wing panels rose higher at the front adjacent to the bonnet shut line and were not interchangeable between the two models. Both were exceptionally handsome motor cars and made a considerable impact at the time of their introduction.*

Above *An early Silver Cloud alongside a Rolls-Royce 'Avon' powered Comet 4 jet airliner.*

Above *Unlike its predecessors, the Silver Cloud and Bentley S Series chassis frame was of welded box section. This is a Silver Cloud chassis fitted with twin master cylinders (introduced May 1956) and splayed frame front end (August 1956) but lacking power-assisted steering. The 'Z' type axle control rod can be seen between the off-side main frame member and the rear axle. The Bentley S Series chassis was identical except for radiator shell and badges, while the long wheelbase version of each marque was similar, but four inches longer. The standard saloon body shell incorporated integral engine compartment side and rear bulkheads, so the chassis illustrated may be assumed to have been destined for special coachwork.*

Left & below *For the first time Rolls-Royce and Bentley models shared identical engines, but for the marque names on the rocker covers. This is an early engine with 1¾ inch S.U. type HD.6 carburetters and no pump for power-assisted steering. The rear extension of the automatic gearbox no longer incorporated a ride control pump as this feature was now electrically operated. The friction disc servo was speeded up on these models to eliminate any trace of 'servo lag'.*

Below *The Silver Cloud and S Series front suspension featured unequal length semi-trailing wishbones, the upper pairs of which doubled as levers of the piston type shock dampers, as on the earlier post-war design. The anti-roll bar can be seen running across the front of the chassis and attached with rubber bushings to the lower wishbone. The flexible hose nearest the wheel is the hydraulic brake line. These were duplicated on later cars with dual master cylinders and split circuit front brakes. The inner hose carries oil from the centralised chassis lubrication system to the kingpin.*

Below *The six-port cylinder head of the Silver Cloud and S Series, showing the very large inlet valves. The head was secured to the block by set-bolts rather than on studs as before.*

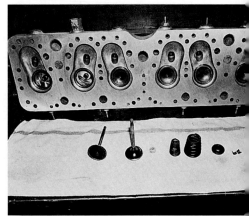

Above, right & left *From mid-1957 2-inch carburetters were fitted. Note the duplicated belts on engines for cars with power-assisted steering, the reservoir and pump for which can be seen on the left-hand side of this engine. The starter motor in this instance is mounted on the right of the engine, for a left-hand drive car.*

Right *The Silver Cloud was equally at home in London or New York, Los Angeles or Sydney – or in English country lanes. The remaining specialist coachbuilders were hard pressed to better either the external lines or interior furnishings. Within four years one firm had ceased coachbuilding, another was building its last bodies and a third had been purchased by Rolls-Royce Ltd, later to be merged with Park Ward.*

Below *A particularly beautiful photograph of a Silver Cloud, showing to full advantage the flawless lines of the standard saloon coachwork – the work of John Blatchley and his Crewe design team. In their fourth decade, these cars still impress. The design lent itself particularly well to two-tone colour schemes.*

Left *This view shows to advantage the alternative Bentley radiator shell, for which more customers opted than the statelier Rolls-Royce type. The winged 'B' mascot was not mounted on a dummy filler cap as it had been on the earlier models, though one could be supplied 'for special mascots' if required.*

Below inset *A test of good styling is how it looks from behind. This three-quarter rear view of a Bentley S illustrates how convincingly John Blatchley's standard saloon passes this test.*

Below *This side view clearly shows the rather complex two-toning arrangement adopted for these cars. It should be noted that normally, though not always, the bonnet top was finished in the lower colour on Bentleys and in the upper colour on Silver Clouds. Cars for Switzerland were supplied without radiator mascots, which probably explains the absence of the winged 'B' on this S Series.*

Above left & right *No less handsome is the standard saloon's interior, the tasteful fascia in particular lending the front compartment an air of unostentatious luxury. The switch on the left of the steering column is for the electrically adjustable rear shock dampers. The 'switchbox' in the centre of the fascia was considerably simplified, with the ignition key now performing the combined functions of the former master switch, master switch lock, ignition switch and starter button. The lighting switch, above the ignition lock, may be locked in the 'off' or 'side & tail' positions by withdrawing the ignition key.*

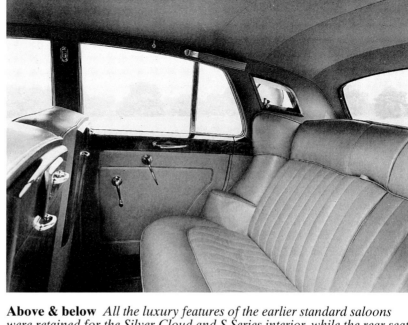

Above & below *All the luxury features of the earlier standard saloons were retained for the Silver Cloud and S Series interior, while the rear seat was even more luxurious than hitherto, with generous corner padding and ample support for shoulders and thighs.*

Above *The front seat was a bench type with separate reclining squabs. The centre armrests shown were absent in the earliest cars. The side armrests are adjustable both fore-and-aft and for height.*

Left *The engine bay of a later 2-inch carburetter car, in this instance a Bentley, fitted with the optional refrigerated air conditioning and power-assisted steering. The oil-bath air filter, with its flexible trunking to the air silencer, indicates an export car destined for a territory with dusty conditions – possibly Australia.*

Below, left & right *These drawings show the layout of the optional refrigerated air conditioning system, with boot mounted refrigeration unit.*

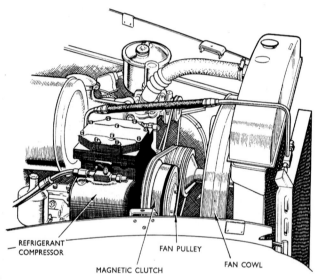

— REFRIGERANT COMPRESSOR

FAN PULLEY

MAGNETIC CLUTCH

FAN COWL

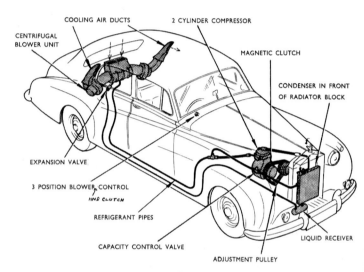

COOLING AIR DUCTS

2 CYLINDER COMPRESSOR

CENTRIFUGAL BLOWER UNIT

MAGNETIC CLUTCH

CONDENSER IN FRONT OF RADIATOR BLOCK

EXPANSION VALVE

3 POSITION BLOWER CONTROL

HAND CLUTCH

REFRIGERANT PIPES

CAPACITY CONTROL VALVE

ADJUSTMENT PULLEY

LIQUID RECEIVER

Bottom opposite, above & right
Continuing an earlier successful theme, Harold Radford (Coachbuilders) Ltd offered a 'Countryman' conversion of the standard saloon that included every conceivable luxury fitting. Each feature was available, and priced, separately so that the customer could choose a uniquely individual package. Thus each 'Countryman' is different and unique. The photograph shows the 'Webasto' sunshine roof, which was one of the more popular Radford modifications. The fine-line painted along the wingline on this car is another feature often applied to Radford cars. John Bull's drawing depicts the picnic requisites, including electric kettle and washbasin, that were among the fittings available for the boot.

Bottom right *In addition to the normal luxury fittings of the standard saloon, the Radford 'Countryman' could be fitted with compartments for glasses, decanters and flasks behind the front seats and/or, as shown here, in the front doors.*

165

THE "SAFARI CAR"

BENTLEY TOWN AND COUNTRY ESTATE CAR

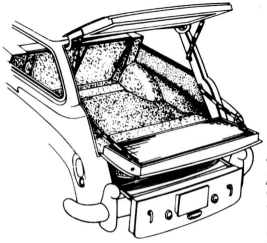

This page *Another Radford conversion of the standard saloon, and a particularly unusual one, was the Town and Country Estate Car. The external modifications were carried out by H. J. Mulliner and Radford did the interiors, which included bi-fold rear seats as was available for the Countryman saloon. Two Estates were built from standard left-hand drive Silver Clouds, chassis LSLG112 and LSMH65, the former of which, believed to be the subject of the photographs, was exhibited at the 1959 New York Motor Show. A further two were built on left-hand drive Silver Cloud Long Wheelbase chassis LCLC38 and LCLC42.*

Left & below *H. J. Mulliner's fully coachbuilt work (as opposed to conversions of the standard saloon) on the Silver Cloud and S Series chassis shared a common wingline and boot shape. This is an early six-light saloon, design number 7401, with turned-out sill line. This was a natural development of their 'Lightweight' saloons on the Mk VI/R chassis, using the same mode of construction – though the end result was far from light! The front wings run right through to the tail in an unbroken line, with the almost vestigial rear wings superimposed on them. Note the rear-hinged doors to the rear compartment – a rare feature on all but formal limousines by the mid-'fifties. 27 of this design were built, with a further 4 examples (design number 7412) on the Silver Cloud I chassis. Note the absence of a radiator mascot and the dummy filler cap, which was supplied for use with 'special mascots' (part number UE.1883). Below is Mulliner designer Herbert Nye's drawing of this saloon.*

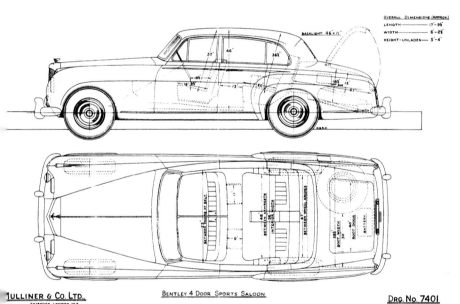

Below, left & right *Another H. J. Mulliner saloon on Bentley S1 chassis B332LEG, owned when the photographs were taken by Dr. C. S. (Sam) Shoup of Tennessee, first President of the RROC (now Inc) and now in the collection of Matthew Sysak (RROC Inc). This car features the 'turned in' sill line of the later examples and was the last of this design before it was discontinued in 1957 in favour of the 'Flying Spur' saloon, which was only built on the Continental chassis.*

Above *Adolph C. Rosner (RROC Inc) owns this H. J. Mulliner saloon on Silver Cloud I chassis SYB30 – one of four such cars built on Rolls-Royce chassis. These fully coachbuilt H. J. Mulliner cars had the wedge-shaped Continental fuel tank with the filler on the opposite side to that of the standard saloons.*

Left *H. J. Mulliner all-metal saloon, 1955 Silver Cloud I chassis SWA76, photographed at Althorp Park, Northamptonshire, by Klaus-Josef Roßfeldt (RREC).*

JACK BARCLAY LTD.

This page *James Young Ltd offered this alternative to the standard saloon, design number SC10 (Rolls-Royce) and B.10 (Bentley). The car in the photograph above is Silver Cloud I chassis SWA52, their 1955 Earls Court Show exhibit. The designer's wash drawing (right) and line drawings (below) show the Bentley version. The knife-edged fin on the rear wing was not present on all examples of this design, some having only a vestigial fin at the rear extremity of the wing.*

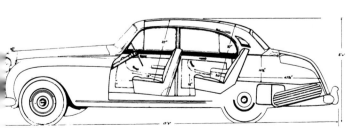
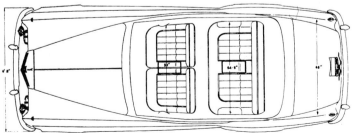

Above & left Hoopers developed their 'new look' for the Silver Cloud and S Series with a rounder look and a very long boot. The Bentley S1 above has semaphore-type trafficators in the centre pillars – very unusual, and possibly unique, for an S Series car. The Silver Cloud I left, showing the rear aspect, is SWA102, owned when photographed by Joe Murphy (RROCA). Note the heavily hooded headlights and non-standard rear lights of this design. The coachbuilder's design number was 8435.

Right The interior of the Hooper saloon could, if required, be fitted with an electrically-operated division as shown here. In this guise, the design numbers were 8444 (Rolls-Royce) and 8443 (Bentley).

Right *For the 1958 model year these designs were modified by incorporating an up-sweep of the wingline over the rear axle, as shown in this photograph of B17EK, owned by the late Andrew Pastouna (RREC). The design numbers were 8506 (Rolls-Royce) and 8497 (Bentley).*

Below *This Hooper saloon, shown in the coachbuilder's line and concept drawings, was never built. The wingline and general lines, however, were used for the design number 8512 saloon for the Continental chassis.*

Above *Freestone & Webb built fewer bodies than the other main coachbuilders, did not batch-build and produced more 'one-off' designs. This six-light saloon on Silver Cloud I chassis SYB24 is a one-off, design number 3224/SC. Note the heavily hooded lights front and rear and the straight-through wingline.*

Left *Freestone & Webb's obviously Hooper-derived styling was carried over from the R-type almost unchanged for the Silver Cloud and Bentley S, even retaining the by now rather old-fashioned razor-edged boot. By this time, Freestone & Webb were nearing the end of their coachbuilding days and these were the last chassis types on which they built bodies.*

Bottom left *The front and rear wing extremities here are characteristic Freestone & Webb of the period, but the wingline is more 'swoopy', lending considerable panache to this one-off fixed head coupé on 1955 Silver Cloud I chassis SWA108, design number 3210/A.*

Above *Another example of Freestone & Webb's interpretation of Hooper's 'new look', this time with two doors. Another one-off, design number 3193 on 1955 Silver Cloud I chassis SWA42.*

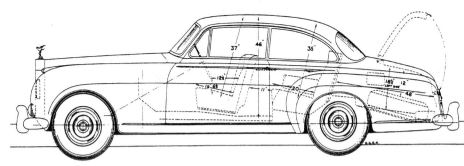

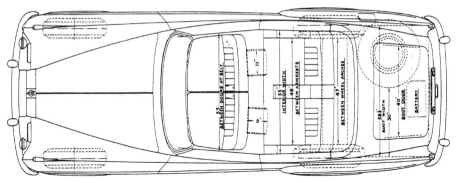

ROLLS-ROYCE SILVER CLOUD 2 DOOR SPORTS SALOON

H.J. MULLINER & CO. LTD.,
CHISWICK, LONDON W.4.

DRG. No. **7408**

Right & below right *Sharing the wingline and boot styling of their six-light saloons, H. J. Mulliner's two-door saloons to design number 7408 (Rolls-Royce) and 7407 (Bentley) are much rarer. The photograph shows an early Bentley S1 and is believed to be B277AP. Note the three-piece wrap-around rear window. The coachbuilder's line drawing shows the Rolls-Royce version.*

Left & bottom right *With a similar styling theme to the closed cars on pages 167, 168 and 173, these drophead coupés were built by H. J. Mulliner until mid-1959, when they changed over to adapting standard saloons to dropheads. Most of these fully coachbuilt dropheads were four-light cars to design number 7410, seen here in left-hand drive Rolls-Royce guise. The black covers over the headlight apertures indicate a U.S. export car – sealed beam headlights being fitted by the dealer after arrival.*

Left *Four-light configuration again, this time a Bentley. Note the slightly flared sill – a small design variation also seen in Mulliner's six-light saloons.*

Bottom left *This two-light variant, on 1958 Silver Cloud I chassis LSGE466, is a one-off to design number 7415. This car also has the turned-out sill line.*

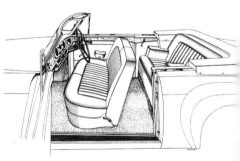

Above & inset *James Young built only three Silver Cloud drophead coupés, to design number SC20. The first of these, on 1958 chassis LSGE448, is seen here in the coachbuilder's official photograph. The raised hood is shown inset.*

Above *This is the third and final James Young design number SC20, a two-seater variant on 1959 chassis LSJF202, photographed in Switzerland by Tom Solley. Note how the two-seater configuration allows the hood to stow flush with the top line of the boot.*

Below & below right *The adaptation of standard saloon bodies to drophead coupés is normally associated with H. J. Mulliner. However, Park Ward carried out the first such adaptation on Bentley S1 chassis B568FA, the subject of these photographs taken by Ian Bennell (RROCA) when he owned the car. Peter Wharton, Park Ward's Chief Draughtsman during the post-war period, recalled that 'the conversion proved so* expensive and the work so protracted that the project was abandoned. In fact, the whole exercise went against the practice of most coachbuilders, who having to design a two-door saloon and a drophead coupé would always design the drophead first, on the principle that one could always convert a drophead to a saloon but never the other way around. When the Mulliner version was announced the lads at Park Ward were, to say the least, a bit vexed – claiming that they had done all the hard work for someone else!'

Top left *H. J. Mulliner's standard saloon to drophead coupé adaptations proved so commercially successful that from early 1959 and right through the Silver Cloud III years their efforts on standard Silver Cloud and Bentley S Series chassis were confined to this design number 7504 style. With the fully-lined hood raised, the car was as comfortable and draught-free as a saloon. The body shells, once converted, were returned to Crewe for mounting on the chassis, using special solid mounts rather than the usual flexible ones, followed by wiring, painting and interior trimming. The hood and its mechanism were then installed by Mulliner.*

Left *With the hood lowered, hood envelope fitted and side windows raised the big drophead was still serene for front seat passengers, though a little draughty in the back!*

Below *Seen here in Rolls-Royce guise, the car was at its most elegant with both hood and side windows down. Power operation of the hood was, at first, optional. It was impossible to detect, even upon the closest and most critical examination, that these dropheads began life with four-door saloon bodies.*

Above *The sedanca coupé was a very rare body style by the mid-'fifties, but James Young built two on left-hand drive Silver Cloud chassis to design number SC20 – curiously enough, a design number shared with the same firm's drophead coupé, despite the two designs scarcely having a single panel in common!*

Below *The rear compartment of the Silver Cloud/Bentley S Series long wheelbase saloon with division is not noticeably roomier than the standard saloon, most of the additional length being taken up by the division and cabinetwork. The centre console houses the radio speaker and controls for heating, air conditioning (when fitted), radio volume, rooflamps and division.*

Above *For the Silver Cloud and S Series chassis, introduced towards the end of 1957, Park Ward were commissioned to produce a lengthened version of the standard saloon. The body shell was extended by adding four inches to the roof and floor pan aft of the centre pillar. Quarter-lights were added to the rear quarters of the body behind the longer rear doors. These long wheelbase saloons were usually equipped with an electrically operated glass division and were aimed at the businessman who required a chauffeur-driven car for business use which could nevertheless be used as an owner-driver family car. Above is the Silver Cloud version and, below, the Bentley S Series.*

JACK BARCLAY LTD.

Top left *The extra four inches of the long wheelbase chassis were used to full advantage by the coachbuilder's designers to create long, graceful designs.*
A. F. McNeil of James Young Ltd designed this handsome six-light saloon with division, design number SC12 (Rolls-Royce), of which seventeen were built and, seen here, design number B.12 (Bentley), of which there were five built.

Left *Hooper's distinctive styling also benefited from the longer chassis. This is their 1957 Earls Court Show exhibit, a saloon with division to design number 8504 on chassis ALC5. Hooper built a total of thirteen similar cars on Silver Cloud I Long Wheelbase chassis, some as owner-driver saloons without division, and a further seven on the Bentley S1 LWB chassis.*

Below left & right *Park Ward adapted their R-type Bentley Continental designs for the S1 Continental with only the most minor of changes other than lengthening to suit the 123in wheelbase of the S1 chassis. Both the two-door saloon and drophead coupé variants were exceedingly handsome cars. The latter is shown outside the Park Ward offices in Willesden.*

Left *A later variant of the saloon had larger rear quarter-lights and a three-piece, wrap-around rear window. The Continental's radiator shell was an inch and a half lower than that of the standard cars.*

Below inset *Inside, the fascia of H. J. Mulliner's S Series Continental recalled the same coachbuilder's R-type Continental, but the seats, in pleated and bolstered style, were noticeably more substantial, adding further weight to what had already become a considerably heavier car than the original Continental concept had called for.*

Below *For the S1 Continental, H. J. Mulliner's famous 'fastback' styling, for the want of a better term, acquired a higher, straight-through wingline with a new swageline on the rear wing. There were actually two designs, with detail differences. The photograph shows the earlier design number 7400. The final twenty cars, design number 7466, differed in having higher swagelines on the wings, sidelights on the tops of the front wings, a slight flare to the wheel arches and detail interior differences, in order to give it a closer family resemblance to the 'Flying Spur' four-door saloon (following pages).*

Top left *Although the Continental chassis was originally intended to be exclusively for two-door cars, Mulliner was eventually permitted, from 1957, to build a Continental four-door saloon. It was a beautifully styled and graceful six-light saloon to which the coachbuilder applied the superb name 'Flying Spur'. The more practical and capacious boot, increased rear compartment headroom and legroom and ease of access all helped to make the 'Flying Spur' the ideal continental touring car. Design number 7443.*

Left *Much rarer was the four-light 'Flying Spur'. This example is chassis BC9FM. Nowadays, this design is often referred to as the 'blind rear quarter' Flying Spur.*

Bottom left *H. J. Mulliner finally succumbed to the need for a more capacious boot for their two-door Continental with this completely restyled car. This is an interesting styling exercise of which only a small number were built, to design number 7560. Except for the prominent tail fins and rather bizarre frontal treatment, the result was aesthetically very successful. In fact, the 'cleaned up' version, design number 7514, became the standard Mulliner two-door design for the S2 Continental and was an outstandingly beautiful car. Note the then-fashionable wrap-around windscreen and rear window.*

Above & right *James Young Ltd, who built twenty bodies on S1 Continental chassis, initially only offered a two-door design. However, when permission was granted to Mulliner to build four-door Continentals, James Young followed suit with a particularly elegant four-light, four-door saloon. The two-door car is easily mistaken for a Park Ward; one of the more reliable distinguishing features being James Young's distinctive door handle with square push-button.*

JACK BARCLAY LTD.

Left *Hooper only built six bodies for the S1 Continental chassis, all to design number 8512 which was a most innovative and distinctive four-door body style. John Bull's drawing shows the unusual profile.*

181

Chapter Six

A new Engine, more Clouds and another Phantom

The Silver Cloud II & III, Bentley S2 & S3 and Phantom V

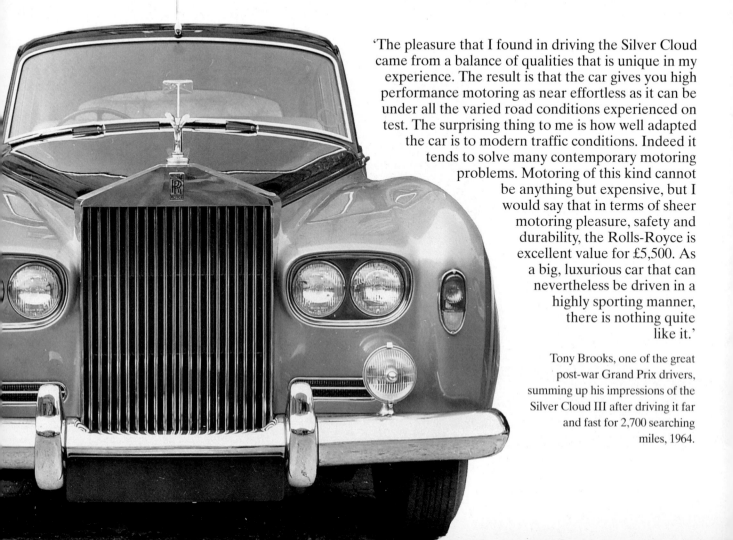

'The pleasure that I found in driving the Silver Cloud came from a balance of qualities that is unique in my experience. The result is that the car gives you high performance motoring as near effortless as it can be under all the varied road conditions experienced on test. The surprising thing to me is how well adapted the car is to modern traffic conditions. Indeed it tends to solve many contemporary motoring problems. Motoring of this kind cannot be anything but expensive, but I would say that in terms of sheer motoring pleasure, safety and durability, the Rolls-Royce is excellent value for £5,500. As a big, luxurious car that can nevertheless be driven in a highly sporting manner, there is nothing quite like it.'

Tony Brooks, one of the great post-war Grand Prix drivers, summing up his impressions of the Silver Cloud III after driving it far and fast for 2,700 searching miles, 1964.

Over the years 1946 to 1959 the six cylinder F-head engine grew in swept volume from 4,257 to 4,887cc. The final version of that power unit, with 8:1 compression ratio and 2 inch S.U. carburetters, represented its practical limit of development. Without serious loss of refinement, when an improvement in that area was being sought, no further significant power output increases could reasonably be pursued. With solid competition, particularly from across the Atlantic, in silence, refinement and weight-saving as well as being clearly outclassed in power output, the in-line six had reached the end of the road. The further requirement called for a power unit that was at least as light as the six, requiring no more bonnet space, while being quieter, more refined and potentially much more powerful. This is precisely what was achieved with the light alloy V-8 announced in August 1959.

This new engine, the outcome of some six years of development work at Crewe, was a 90° over-square vee unit of 6,230cc, built largely of aluminium and weighing around the same as the old six, but capable of producing considerably more power. Since Rolls-Royce do not normally reveal the power output of their car engines, preferring instead to describe it, rather infuriatingly as 'adequate', no published figures are available from the Company to illustrate precisely how big an improvement the V-8 actually represented. However, 160 bhp for the final version of the six as installed would be a reasonably accurate estimate, since it is known to have produced 178 bhp with open exhaust on the test bed. In its September 23rd., 1959 issue, *The Motor* boldly stated that the V-8's 'maximum power output must comfortably exceed a genuine 200 bhp' – though information that has more recently come to light reveals that the last of the 6,750cc carburated versions gave just

under that figure at 4,000 rpm. Therefore, the early V-8, with smaller carburetters and a rather less efficient exhaust system, would also have developed around 200 bhp. It can thus be safely assumed that the Silver Cloud II and Bentley S2, announced in August 1959, enjoyed a bonus of some 25% in the power department over the last of the six cylinder cars.

In the interests of silence and ease of maintenance, the new power unit's tappet clearances were maintained hydraulically. Like the automatic gearbox, the hydraulic tappets were at first 'bought out' from Detroit – in this instance from Chrysler – and later put into production at Crewe. It was not the first time Rolls-Royce had used hydraulic tappets in a motor car – they had been tried as long ago as 1935 for the V-12 Phantom III. Unfortunately the pre-War experience was not an unqualified success; in fact the final (D) series PIIIs appeared with solid tappets and most of the earlier cars were converted retrospectively. The cause of the trouble had been sludge narrowing or blocking the passages leading to the hydraulic plungers, preventing the hydraulic tappet from functioning correctly and consequently leading to severe cam wear. This problem disappeared with the advent of the modern engine oils and better filters and a similar system was employed with complete confidence for the V-8.

The cylinder liners were of cast iron, pressed into the aluminium block and in direct contact with the inhibited glycol coolant – i e. 'wet' liners. For the first time in a Rolls-Royce or Bentley the bore dimension exceeded that of the stroke, the actual ratio being 0.876:1. As if to deliberately restrict the initial power output of the V-8, the choice of carburetter – 1¾ inch S.Us – represented a return to pre-1957 practice. The induction manifolding was arranged so that each carburetter

served cylinders 1 and 4 of one bank and 2 and 3 of the other bank.

Few chassis modifications were necessary to accommodate the new engine. Some transmission components were strengthened and provision was made for new engine mountings. Additionally, because the steering box had to be moved outside the frame to make way for the wider engine, it was necessary to add a pair of pinions at the base of the column in order to maintain the same lateral position of the steering wheel. The steering column was also more steeply raked and the smaller, thinner rimmed steering wheel was positioned slightly closer to the fascia. At the rear of the chassis the only changes were a higher final drive ratio and a modified Z-type axle control rod which was rubber bushed to serve as a radius rod only,* to prevent spring wind-up due to torque reaction. A significant break with tradition was the abandonment of what remained of the 'one-shot' centralised chassis lubrication system in favour of long-life grease lubrication at 21 points.

The Silver Cloud II and Bentley S2 standard saloons were externally virtually indistinguishable from their six-cylinder counterparts. The only noticeable changes were confined to the interior, with subtle alterations to the fascia layout and new face-level adjustable louvred openings in the fascia capping rail as the only visible evidence that the heating and ventilation system had been completely revised. The improved driving position due to the repositioned, smaller and more comfortably thin rimmed steering wheel was also readily apparent. The direction indicator switch on the fascia capping rail with its clockwork

* The modification of the Z-bar, to relieve it of its anti-roll duties, was introduced first for the S1 Continental and was found to improve directional stability.

timed self-cancelling mechanism gave way to a conventional steering column mounted stalk, which on later cars doubled as a headlamp flasher.

With their more powerful engine and final drive ratio raised to 3.08:1, the Series II cars comfortably out-performed their predecessors, with a top speed in the region of 115 mph and acceleration to 70 mph around four seconds quicker. Use of this enhanced performance naturally brought an increase in fuel consumption, but *The Motor* magazine's road tests showed that at a constant 80 mph the Silver Cloud II was the equal of its six cylinder equivalent in fuel economy and marginally better at higher speeds, at which the six would obviously have been working rather harder.

The Bentley S2 Continental differed from the standard chassis in having a still higher final drive ratio* (2.92:1), tyres of slightly narrower section and new four-shoe front brakes. In order to blend with the sleek coachwork customarily built on the Continental chassis and to present a reduced frontal area, a new, lower radiator shell was fitted. As a further departure from the traditional tall, slightly raked Bentley radiator, the new version was mounted with a slight forward lean. Most of the efforts of the coachbuilders were concentrated on this chassis, and, to a lesser extent, on the Silver Cloud II and Bentley S2 Long Wheelbase chassis.

The demand for a really stately limousine was largely met until 1958 by the Silver Wraith, which had remained in production in long wheelbase form alongside the Silver Cloud, sharing the same 4.9 litre engine from 1956. The remainder of the Silver Wraith chassis was, however, of basically 1946 design, as were some of the body styles mounted thereon. It

Standard (3.08:1) ratio from chassis number BC100BY onwards.

was not quite long enough to carry limousine coachwork combining really huge rear compartments with long, capacious luggage boots. Really spacious seven-seater limousines on the Silver Wraith chassis all suffered from stunted luggage boots that not only limited the luggage carrying capacity of the car but all too often marred the otherwise graceful lines.

The introduction of the V-8 engine in 1959 allowed the Silver Wraith to be discontinued and replaced with the Phantom V, which with a wheelbase over twelve feet and overall length within two inches of twenty feet, was ideally suited to limousine coachwork. For the first time coachbuilders were able to combine extraordinarily spacious rear compartments with long, shapely tail treatment.

The Phantom V chassis was a much-lengthened version of the Silver Cloud II chassis, with an enormous longitudinal tubular section and an additional box-section cross member added into the cruciform bracing. The radius rod provided on the Silver Clouds for rear axle control was deemed unnecessary on the Phantom and was not fitted, its function being taken care of by mounting the axle asymmetrically on the longer springs. All other chassis details were similar to those of the Silver Cloud II and from the VA series onwards, to those of the Silver Cloud III. As a concession to the vastly larger and heavier coachwork carried and to the likely nature of the cars' use, the rear axle ratio was 3.89:1 as opposed to the 3.08:1 of the V-8 Silver Clouds. This was sufficient to endow the huge Phantom with a quite astonishing performance for so huge a motor car, with a top speed in excess of 100 mph and acceleration capabilities not far short of those of its smaller stablemates. It is pertinent to point out that the same chassis design only just ceased production – as the

Phantom VI – in 1990 and in fact only began to receive the Silver Shadow-type three-speed automatic transmission as recently as 1978. In this sense the Phantom V/VI is easily the longest-lived of all Rolls-Royce chassis designs, as well as the largest.

By the time the Phantom V appeared, Freestone & Webb had ceased coachbuilding and Hoopers were in the closing stages of winding down their coachbuilding operations. Mulliners turned out their own design for the Phantom V prior to their integration with Park Ward. This was an extremely handsome car with a wingline very reminiscent of the Flying Spur and other Mulliner S Series designs of the period, but with razor-edged lines to the roof and boot. The remaining eight Mulliner limousines were built after the amalgamation with Park Ward and were pure Park Ward below the waistline. This was intended to be a standard Touring Limousine design to compete with the James Young edition, but was never put into full scale production.

Park Ward's standard offering on the Phantom V chassis was their 7-passenger Limousine. This design, with some Mulliner-inspired changes to the upper body panels, survived into the nineties as the Phantom VI 7-passenger Limousine by Mulliner Park Ward.

Perhaps the most aesthetically pleasing of all Phantom V coachwork was the elegant work of James Young Ltd. These cars somehow contrived, in spite of their huge size, to be quite extraordinarily graceful of line, particularly when compared to other large cars of the period such as the 'Grosser' Mercedes 600. There were several versions of this coachwork – a 7-passenger Limousine with forward-facing occasional seats, a closer-coupled Touring Limousine with sideways-facing occasionals and (rather rare) a sedanca de ville. A small number even appeared as owner-driver saloons without the almost obligatory glass division – and there was even a brace of two-door cars.

At the 1965 Earls Court Motor Show, James Young Ltd were awarded the Gold and Bronze medals for their Touring Limousine and sedanca de ville respectively, in the Institute of British Carriage and Automobile Manufacturer's coachwork competition. H. J. Mulliner, Park Ward were awarded the Silver Medal for their 7-passenger Limousine.

A rare edition of the Phantom V was the Park Ward (and later Mulliner Park Ward) Landaulette. This was actually produced in two versions – the State Landaulette, with fully opening rear compartment, and an earlier alternative, of which only a handful were built, with opening rear quarter only. Even more scarce are the Hooper designs, since only one body on a production Phantom V chassis emanated from that coachbuilder's works, though they had built a similar body on an experimental chassis in 1957. This latter was chassis number 44EX – one of two prototype Phantom Vs. The year 1959 saw the end of Hoopers as coachbuilders, but the flare and genius of Osmond Rivers, their Chief Designer, manifested itself in another Phantom V built by Henri Chapron of Paris under Mr. Rivers' direct supervision.

The final changes to the Silver Cloud and Bentley S Series cars took place with the introduction of the Silver Cloud III and Bentley S3 in October 1962. These models could be dismissed as merely face-lifted series II cars but in fact they represented a considerable advance over their outwardly more conservative predecessors. The most obvious change to the casual observer was, of course, the twin headlamp arrangement. The changes and improvements introduced for the Silver Cloud III went beyond

mere external appearance, however, and may be summarized as follows:

- Four headlamp system for more illumination at a greater distance ahead and to more effectively light the sides of the road;
- $1\frac{1}{2}$ inch lower radiator shell with consequent increased slope to the bonnet for improved forward vision;
- Re-styled front wings without sidelamps let into their tops;
- Flashing indicators and sidelamps combined in a single unit mounted in the noses of the front wings;
- New, smaller bumper overriders (except for Nth. America, and some coachbuilt cars, for which the older pattern was retained);
- Black leather covering to the fascia capping rail, with token padding;
- Individual front seats (as opposed to the bench type seat with separate squabs of the Silver Cloud II) designed to give better lateral support for the driver and front seat passenger;
- A more upright squab and less prominent side padding to the rear seat for more legroom and greater effective width;
- A new Lucas distributor with vacuum advance;
- 9:1 compression ratio for the home market and other countries where 100 octane petrol was readily available;
- Larger (2 inch in lieu of $1\frac{3}{4}$ inch) S.U. carburetters;
- Improvements to the power assisted steering which rendered cars still lighter to park and manoeuvre without robbing the driver of 'feel' at speed.

The use of 2 inch S.U. carburetters, like those of the later six cylinder cars, together with the increase in compression ratio to 9:1 gave the new models a slight edge in acceleration, particularly above 60 mph, and a slightly higher top speed. An improve-

ment in fuel economy was attributed to the new vacuum advance Lucas (previously Delco-Remy) distributor.

One hears opposing views as to whether or not the revised frontal appearance was actually in keeping with the otherwise rather –conservative Silver Cloud body style. From their maker's point of view the change was almost certainly aimed at subtly preparing their customers for the radically new styling of the Silver Shadow that was to follow three years later. However, the fact that the cars sold well at the time and their comparatively bouyant value on today's market both strongly suggest that the frontal appearance was and remains an appealing feature. Other enthusiasts are attracted to the fact that, other than the Phantoms V and VI, these were the last Rolls-Royce and Bentley cars with a body mounted on a separate chassis. With the same exceptions, they were also the last to have drum brakes and live rear axle. This attracted criticism that Rolls-Royce cars were old-fashioned, which ignored the fact that most other cars of the period were downright crude in comparison.

The Bentley Continental in S3 guise no longer had a more powerful engine or higher gearing than the standard cars, nor did it need to, for the standard specification was more than adequate to see off not only virtually all saloon cars of the period, but most sports cars, too! The differences that distinguished the Continental chassis were few and of a minor nature and it was the coachwork more than anything else that made the Bentley Continentals so special, along with their special comprehensive instrumentation, complete with rev counter. Coachbuilders offering designs for the S3 Continental were down to two surviving firms, and one of these, James Young Ltd, was only destined to last another five years. H. J. Mulliner and Park Ward, by now combined as a single entity – H. J. Mulliner, Park Ward Ltd – offered two-door and four-door saloons and a drophead coupé, all derived from the designs of the two constituent companies.

Several coachbuilt designs were offered on the Silver Cloud III chassis. H. J. Mulliner, Park Ward continued to offer their drophead coupé adaptation of the standard saloon for the first few months of production, after which a policy decision was made allowing the Bentley Continental body styles to be built on Rolls-Royce Silver Cloud III chassis. Special chassis were built for this purpose with the lower Bentley Continental steering column rake and some other minor Continental features – though the fascias were modified to take the simpler Rolls-Royce instrumentation. James Young followed suit in offering their Continental body styles on the Silver Cloud III chassis. Unfortunately, all this has given rise to the incorrect practice of referring to these coachbuilt Silver Cloud IIIs as 'Continentals', particularly in the U.K. used car trade. They were never marketed as Continentals and are not Continentals. In fact, in the post-war years, the Company has never applied the Continental name to any model that is not a Bentley. Unfortunately, though, the damage to historical accuracy will be difficult to undo.

Like the earlier Silver Clouds and S Series cars, the Silver Cloud III and Bentley S3 were available in long wheelbase guise. The chassis was four inches longer than standard and was fitted with a suitably lengthened standard saloon body, usually with a division. The task of extending the bodies was entrusted to H. J. Mulliner, Park Ward in London with the painting, interior trimming and finishing work being carried out at Crewe on the standard saloon build lines. There was

also a particularly handsome but much more expensive coachbuilt version by James Young.

Even thirty years on, few cars are as ideally suited to fast, fatigue-free, long distance motoring as a Silver Cloud III or Bentley S3 standard saloon. The lofty driving position and commanding view over the elegant bonnet, excellent handling and road-holding, smooth but firm ride, a virtually flat floor and beautifully finished interior furnishings and fittings all contribute to the pleasure of driving, while for the comfort of the back seat passengers they have few rivals, fewer equals and no betters.

The Silver Cloud III and Bentley S3 remained in production for just three years, before the highly sophisticated Silver Shadow series superseded them, though deliveries of chassis with special coachwork continued for a few months. Like all Rolls-Royce products they were built to last, so the overwhelming majority having survived in good to excellent condition.

TECHNICAL SPECIFICATION

Rolls-Royce Silver Cloud II & III, Bentley S2 & S3, Phantom V

Engine

Dimensions
Eight cylinders in 90 degree vee formation. Bore 4.1 inches (104.14mm), stroke 3.6 inches (91.44mm), cubic capacity 380 cu. in. (6,230cc) Compression ratio 8:1 (Silver Cloud III, Bentley S3 and Phantom V from VA series onwards, 9:1 standard, 8:1 for countries where 100 octane fuel not available).

Cylinder block/Crankcase
High silicon content aluminium alloy block with cast iron wet cylinder liners.

Crankshaft
Nitride hardened chrome molybdenum steel, with integral balance weights, running in five main bearings.

Pistons
Aluminium alloy. Three compression rings and one oil control ring.

Cylinder heads
Aluminium alloy with austenitic steel valve seats.

Valve gear
Overhead valves. Monikrom cast iron camshaft driven by helical gears, four bearings. Hydraulic tappets.

Carburetters
Two S.U. type HD.6 (1¾ inch) carburetters with automatic choke. Acoustic air intake silencer incorporating micronic air filter. Silver Cloud III, Bentley S3 and Phantom V from VA series onwards, type HD.8 (2 inch) carburetters with paper or oil wetted wire mesh air filter element.

Ignition system
Ignition by high tension coil and Delco-Remy distributor with twin contact breaker points. Silver Cloud III, Bentley S3 and Phantom V from VA series onwards, Lucas distributor with vacuum advance. Firing order A1, B1, A4, B4, B2, A3, B3, A2.

Lubrication system
Helical gear oil pump in crankcase driven by skew gear from crankshaft. Oil pick-up in sump incorporating gauze strainer. Full-flow filter on side of crankcase. Pressure relief valve regulates oil pressure at approximately 40 lb/sq. in. Sump capacity 12.5 pints (15 U.S. gallons, 7.1 litres).

Cooling system
Pressurised system operating at 7 lb/sq. in. Temperature control by thermostat at the front of engine. Belt driven centrifugal coolant pump and fan.

Chassis

Dimensions
Overall length, standard and Bentley Continental 17' 8" (5,435mm)
Overall length, long wheelbase 18' (5,486mm)
Overall length, Phantom V 19' 10" (6,045mm)
Wheelbase, standard and Bentley Continental 10' 3" (3,124mm)
Wheelbase, long 10' 7" (3,226mm)
Wheelbase, Phantom V 12' 1" (3,683mm)
Front track 4' 10½" (1,486mm)
Rear track 5' (1,524mm)
Front track, Phantom V 5' ⅞" (1,546mm)
Rear track, Phantom V 5' 4" (1,625mm)
Note: for overall lengths of Silver Cloud III and Bentley S3, except for Nth American exports and certain coachbuilt cars, subtract 1" (2.5mm) from the above figures, due to the smaller overriders fitted. This also applies to a small number of VA series and later Phantom Vs.

Frame
Closed box section frame of welded steel construction with cruciform centre bracing and crossmembers. Phantom V had additional tubular member and an additional cross-member in the middle of the cruciform.

Suspension
Front: independent by coil springs and rubber bushed wishbones, double acting hydraulic dampers and anti-roll bar.
Rear: semi-elliptic leaf springs protected by leather gaiters. Controllable hydraulic dampers by solenoid operated by switch on left side of steering column. 'Z' type axle control rod (except Phantom V).

Steering
Power assisted cam and roller, Hobourn Eaton belt driven pump. Three-piece track linkage. Turns lock to lock, 4¼.

Transmission
Rolls-Royce automatic gearbox and fluid coupling with selector mounted on the right of the steering column.

Four forward speeds and reverse. Ratios: Top 1:1, Third 1.45:1, Second 2.63:1, First 3.82:1, Reverse 4.3:1. Divided propeller shaft with Detroit type front universal joint, needle roller bearing Hardy-Spicer type rear universal joint and flexibly mounted centre bearing.
Rear axle: semi-floating type with hypoid bevel gears. Ratio, standard, long wheelbase and Bentley Continental S2 from chassis BC100BY onwards 3.89:1. Bentley Continental S2 to chassis BC99BY 2.92:1. Phantom V 3.89:1.

Brakes
Hydraulic front, hydraulic and mechanical rear, drum brakes. Operation by means of friction disc servo on the offside of the gearbox, which applies the brakes through

Coachwork

Standard four-door factory saloon body, except as indicated in the following table. All Bentley Continental and Phantom V cars were coachbuilt.

Coachbuilder	Silver Cloud II	Silver Cloud II lwb
H. J. Mulliner	107*	1
James Young	–	38
Hooper	–	1
Totals	107	40

* drophead coupé adaptations of standard saloons.

Coachbuilder	Bentley S2	Bentley S2 lwb	Bentley Continental S2
H. J. Mulliner	15*	–	221†
Park Ward	–	–	125†
James Young	–	5	41
Totals	15	5	388

* drophead coupé adaptations of standard saloons.
† H. J. Mulliner, Park Ward Ltd was formed in 1961 and some of these bodies were strictly speaking built by that firm. However, these figures are for the two constituent company's designs.

Coachbuilder	Silver Cloud III	Silver Cloud III lwb
H. J. Mulliner, Park Ward	302*	5†
James Young	26	42
Totals	328	47

* includes 38 drophead coupé adaptations of standard saloons. All bodies were of Park Ward and H. J. Mulliner derivation and were fitted with builder's plates bearing the individual firm's names until well into 1963.
† cabriolets of H. J. Mulliner design and fitted with H. J. Mulliner builder's plates.

Coachbuilder	Bentley S3	Bentley S3 lwb	Bentley Continental S3
H. J. Mulliner, Park Ward	1	–	291*
James Young	–	7	20
Graber	–	–	1
Totals	1	7	312

* all of Park Ward and H. J. Mulliner derivation. Builder's plates bearing the individual firm's names were fitted until well into 1963.

two master cylinders and dual hydraulic circuits and assists the mechanical application of the rear brakes. Handbrake on rear wheels by pull-and-twist handle under fascia through a cable and mechanical linkage. Cast iron drums.

Exhaust system
Single system with three expansion boxes, each tuned to absorb a different range of frequencies.

Lubrication system
Long life grease lubrication by nipples at 21 points.

Fuel system
Rear mounted petrol tank, capacity 18 gallons (21.6 U.S. gallons, 81.8 litres). Phantom V 23 gallons (27.6 U.S. gallons, 105 litres). Twin S.U. electric fuel pump mounted in the frame.

Electrical system
12 volt negative earth system. Lucas special equipment dynamo and starter motor with pre-engagement pinion. Lucas built-in headlamps (twin headlamps Silver Cloud III, Bentley S3 and Phantom V from VA series onwards). Twin Lucas fog lamps. Medium wave/Long wave or Medium wave/Short wave Radiomobile radio with push-button tuning and three speakers. An electrically operated wing mounted aerial was available at extra cost. Direction indicators built into fog lamps (in noses of front wings combined with sidelamps, Silver Cloud III, Bentley S3 and Phantom V from VA series onwards), operated by switch mounted on left of steering column. Electrically operated windscreen washer. Triplex heated rear window. Refrigerated air conditioning and electric windows available at extra cost.

Road wheels and tyres
15 inch steel disc wheels on five studs, carrying 8.20 x 15 tyres. Phantom V 8.90 x 15 tyres. Tyre pressures 22 lb/sq. in. front, 27 lb/sq. in. rear. Phantom V 30 lb/sq. in. rear.

Coachbuilder	Phantom V: Chassis series AS to CG:	Phantom V Chassis series VA to VF:
Park Ward*	195	–
H. J. Mulliner*	9	–
H. J. Mulliner, Park Ward	–	112
Hooper	1	–
James Young	71	125
Chapron	2	–
Woodall Nicholson	–	1†
Totals	278	238

* Park Ward and H. J. Mulliner designs are attributed to the individual firms up to the end of the CG series, at which point the designs of the combined firm H. J. Mulliner, Park Ward Ltd were introduced.
† hearse.

Chassis and engine numbers

Silver Cloud II
Chassis sub-series starting with 1 use odd number only, those starting with 2 use even numbers only. Engines are numbered consecutively. The number 13 was omitted from chassis numbering.

Series	Chassis numbers	Engine numbers
A	SPA2-362, SRA1-325	2AS-325AS
B	STB2 -500, SVB1-501	1BS-500BS
C	SWC2-730, SXC1-671	1CS-700CS
D	SYD2-550, SZD1-551	1DS-550DS
E	SAE1-685*	1ES-342ES

* Plus experimental car 30B, later renumbered SAE687.
Total: 2,418 cars.

Bentley S2
Chassis sub-series starting with 1 use odd number only, those starting with 2 use even numbers only. Engines are numbered consecutively. The number 13 was omitted from chassis numbering.

Series	Chassis numbers	Engine numbers
A	B1AA-B325AA, B2AM-B326AM	1AB-325AB

Series	Chassis numbers	Engine numbers
B	B1BR-B501BR, B2BS-B500BS	1BB-500BB
C	B1CT-B445CT, B2CU-B756CU	1CB-600CB
D	B1DV-b501DV, B2DW-B376DW	1DB-438DB

Total: 1,863 cars.

Silver Cloud II long wheelbase
Chassis and engines are numbered consecutively, omitting 13 from chassis numbering.

Series	Chassis numbers	Engine numbers
A	LCA1-76	LC1A-LC75A
B	LCB1-101	LC1B-LC100B
C	LCC1-101	LC1C-LC100C
D	LCD1-25	LC1D-LC24D

Total: 299 cars.

Bentley S2 long wheelbase
Chassis and engines are numbered consecutively, omitting 13 from chassis numbering.

Series	Chassis numbers	Engine numbers
A	LBA1-26	LB1A-LB25A
B	LBB1-33	LB1B-LB32B

Total: 57 cars.

A NEW ENGINE, MORE CLOUDS AND ANOTHER PHANTOM

Bentley Continental S2
Chassis and engines are numbered consecutively, omitting 13 from chassis numbering.

Series	Chassis numbers	Engine numbers
A	BC1AR-BC151AR	A1BC-A150BC
B	BC1BY-BC101BY	B1BC-B100BC
C	BC1CZ-BC139CZ	C1BC-C138BC

Total: 388 cars.

Phantom V
Chassis series and sub-series starting with 1 use odd number only, those starting with 2 use even numbers only. Engines are numbered consecutively. The number 13 was omitted from chassis numbering.

Series	Chassis numbers	Engine numbers
A	5AS1-5AS101, 5AT2-5AT100	PV1A-PV100A
B	5BV1-5BV101, 5BX2-5BX100	PV1B-PV100B
C	5CG1-5CG79	PV1C-PV39C
A	5VA1-5VA123	A1PV-A61PV
B	5VB1-5VB51	B1PV-B25PV
C	5VC1-5VC51	C1PV-C25PV
D	5VD1-5VD101	D1PV-D50PV
E	5VE1-5VF51	E1PV-E25PV
F	5VF1-5VF183	F1PV-F91PV

Total: 516 cars.

Silver Cloud III
All chassis series start with 1 and use odd numbers only, omitting 13. Engines are numbered consecutively.

Series	Chassis numbers	Engine numbers
A	SAZ1-61	SZ1A-SZ30A
	B series was omitted	
C	SCX1-877	SX1C-SX438C
D	SDW1-601	SW1D-SW300D
E	SEV1-495	SV1E-SV247E
F	SFU1-803	SU1F-SU401F
G	SGT1-659	ST1G-ST329G
H	SHS1-357	SS1H-SS178H
J	SJR1-623	SR1J-SR311J
K	SKP1-423	SP1K-SP211K
Coachbuilt	CSC1B-CSC141B*	B1CS-B70CS
Coachbuilt	CSC1C-CSC83C‡	C1CS-C40CS

Total: 2,555 cars.

* Omitting CSC83B.
‡ The final number in this series was to have been CSC83C but an additional (left-hand drive) chassis LCSC83C was added. This car was built for the Shah of Iran as a Bentley Continental S3 (BC56LXE) and exhibited at the 1965 Frankfurt Motor Show, but was delivered in Rolls-Royce guise to the Iranian Ambassador, London.

Bentley S3
All chassis series start with 2 and use even numbers only. Engines are numbered consecutively.

Series	Chassis numbers	Engine numbers
A	B2AV-B26AV	BAV1-13
	B series was omitted	
C	B2CN-B828CN	BCN1-414
D	B2DF-B198DF	BDF1-99
E	B2EC-B530EC	BEC1-265
F	B2FG-B350FG	BFG1-175
G	B2GJ-B200GJ	BGJ1-100
H	B2HN-B400HN	BHN1-200
J	B2JP-B40JP	BJP1-20

Total: 1,286 cars.

Silver Cloud III long wheelbase
All chassis series start with 1 and use odd numbers only, omitting 13. Engines are numbered consecutively.

Series	Chassis numbers	Engine numbers
A	CAL1-83	CL1A-CL41A
B	CBL1-61	CL1B-CL30B
C	CCL1-101	CL1C-CL50C
D	CDL1-95	CL1D-CL47D
E	CEL1-105	CL1E-CL52E
F	CFL1-41	CL1F-CL20F
G	CGL1-29	CL1G-CL14G

Total: 254 cars.

Bentley S3 long wheelbase
All chassis series start with 2 and use even numbers only. Engines are numbered consecutively.

Series	Chassis numbers	Engine numbers
A	BAL2-30	BL1A-BL15A
B	BBL2-12	BL1B-BL6B
C	BCL2-22	BL1C-BL11C

Total: 32 cars.

Bentley Continental S3
All chassis series start with 2 and use even numbers only. Engines are numbered consecutively.

Series	Chassis numbers	Engine numbers
A	BC2XA-BC174XA	1ABC-87ABC
B	BC2XB-BC100XB	1BBC-50BBC
C	BC2XC-BC202XC	1CBC-101CBC
D	BC2XD-BC28XD	1DBC-14DBC
E	BC2XE-BC120XC*	1EBC-60EBC*

Total: 311 cars.

* Omitting chassis BC56XE and engine 28EBC (car completed and delivered as Rolls-Royce Silver Cloud III chassis LCSC83C).

189

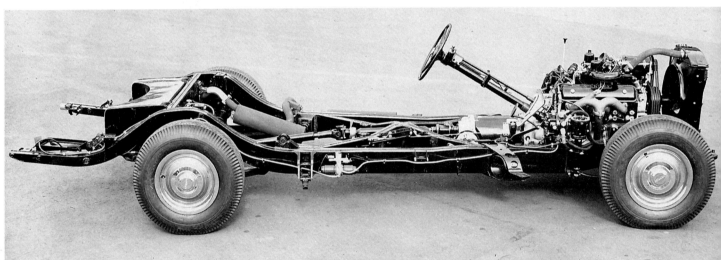

Left: *Two photographs of the S2 chassis in which some of the detail differences between that model and the earlier 6-cylinder chassis may be discerned. Apart from the self-evident one – the 6,230cc V-8 engine – none of these are very obvious, but in the centre photograph it can be seen that the steering box had been relocated to a position outside the frame and that it was mounted vertically instead of at the steering column angle. A transfer box with a pair of spiral pinions was provided to maintain the lateral position of the column, which was more steeply raked than hitherto. This, together with the fact that the steering wheel was an inch smaller in diameter, with a thinner rim and mounted closer to the fascia, made for a more comfortable driving position. The rear axle control rod, or 'Z' bar, visible in the upper photograph, being deemed no longer necessary in its role of modifying rear roll stiffness, was now rubber bushed and the arm at the axle end was shortened. The projection below the radiator is the hydraulic actuating cylinder of the by now standard power assisted steering. Though the radiator shell had not been fitted when the photographs were taken, this normally being done after the fitting and painting of the body, the name on the wheel discs and valve rocker covers indicates that this is a Bentley S2 chassis, the Rolls-Royce Silver Cloud II being otherwise identical. The Silver Cloud II and Bentley S2 long wheelbase chassis was similar to that of the standard cars, but four inches longer. The Bentley S2 Continental chassis was also similar in appearance except that it was supplied with engine compartment rear bulkhead and side panels, as was the huge Phantom V chassis shown in the bottom photograph. This also clearly shows the additional frame cross-member and 21 inch long tubular member let into the cruciform. These provided the additional stiffness needed for this 145 inch wheelbase car. The absence of a rear axle control rod on this model will be noted.*

Above *The 6,230cc V-8 engine – painted in grey for photographic purposes – as fitted to the Silver Cloud II, Bentley S2 and AS to CG series Phantom V. The carburetters are 1¾ inch S.U. type HD.6, similar to those of the early six cylinder Silver Cloud/S Series engine. The engine is fitted with the pump and reservoir for the standard power assisted steering and compressor for the optional refrigerated air conditioning. Note the take-off on the gearbox rear extension for the brake servo.*

Right *At left is Harry Grylls (Gry), Chief Engineer, with Ronald West (Wst), head of Engine Development at Crewe, admiring a prototype 'narrow' V-8 engine which was ultimately to power every Rolls-Royce and Bentley car from late 1959 to the present – some 80% of all Rolls-Royce-built motor cars. Both venerable gentlemen have since passed away.*

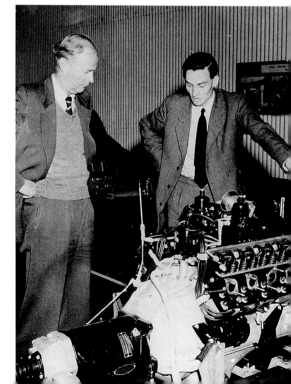

191

Above left & right *Two factory photographs of V-8 engine detail. The left photograph shows the massive five-bearing crankshaft with its integral balance weights. The valve gear, in accordance with previous Rolls-Royce practice, and Royce's own preference, is driven by gears rather than by chains as lesser makes are wont to use. In the right photograph it can be seen that no provision is made for tappet clearance adjustment, this being taken care of by hydraulic self-adjusting tappets, initial production of which came from Chrysler in Detroit.*

Right *These two views of the V-8 engine as installed in the car, unfortunately distorted by wide angle photography, show that there was little room to spare under the S Series bonnet. This particular car is fitted with refrigerated air-conditioning, the compressor for which can be seen in both photographs. Note how the large air intake silencer and cleaner may be swung up to allow access to other under-bonnet components. This immaculate 1960 Bentley S2, chassis B25CT, has been owned since nearly new by John and Isobel Salter (RROCA).*

Top right & below *Externally, there were no changes to the standard saloon coachwork – and why should there have been? – its beauty of line was immune to the dictates of fashion and spoke for itself. These two photographs show how well the design lent itself to two-tone paint schemes. Note that in the case of the Bentley, the bonnet top was normally finished in what was otherwise the lower of the two colours, with the upper colour extended along the bonnet side mouldings. It should be said, however, that this was not a hard and fast rule. On cars fitted with the optional refrigerated air-conditioning, customers were discouraged from choosing dark colours for the upper part of the body.*

Below left *A set of specially tailored 'Antler' fitted suitcases could be supplied as one of the many extras offered for the Silver Cloud II and Bentley S2. These were timber framed, covered with 'Arlinghide', a light, durable material of pleasing appearance, lined with quilted taffeta with patent 'Antler' soft handles and locks and other fittings in brass. The set for the standard car consisted of nine cases (shown) while a set of six cases could be supplied for cars fitted with the boot mounted refrigeration unit.*

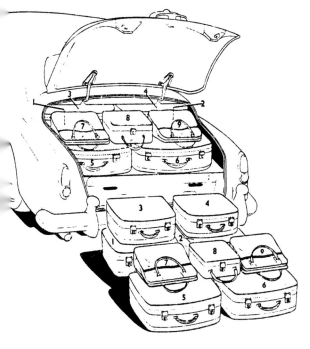

Above *There were no true coachbuilt bodies on either the Silver Cloud II or Bentley S2 standard chassis, the work of the coachbuilders being confined to the long wheelbase chassis and, to a greater extent, the Bentley Continental chassis. However, H. J. Mulliner continued to adapt the standard saloon body shells to present this beautiful and highly desirable drophead coupé form. Perfect for that weekend trip to the South of France or Florida! No fewer than 107 Silver Cloud IIs were built in this form, plus a further 15 Bentley S2s.*

Left & above *The long wheelbase adaptation of the standard saloon, carried out by Park Ward, was continued for the Silver Cloud II range. The cabinetwork and other details of the interior, below, withstood critical comparison with the best coachbuilders' work.*

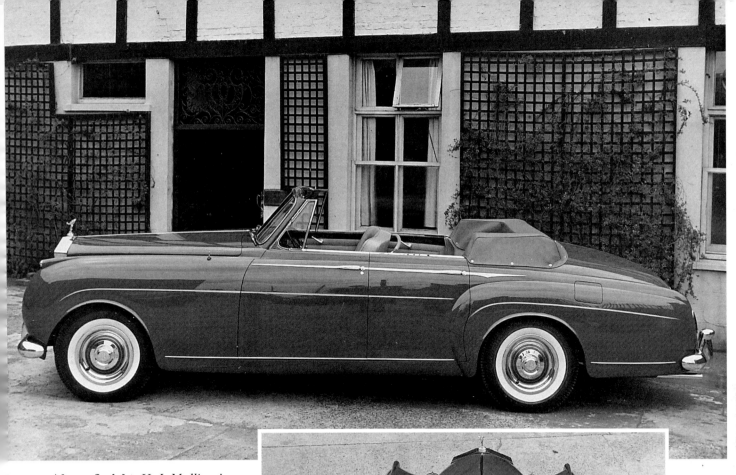

Above & right *H. J. Mulliner's work on the Silver Cloud II long wheelbase chassis was confined to a solitary, superb cabriolet on Chassis No. LLCB16, photographed outside the Park Ward offices in Willesden, which were at that time used by the combined firm H. J. Mulliner, Park Ward Ltd, but sadly demolished in 1982. Design number 7484, it is an obvious continuation of their saloon, fixed head coupé and drophead coupé theme illustrated in the previous chapter. Even this was not the end for this attractive styling, as five more cabriolets to the same design were built on lwb Silver Cloud III chassis. The unusual rear view, taken from above, shows some of the interior details, including the one-piece grab rail in the rear compartment, for processional use.*

Top left *The rear view of Park Ward's S2 Continental emphasises just how significant a break with styling tradition this coachwork represented. The leather loop and metal catch visible in the centre of the rear seat squab indicate that the seat may be folded flat to form a platform for additional luggage – a feature not new to Park Ward Bentleys. The hood was electro-hydraulically power operated and the backlight was secured by means of a zip fastener so that it could be opened. Extensive use of welded steel for the frame and fixed panels, using aircraft construction methods, was a first for the British coachbuilding trade and formed the basis of the construction principles employed for the later Silver Shadow/Bentley T Series two-door cars and the subsequent Corniche and Camargue models.*

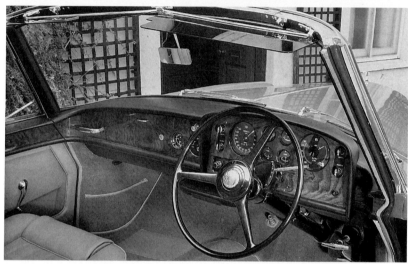

Left *This interior view of the Park Ward S2 Continental drophead coupé shows the customarily comprehensive Continental instrumentation grouped within a leather surrounded walnut veneered nacelle in front of the driver. The rigid Perspex sun visors, it is thought, would not satisfy present day safety design standards!*

Below *H. J. Mulliner's 'Flying Spur' saloon remained unchanged for the S2 Continental except that the bonnet was lowered at the front to suit the squatter radiator shell and the bootlid was extended downwards to eliminate the loading lip, with the number plate and reverse lights being moved from the body onto the bootlid. The final series of these cars had the standard S3-pattern rear lights in lieu of the special H. J. Mulliner 'cathedral' type.*

Above *The H. J. Mulliner two-door Continental lost its former familiar 'fastback' outline and adopted the lines of the much rarer car shown on page 180, though mercifully without the rather bizarre front and rear wing embellishments. The result was this strikingly handsome sports saloon which despite the now dated looking wrap-around front and rear glass is arguably the best-looking of all Bentley Continentals.*

Right *This photograph, taken in the Berkeley Square showroom of parent company Jack Barclay Ltd, shows how James Young's four-door sports saloon coachwork for the S2 Continental had developed into a six-light design, though retaining unchanged the wingline of the six cylinder car. Design number CV100.*

Bottom right *Hooper's only body for a Bentley S2, and their final Bentley body, Continental chassis No. BC1AR. The styling was unchanged from their S1 Continental design.*

Left & below *This is design number 980, Park Ward's standard seven-passenger limousine design for the Phantom V up to and including the CG series. This car is chassis number 5AS7, the second of a design which eventually totalled 150 cars. The wingline of this design is traceable to that of the same coachbuilder's R-type and S1 Bentley Continentals and has, in fact, remained substantially unchanged right to the subsequent Phantom VI, the last of which was completed as recently as 1992. Styling was the work of John Blatchley and his Crewe-based design team.*

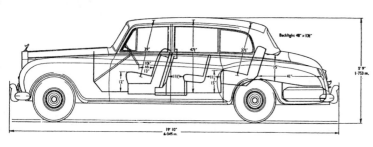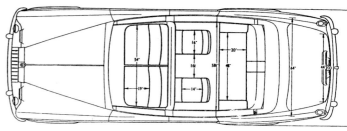

Below left & right *Park Ward design number 980, Phantom V. The wheelbase of 12ft 1in and overall length of 19ft 10in allowed the rear compartment to be unusually spacious without sacrificing luggage capacity or graceful lines. The cabinet work behind the division incorporated a cocktail cabinet and radio speaker. The switches in the right-hand armrest were, from front to back, for operation of the fresh air booster fan, refrigerated air conditioning (optional) and under-seat heater. The radio was located in the left-hand armrest. Electrically operated windows were an option that most purchasers specified. Upholstery for the rear compartment was leather, West of England cloth or twill to choice. The interior design could be varied considerably to suit individual owner's requirements.*

This page *Often regarded as the most elegant of the coachwork on the Phantom V was that by James Young Ltd, the very long chassis allowing A. F. McNeil's outstanding styling skills to be given free rein. On these pages we see their interpretation of the 7-passenger limousine, design number PV15, which like Park Ward's version had face-forward occasional seats in a huge rear compartment. The upholstery shown is leather, though West of England cloth was often specified for the rear compartment. In the garnish rail below the quarter light are the radio, switch for the electrically operated aerial and a pair of pushbuttons to raise and lower the division. Ashtrays and cigar lighters are in the leading edges of the generous side armrests, and there is a swivelling reading light above the vanity mirror in the rear quarter. Note the luxurious rug over the usual carpets.*

This page *Extraordinarily elegant, with its closer-coupled body and steeper slope to the tail, was James Young's design number PV22 touring limousine. The Phantom V chassis was of sufficient length to allow even this body type to have an exceptionally spacious rear compartment with occasional seats – in this instance sideways facing and obviously intended for more infrequent use than the more substantial occasionals of the seven seater on the previous page. Typically James Young, the cabinetwork behind the division is truly magnificent.*

This page *Rare Phantom V coachwork. The top picture shows H. J. Mulliner's design number 7516 touring limousine, an interesting design built at Chiswick works of H. J. Mulliner just prior to their move to the Willesden works of Park Ward. The eight cars to this design were built on Park Ward base frames including front, centre and rear quarter pillars, wheel arches and all panel work below the waist rail. The object of this exercise was to produce a touring limousine to put the emerging combined firm H. J. Mulliner, Park Ward Ltd on an even footing with James Young, who offered both 7-passenger and touring limousine versions. It is not clear why this was not proceeded with beyond the initial eight cars. This is an artist's impression from a contemporary brochure. Right (middle) from the talented hand of John Bull, is H. J. Mulliner's design number 7515, their first body on a Phantom V and a one-off, on chassis 5LAS3. This was their 1959 Earls Court Show exhibit and had an obvious family resemblance to their Bentley Continental 'Flying Spur' saloon, though of course much longer.*

Below *For royalty and heads of state only, the Park Ward landaulette was a rare variant of their limousine design number 980. Only three were built – two design number 1000, and one, this car, design number 1104 on chassis 5CG37 for H.M. The Queen Mother. Note the blue 'police light' above the windscreen.*

Above A coachbuilder's artist's impression, by Park Ward Chief Draughtsman Peter Wharton, of the high roofed, Perspex-panelled Phantom V design for H.M The Queen. Two were built, on chassis nos. 5AS33 and 5AT34, known respectively as 'Canberra II' and 'Canberra I'. (Somewhat confusingly, 'Canberra II' has the earlier chassis number and vice versa.) A further body of this concept, on a Phantom VI chassis, was delivered to Her Majesty in 1977.

Above The rare sedanca de ville variant of James Young's design number PV22 touring limousine. This is their design number PV22SD on chassis no. 5BX44, the 1st Prize winning car at Blenheim Palace, June 1962. James Young Ltd also took 2nd Prize in the coachwork competition for their Long Wheelbase Silver Cloud II.

Below left & above right The practice of sending Rolls-Royce chassis to foreign coachbuilders had become rare by 1960, only two Phantom V chassis being so treated. Both were bodied by Henri Chapron of Paris as a direct result of Hooper ceasing coachbuilding. Hooper had built a body of non-traditional lines for the experimental Phantom V 44EX and another similar body for a production Phantom V before the firm's coachbuilding activities came to an end in 1959. However, a further order, from Marty Martyn and his wife Margi, was received just as the decision to end coachbuilding had been reached by the Hooper board, so arrangements were made for Chapron to build the body for the American couple. Hooper's Chief Designer Osmond Rivers commuted between London and Paris to supervise the car's

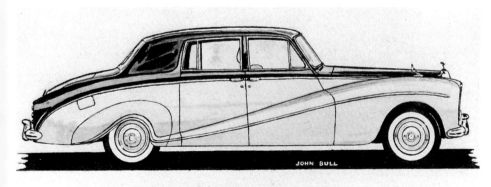

construction on chassis 5LAT4. The photograph and John Bull's drawing show the characteristically Rivers lines, in fact a longer version of the Silver Cloud on page 197. The close-coupled four-light configuration is extremely unusual for a Phantom V and made for a truly enormous luggage capacity.

Right With Mr Rivers' consent, Chapron used the working drawings of the Martyn car as the basis of a second car, on chassis 5LAT50, for another American client, Mrs. Katherine Milbank of New York City. The photograph shows that although the frontal appearance was similar to that of the earlier car, it differed markedly in external lines, being a six-light design with a higher wingline and distinct rear wings. According to the late Osmond Rivers, and contrary to oft-published claims, neither of these Chapron-Rivers cars was ordered by or delivered to Mr. Nubar Gulbenkian. However, Mr. Rivers did reveal that at the time he was consulted by the famous Armenian oil magnate, who was a valued client of both Rolls-Royce and Hooper, on a Phantom V project, but this did not materialize and eventually emerged as a specially modified Mercedes 600 – again a Chapron-Rivers effort.

Below James Young built a pair of two-door cars on Phantom V chassis 5LBV69 and 5LBX76, of which the picture is believed to be of the latter car. They were a two-door version of their touring limousine and in fact shared the same design number (PV22) and were called 'two-door touring limousines'.

This page *In October 1962 the Silver Cloud III and its sister car the Bentley S3 replaced the Silver Cloud II and Bentley S2. The main mechanical changes were larger S.U. type HD.8 carburetters, Lucas distributor with vacuum advance, 9:1 compression ratio (mainly for home market cars), improved power assisted steering, revised exhaust system and lower radiator to suit the changed frontal appearance. The Silver Cloud III chassis above was prepared for exhibition at the 1963 Earls Court Motor Show and is now housed at the Sir Henry Royce Memorial Foundation headquarters at Paulerspury. The Bentley S3 chassis was identical except for badging – the radiator shell not normally being fitted until the later stages of finishing the body. Chassis for Bentley Continentals and coachbuilt Silver Cloud IIIs had a lower steering column rake and self-contained engine bay side and rear bulkheads. The 'X-ray' view, from the Silver Cloud III/Bentley S3 brochure, shows some of the detail not visible in the chassis photograph. The photograph (right)*

shows the V-8 engine installation as revised for the Silver Cloud III and Bentley S3 – in this instance the latter. The larger, 2in choke type HD.8 carburetters are the main recognition feature. Except for the reduced height radiator, all the new features of the Silver Cloud III were adopted for the Phantom V from the VA series, a left-hand drive example of which is shown below. Note that on these later chassis the exhaust system passes through apertures in the framing rather than over the frame.

This page *The appearance of the Silver Cloud III standard saloon was unmistakable. The radiator shell was 1½ inches lower than that of the earlier Silver Clouds. This, together with the horizontally paired headlamps, made for a lower, wider frontal appearance – though in fact the width of the car remained unchanged. The sidelamps and direction indicators were combined in new units mounted in the noses of the front wings, which meant that the foglamps no longer needed to double as flashing direction indicators as they had on the I and II. The smaller bumper overriders were new, though the older pattern was retained for North American exports. From March 1964 the headlamp surrounds carried a Rolls-Royce (or Bentley) monogram. Identification from the rear is less easy. In our photographs the smaller overriders are a clue, but as these were not used for North American export cars, not a reliable one. The larger, two-colour rear light lenses are also not a reliable recognition point as the final batch of series II cars were similarly fitted. All but the earliest Silver Cloud IIIs, however, carried a distinctive motif (below) on the lower right-hand corner of the bootlid. Bentleys had an 'S3' motif.*

This page *The re-styled standard saloon coachwork was no less handsome in Bentley form. Here we see the Bentley S3 which, as in the case of previous versions, looks very smart in two-tone paint schemes. Again it will be noted that it was customary to finish the bonnet top in the lower colour on Bentleys rather than in the upper colour as on their square radiatored counterparts. Any departure from this is non-standard, though not necessarily non-original. The front compartment interior photographs clearly show the individual seat cushions and black leather covering to the fascia capping rail. It is suggested that the latter feature was aimed more at solving the problem of the timber veneer being adversely affected by the sun than at the safety aspect, the padding being of a somewhat token nature. The rear vision mirror was hung from the windscreen top rail on later cars and those for certain export markets. The knob above the windscreen is to turn the radio aerial down parallel with the screen to avoid low garage doorways. An electrically operated wing-mounted aerial was optional, the switch for which was mounted below the 'switchbox' between the radio and front speaker. The lower picture shows one of the switches for the electric windows. Silver Cloud III and Bentley S3 standard saloon interiors were identical except for the motifs on the instruments and brake pedal pad.*

This page *H. J. Mulliner, by now fully integrated with Park Ward as H. J. Mulliner, Park Ward Ltd, continued to adapt the standard saloon to produce the highly desirable drophead coupé shown above. 38 Silver Cloud IIIs and a solitary Bentley S3 were so treated between October 1962 and September 1963 when the design was discontinued in favour of that shown below. The origin of the coachwork of this car and those on the following page may be traced to Park Ward's drophead coupé design on the S2 Continental chassis. The centre car is an S3 Continental, design number 2006. The paired headlights, set at an angle in the extremities of the front wings, are the main feature distinguishing these cars from the earlier S2 Continentals. Though built by the combined firm H. J. Mulliner, Park Ward, these cars were of pure Park Ward design and continued to carry Park Ward sillplates until well into 1963, when H. J. Mulliner, Park Ward plates began to appear on the designs of both constituent companies. At the 1963 Earls Court Motor Show the same body style, as design number 2045, first appeared on a specially adapted Silver Cloud III chassis with Bentley Continental-type lower raked steering column. The standard Silver Cloud III instruments were grouped in the panel in front of the driver, whereas the Bentley retained its customary Continental instrumentation, complete with revolution counter. The close-up view of the rear of one of these cars shows the distinctive and unusual tail-fins and rear-lamp clusters.*

This page *The styling of the
drophead coupés on the previous
page was the basis of these two-
door saloons. Design number 2035,
the Bentley S3 Continental version
(top) looks a little slab-sided
without the chromium embellishing
strip fitted to the design number
2041 Silver Cloud IIIs in the other
three photographs. The bottom
right car is Silver Cloud III
SEV117, the Rolls-Royce London
Sales Department demonstrator.
This photograph, in a rural village
setting, shows off the unusual rear
aspect, which featured 'fins' and a
full-width, slightly hooded rear
window – neither of which were
usually associated with Rolls-Royce
cars but which somehow suited
these designs, which were known
within the coachbuilder's works as
the 'Koren coupés' – V. Koren being
the name of their Swedish freelance
designer. They represent, together
with the drophead versions on the
previous page, the overwhelming
majority of S3 Continental and
Silver Cloud III (standard
wheelbase) special coachwork.
Construction was of steel with
aluminium bonnet and boot lids
and doors. The lower left
photograph on this page also shows
the unusual tail treatment. The use
of the term 'Continental' for these
coachbuilt Silver Cloud IIIs, as
popularised by the used car trade,
has no foundation in fact and they
were never marketed or designated
as such by their makers.*

This page *H. J. Mulliner's 'Flying Spur' saloon was continued by H. J. Mulliner, Park Ward for the S3 Continental, though with the revised frontal appearance which, it is felt, suited it particularly well. An extremely handsome car with performance to match. From the 1963 Earls Court Motor Show this design also became available on specially modified Silver Cloud III chassis, though it could be said that the shape blended better with the Bentley radiator with which it was originally conceived than with the Rolls-Royce radiator (right). The standard Silver Cloud instruments, too, were less impressive (lower photograph) in the fascia which had been designed for the more comprehensive Bentley Continental instrumentation. The large accelerator pedal was standard on all post-war left-hand drive cars and the larger than standard brake pedal shown here appeared on left-hand drive Silver Cloud IIIs, becoming standard for the later Silver Shadow range and is still unchanged on the current models.*

This page *The cars on this page are a very rare 'Flying Spur' variant with small rear quarter-lights, in this instance still a six-light body unlike the four-light 'Flying Spur' seen in Chapter 5 and (below) another rare S3 Continental, the H. J. Mulliner two-door saloon which was an adaptation of their S2 Continental two-door design. This was a car for those who, whilst requiring a two-door car, could not countenance the more radical styling of the 'Koren' coupés (see preceding page), which had been standardised for two-door coachwork but which was not to everybody's taste. The interior view serves to illustrate the Bentley Continental instrumentation and consequent different fascia layout to that of the Silver Cloud III (previous pages). Note how massive the front seats appear – an approach to luxury that would not have been countenanced for the lightweight R-type Continental!*

This page *Three photographs of James Young coachwork. Like the Park Ward and H. J. Mulliner designs, these remained unchanged from their previous designs apart from frontal appearance. Again, while this style of coachwork was originally conceived for the Bentley Continental (top), some examples found their way onto special Silver Cloud III chassis for the benefit of those who craved the sleek Continental shape while preferring the Rolls-Royce frontal appearance as seen in the other two photographs. At upper right is Silver Cloud III SEV121, the 1963 Earls Court Show James Young stand exhibit. Below right we have another Silver Cloud III, on chassis SHS313C, owned by Thorn Electrical Industries from new in 1964 until 1976 when it was acquired by Thomas T. Solley (RREC). All three photos clearly show the wrap-around rear glass on these cars. Note also that the door handles, with their characteristic James Young square push-buttons, extend into a chromium waist moulding on the Silver Cloud IIIs but not on the Bentley Continental, and that while SEV121 has the standard Silver Cloud III bumper overriders, SHS131C and the Bentley both have the earlier pattern, which were fitted to many of the coachbuilt cars as well as routinely to North American exports.*

Above *A rare two-door variant of the James Young saloons on the previous page. Only six were built on the Silver Cloud III chassis, of which this is the first, chassis SGT609C, the 1964 Earls Court Show exhibit. Curiously, these two-door cars and their four-door counterparts shared the same design number, SCV100.*

Below & right *The Silver Cloud III and Bentley S3 Long Wheelbase Saloon with Division was intended for the owner who required a car for business use, chauffeur driven, which could nevertheless be used as a private family car at weekends and on holiday.*

This page *James Young accounted for the vast majority of special coachwork on long wheelbase Silver Cloud III and Bentley S3 chassis, their superbly proportioned design number SCT100 touring limousine being the dominant design. First introduced for the Silver Cloud II long wheelbase chassis, it was modified with the new frontal appearance for the Silver Cloud III and Bentley S3. In the twilight of their coachbuilding years, James Young had reached the pinnacle with these cars in terms of elegance. The styling was similar to that of their famous Phantom Vs, a fact which gave rise to the term 'mini-Phantom' for these cars in the trade. The top photo is a well known Jack Barclay Ltd publicity shot of CAL3, the 1962 Earls Court Show car, while the middle photograph shows the elegant flowing lines of the rear of CCL57. John Bull's ink and wash drawing (bottom) shows the profile of the Bentley version, design number B3.100.*

Above & left *Two-door coachwork on the long wheelbase chassis is extremely rare and each of the two James Young cars on this page is unique in its own right. Both are to design number SCT200 and represent the only two examples of the design. The upper car is LCDL1, built for King Hassan II of Morocco. Note the royal crest on the door and flag-masts on the front wings. The lower car is CEL19, which may be instantly recognised by its Hooper-style quarter lights.*

Opposite page bottom & this page top right *H. J. Mulliner, Park Ward built five cabriolets to design number 2033 on the Silver Cloud III long wheelbase chassis. These were extremely unusual in that the paired headlamps, normally a distinguishing feature of the Silver Cloud III, were absent – the frontal appearance remaining exactly as it had for the example built by H. J. Mulliner on a Silver Cloud II chassis (page 195), right down to the taller radiator shell and sidelights on the tops of the front wings. The subject of our photograph is CAL37, one of a pair, the other being CAL39, built for the Australian Government in 1962. Both featured separate rear seats that could be raised so that the occupants, ranging from royalty, through U.S. astronauts to the America's Cup (right) could be brought into public view. Three more were built after the Australian cars but these differed in having the standard Silver Cloud III rear lights in lieu of the distinctive 'cathedral' type. These cabriolets represent the final examples of a styling theme which began on the Silver Cloud I and Bentley S1 chassis (Chapter Five).*

Right & bottom right *From the Phantom V 'VA' series onwards the Park Ward 7-passenger limousine became the H. J. Mulliner, Park Ward 7-passenger limousine, design number 2003. The panelwork below the waistline remained much as before but modified to incorporate the paired headlamps and new sidelamp and rear lamp assemblies. From the waistline up, however, it was all change. The windscreen was a different shape while the formerly rounded rear quarters and boot gave way to razor edges and the former heavy, painted frames to the door windows disappeared in favour of slim chromium plated frames. The combined overall effect of this 'face-lift', carried out by Martin Bourne, one of John Blatchley's Crewe body design team, was aesthetically very pleasing. This version of the Phantom V was known within the Company as 'Phantom V½', and the design*

remained essentially unchanged, as the Phantom VI, until 1990 when construction of the final example commenced, making it the longest-lived body design of all time. The view of the rear compartment interior shows that the layout and fittings remained virtually unchanged from those of the earlier Park Ward design. Leather upholstery is shown, but West of England cloth, twill or other materials could be specified for the rear compartment, the front normally being leather regardless of the rear upholstery material.

217

Above This landaulette, to design number 2047, is an obvious development of Park Ward's design number 1000. Only two of these were built, one for the Ruler of Bahrain and this one, on chassis 5VD51, for the Government of East Nigeria. Note the fitting attached to the radiator mascot for mounting a flag mast.

Below The design represented by the brace of landaulettes described in the previous caption was replaced by the much more satisfactory State Landaulette, design number 2052, seen here. The second of these, on chassis 5VD83, is the subject of our photograph. It was exhibited by Rolls-Royce at the 1965 Earls Court Motor Show alongside the all-new Silver Shadow. Note that the styling of the boot reverted to that of the Park Ward design numbers 980/1000/1104 for this model, a pleasing solution to the problem of blending the folding hood with what would otherwise have been a razor-edged boot. The State Landaulette was intended for Heads of State and foreign governments. The first car built went to the President of Tanzania, on chassis 5VD99 – a later chassis number than the second car, 5VD83 (this car) which was sold to the Ruler of Bahrain. A further two went to the governments of Persia and Romania, with a fifth, on the final Phantom V chassis, to a private owner. The interior design closely follows that of the Limousine, except that the rear seat could be raised three inches electrically and there was a grab-rail above the division for processional use. Note the flag masts on the front wings.

coachwork on specially modified base units. The base units were supplied by Pressed Steel Fisher of Oxford while the external panels were bought in from various outside suppliers, welded onto the base unit and finished to Rolls-Royce standards ready for painting.

Left *Another major role played by H. J. Mulliner, Park Ward was the construction of coachwork for the huge Phantom V chassis. At the end of 1968 this model was replaced by the Phantom VI, the chassis of which was, to all intents and purposes, the same as far as the coachbuilder was concerned. The H. J. Mulliner, Park Ward designs remained much as they were, as did the method of construction, which was strictly traditional coachbuilding. The photographs in the following series show some of the construction processes, starting with the body frame, which was hand-built from galvanised steel and is seen here mounted on a dummy 'chassis' frame.*

Below left *Construction of a Phantom VI was an unhurried process. All panels were made by hand from aluminium sheet. Here we see John McKenzie (left) file finishing a completed front wing. Note the wooden 'buck' over which the front wing (right) is being formed by Ian Brown (back to camera).*

Below right *A closer view of the wooden buck on which, in this instance, a right-hand front wing is partly formed. In the background are two wheeling machines used to form curved panels.*

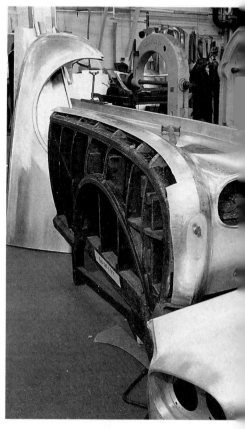

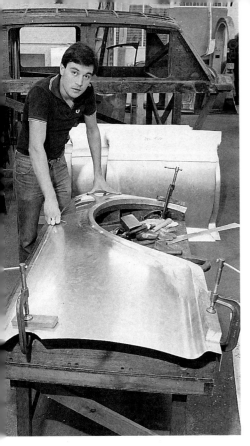

Above *Carl Ashworth working on a partly formed front wing. In the background is the main body 'buck'. This did not form part of the car but is the former on which the various panels were shaped.*

Above right *Arthur Noyes file-finishing a rear wing.*

Right *Dennis Lawes making adjustments to the rear door shut line on a nearly completed Phantom VI body shell. Dennis joined H. J. Mulliner & Co. in 1950 and finished his career building Phantoms, retiring after the last Phantom was delivered in early 1992.*

Bottom right *Removed from its dummy chassis and supported by wooden trestles, this Phantom VI body is ready for fitting to its actual chassis. The black paint is a 'guide coat' which will be rubbed down to reveal slight imperfections for attention before the finishing coats are applied.*

Left *Phantom builders. From left to right are Jack Giles, Gary Jackson and foreman Jim Davis.*

Below *The body mounted on its chassis, this Phantom VI is nearing completion. Body finisher John Martin fitting the electric window equipment. Trimmers are at work on the interior at this stage.*

Above *The front wings and bonnet were the last parts of the coachwork to be fitted. The car on the hoist behind is nearly finished.*

Right & below *These two photographs show a car nearly ready for delivery. The brightwork is being wrapped in readiness for shipping overseas and the paintwork is receiving some last minute rectification. The type of rear light cluster shown was fitted to a small number of Phantom VIs. Early cars had the Silver Cloud III type and most later cars had the Corniche type. Note the Silver Cloud style bumpers, overriders and boot lid hardware, all of which date from the mid-1950s.*

Chapter Eight

Cloud OverShadowed

The Silver Shadow, Bentley T Series and derivatives, and the Phantom VI

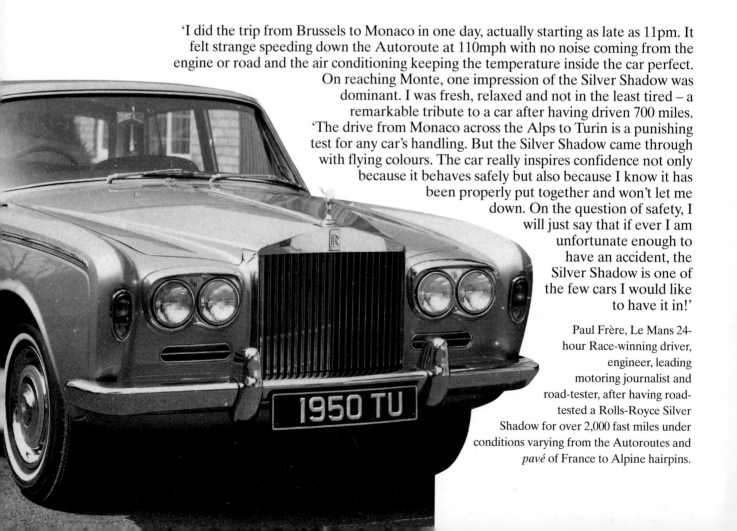

'I did the trip from Brussels to Monaco in one day, actually starting as late as 11pm. It felt strange speeding down the Autoroute at 110mph with no noise coming from the engine or road and the air conditioning keeping the temperature inside the car perfect. On reaching Monte, one impression of the Silver Shadow was dominant. I was fresh, relaxed and not in the least tired – a remarkable tribute to a car after having driven 700 miles. 'The drive from Monaco across the Alps to Turin is a punishing test for any car's handling. But the Silver Shadow came through with flying colours. The car really inspires confidence not only because it behaves safely but also because I know it has been properly put together and won't let me down. On the question of safety, I will just say that if ever I am unfortunate enough to have an accident, the Silver Shadow is one of the few cars I would like to have it in!'

Paul Frère, Le Mans 24-hour Race-winning driver, engineer, leading motoring journalist and road-tester, after having road-tested a Rolls-Royce Silver Shadow for over 2,000 fast miles under conditions varying from the Autoroutes and *pavé* of France to Alpine hairpins.

The Rolls-Royce Silver Shadow and its Bentley counterpart the T Series were announced in October 1965 as 'the most radically new Rolls-Royce cars for 59 years.' It was certainly true that no previous model had even hinted at chassis-less construction, all-independent self-levelling suspension, disc brakes, high-pressure hydraulic system for brakes and levelling and electrically operated seat adjustment and gear range selection. Moreover, no previous model, not even the Phantom III, had ever introduced so many new features at a single stroke. The fact that these cars remained fundamentally unchanged for a fifteen year model run, together with the fact that more than 37,000 cars were built during that time, amply testifies to the 'rightness' of the original concept. Though it is perhaps open to argument to what extent this outstanding success was attributable to the underlying affluence of the times and other economic factors as opposed to any increased appeal of the cars, the fact remains that the Silver Shadow and its derivatives were far more widely accepted than, and handsomely outsold, all previous models. The only possible negative aspect was the sad but inescapable fact that the Bentley marque was allowed to all but die out, seemingly as a deliberate act of Company policy. For some years the availability of a Bentley alternative was not even mentioned in Silver Shadow publicity brochures and as a result the Bentley T Series is a comparative rarity. The T2 and Bentley Corniche even more so. Happily, with the introduction of the following Silver Spirit range came a new-found enthusiasm for the Bentley marque and the decline was comprehensively reversed.

Among the most important considerations in the styling of the Silver Shadow was that it should withstand the ravages of time. Obviously a firm such as Rolls-Royce, with a relatively modest output, cannot afford the luxury of frequent styling changes. Therefore, styling features that are liable to date quickly need to be avoided. As a result, the fifteen years of Silver Shadow production saw only minimal changes to the standard saloon body, with the most obvious of the few changes that did occur being confined almost entirely to the interior. The body style that resulted from these aims and constraints was fairly conservative but quite timeless. It is difficult for the untrained eye to date a Silver Shadow or T Series at a glance – a 1966 example looking substantially the same as a 1972 or 1976 – and they do not look unduly dated even today. The writer's 1966 T Series has been mistaken for 'newish' on more than one occasion. Only the Silver Shadow II and its companion Bentley T2, with their black polyurethane-faced bumpers are easier to distinguish, though the bumpers themselves are not a reliable clue as these were fitted to certain U.S. export cars as early as 1973.

Beneath this conservative (one hesitates to say ordinary) exterior lay a technical specification that was second to none for sophistication and innovation. When first introduced in 1965 these cars were easily the most technically advanced in the world, and without any fundamental changes having been made, there is little risk of contradiction in stating that in many ways they still were when discontinued in 1980. In fact, the same design concept still forms the basis of the current range of cars.

Unlike their predecessors the Silver Shadow series had no separate chassis, the extremely rigid monocoque body being mounted on front and rear sub-frames that carried the engine, gearbox, front suspension and steering equipment, and rear axle and rear suspension respectively. Suspension was all-independent with front anti-dive and rear anti-lift characteristics to resist nose-diving under heavy braking. Superimposed on the suspension, but playing no part in the actual springing or damping, was a sophisticated high pressure hydraulic self-levelling, or height control, system to maintain optimum ride height and attitude regardless of load and load distribution. This system, certain features of which were covered by Citroën patents, operated at two speeds, fast levelling taking effect when a door was open or neutral selected. The hydraulic pressure for the levelling and brakes, at 2,500 pounds per square inch, was (and still is on current models) supplied by a pair of camshaft-driven piston pumps and stored in spherical accumulators. Rams above each coil spring, with one inch of travel at the front and three inches at the rear, were supplied by hydraulic fluid under pressure by height control valves, or sensors, one for the front pair of rams and two for the rear pair.

The four-wheel disc brake system incorporated two independent powered circuits, using high pressure hydraulics from the same pump and accumulator that supplied the height control system for one circuit, the second pump and accumulator for the second circuit, with a third, conventional master cylinder circuit connected directly to the pedal. One powered circuit provided 46% of the total braking, operating one caliper on each front disc and part of the rear braking, while the other powered circuit provided 31% of the total braking, operating the second caliper of each front disc. The direct master cylinder circuit provided the remaining 23% of braking and served the same purpose as the direct mechanical linkage in the old brake system, i.e. to introduce positive 'feel' into the pedal. A deceleration-conscious pressure-limiting valve, or 'G-valve', was provided to prevent premature wheel locking.

Power-assisted steering was by Saginaw (U.S.) recirculating ball steering box with integral ram – as opposed to the external ram of the Silver Cloud/S Series system – supplied with hydraulic pressure by a Hobourn-Eaton* belt-driven pump as on the earlier models. For the first time on a Rolls-Royce or Bentley the steering column was collapsible, for safety, and the steering wheel was a new two-spoke design with the same diameter and rim section as that of the Silver Clouds II and III and a central horn button.

The engine used for the Silver Shadow series was, at first, basically the same 6,230cc unit first introduced in October 1959, though with redesigned cylinder heads which gave a more efficient combustion chamber shape and brought the spark plugs up to a more readily accessible position above the redesigned exhaust manifolds. Likewise, the automatic gearbox, at least on right-hand drive cars, was still the four-speed Rolls-Royce 'box with fluid coupling as first introduced in 1952, though with aluminium alloy in lieu of cast iron for the main casing and some internal parts and with a freewheel incorporated for first and second gears – this feature being inoperative with '2' selected in order to provide engine braking when required. Cars for North America, however, had a three-speed automatic transmission with torque converter, bought in complete from General Motors in Detroit and fitted unmodified – such was the state of the art of automatic transmission manufacture in the U.S. In both cases, range selection was electrically operated, thus eliminating a possible noise path and providing light finger-tip action.

The opportunity for the remaining coachbuilders to express their traditional arts was severely curtailed by the monocoque mode of construction of the Silver Shadow, though this did not discourage James Young Ltd from embarking on a series of fifty two-door cars based on standard Silver Shadow and Bentley T Series body shells. These cars were, it must be said, somewhat plain looking, but apart from a solitary car from Pininfarina, they represented the only effort by a coachbuilder outside the Rolls-Royce empire on the Silver Shadow models. James Young bowed out gracefully very soon after that exercise, as the last independent coachbuilder for Rolls-Royce and Bentley cars. As a subsidiary of Rolls-Royce Ltd, H. J. Mulliner, Park Ward were better placed to fulfil the demand for coachbuilt cars, even if they were no longer really coachbuilt in the previously accepted sense, and the task of turning out a truly distinctive two-door car fell to that firm. For a while, during the latter part of 1965 and early 1966, they continued to build specialist coachwork for Bentley S3 Continental and special Silver Cloud III chassis, though these soon gave way to sleek new two-door saloon and drophead coupé designs for the new models. These cars, like the Standard Saloon, were designed by John Blatchley's styling team at Crewe and were built in a manner that was more body engineering than coach-building, though the interior trimming and finishing remained traditional coachbuilding tasks. They were built on special base units supplied by Pressed Steel Fisher, using panels supplied in roughly finished state by various companies such as Albany Jig & Tool, Paul & Airflow Streamlines and Dowty Doulton. They formed the basis of what was to become the Corniche.

A surprising omission from the range, at first, was a long wheelbase version. The chassisless construction appears to have been the main stumbling block, though the solution eventually adopted – cutting a standard body shell in half and letting in an extra four inches just aft of the centre pillars – was remarkably simple and worked well. This work was carried out at the Willesden works of H. J. Mulliner, Park Ward. After being modified to Long Wheelbase specification, the body shells were transported to Crewe where they were fed onto the production line for finishing. Unlike the long wheelbase conversions of Silver Cloud and S Series Standard Saloons, the Silver Shadow Long Wheelbase Saloon, introduced in May 1969, retained the standard car's four-light body configuration.

During the fifteen year production run of the Silver Shadow and its derivatives, over 2,000 individual technical and coachwork changes were introduced, culminating in the introduction of the Silver Shadow II range in February 1977. Most of the changes were mere details, though there were many more notable ones and these are outlined in the technical specification at the end of this chapter. Perhaps the most important change, apart from those that came with the Silver Shadow II range of which more anon, was the enlargement of the engine capacity from 6,230cc to 6,750cc. This change took place in July 1970 and was accomplished by lengthening the stroke from 3.6 to 3.9 inches. The increase in power output that could reasonably have been expected to result from this change was largely absorbed by the exhaust emission control equipment that was required to be fitted, firstly on cars for California and later for the remainder of North America and other countries, notably Australia and Japan. The three-speed G.M. automatic transmission fitted to North American models began to appear on right-hand drive cars during 1968 and was standard by November of that year. In May 1969 the front height control valve and levelling rams

248

were deleted, with automatic height control remaining on the rear only, where experience had shown that it had been doing nearly all the effective levelling work. Most of the earlier cars have had their front height control equipment disconnected and blanked off.

Corniche

On February 4th, 1971 Rolls-Royce Ltd went into receivership following an unmanageable blow-out in the development costs of the RB211 jet engine, a new, larger engine which the Company was developing for the new generation of wide-bodied jets, including the Lockheed Tristar. Motor car production, however, continued without interruption on the specific instructions of the Receiver, E. R. Nicholson, who subsequently separated the motor car and diesel engine divisions from the aero engine business. In May 1973 a new public company, Rolls-Royce Motors Ltd, was formed.

Within two weeks of the Company going into receivership a new model was announced. More accurately, an existing model had been significantly revised and given a distinctive new model name. The H. J. Mulliner, Park Ward coachbuilt Silver Shadow and T Series cars became the Corniche – a name shared by the Rolls-Royce and Bentley variants. This was the start of a policy of giving model names to body styles rather than to chassis types, which was perhaps inevitable given the absence of a separate chassis under all Rolls-Royce and Bentley cars other than the huge Phantom VI. This policy eventually saw in separate model names for each body style and wheelbase. The choice of the model designation Corniche was not a difficult one for the Company. As related in Chapter Three, Corniche was a name first registered by Rolls-Royce Ltd in 1939, when it was applied to a high-

performance derivative of the Bentley Mk V which never saw series production due to the outbreak of World War II. Also, the prototype post-war Bentley Continental was known within the Experimental Department as 'Corniche II'. Despite the clear Bentley connotations of the name Corniche, both Bentley and Rolls-Royce versions of the new model were offered. Moreover, customers opting for the Bentley were outnumbered twenty to one by those specifying the Rolls-Royce – a fact that has made the Bentley Corniche a rare and desirable collectors' item. Also, it is difficult to escape the conclusion that an opportunity was missed in that the evocative name Continental was not applied to the Bentley. This sad situation was not corrected until 1984 when the Continental name was revived for the Bentley version of the Corniche.

Modifications to the valve and ignition timing, a more efficient air intake silencer and a low-loss exhaust system increased in bore from 2" to 2¼" all contributed to the enhanced performance of the Corniche over that of the Standard Silver Shadow models. Traditionally, Rolls-Royce do not disclose the power output of their motor car engines, preferring to describe it as 'adequate' or 'sufficient'. However, in the case of the Corniche it was a case of 'adequate plus ten per cent'; sufficiently adequate, in fact, to give the big coupés a top speed in excess of 120mph, with acceleration capabilities, particularly from speeds above 50mph, considerably better than those of the standard car, itself no sluggard, and indeed better than those of the average 'sports car' of the period! The engine modifications did not apply to the Corniche for export to the United States, due to the need to comply with emission regulations.

Visually, the Corniche differed from the coachbuilt Silver Shadow and Bentley T Series cars from

which it was derived by having new distinctive spun stainless steel wheel trims – designed to allow better air flow around the brakes – and a new fascia with comprehensive instrumentation which included a rev counter and a fifteen inch diameter wood-rimmed steering wheel with leather-covered spokes (soon deleted on safety grounds in favour of the standard sixteen inch Silver Shadow wheel). The radiator shell was slightly but noticeably deeper (measured front to rear) and a CORNICHE badge on the bootlid distinguished the new model.

An interesting technical innovation, first introduced on the Corniche but later standardised on all models, was the automatic speed control, or 'cruise control'. The controls for this were mounted on the fascia below the rev counter and maintained any desired speed regardless of gradient, to within 1mph or so. The system could be overridden by pressing the accelerator or disengaged by using the brake pedal after which the selected cruising speed could be resumed by pressing a 'Resume' button. Similar systems are relatively common today, even on lower-priced cars, but it was practically unknown on other British cars in the early 1970s.

The drophead coupé version of the Corniche, actually marketed as the Convertible, using the American terminology, is surely the ultimate in high-performance open air motoring. It has been so successful that it is still a current model, though only to special order and with much more modern technical specification nowadays. The body styling dates from September 1967, when it was introduced as the Silver Shadow Drophead Coupé. In closed form it dates from eighteen months before that.

Camargue

In March 1975 a second luxurious two-door coachbuilt car was added to the range. This was the Pininfarina-styled Camargue – a name which, like Corniche, has its origins in the South of France, a part of the world with close associations with Sir Henry Royce, who carried out much of his design work at his winter home La Villa Mimosa at Le Canadel.

In October 1969 the Italian stylist had been commissioned to design a car which would be suitable for production by H. J. Mulliner, Park Ward and which could be based upon the standard mechanical units and base platform of the Silver Shadow. It was specified that the car should be a two-door saloon offering superior passenger and luggage accommodation to the Silver Shadow two-door saloon (which, in developed form was known, from March 1971, as the Corniche).

Construction of the first prototype Camargue was commenced by Mulliner Park Ward during 1971 and it was on the road by July 1972. It was the first model designed on a metric basis and much to the consternation of Bentley enthusiasts was intended to be a Rolls-Royce only, though the experimental prototypes appeared in Bentley guise for testing purposes and a Bentley version, with turbocharged engine, was once contemplated. Managing Director David (now Sir David) Plastow was once quoted as saying 'If anyone asked us for a Bentley, we would certainly quote him a price.' Only one Camargue customer took up this offer.

The styling was characteristically Pininfarina and the car looks much larger than the Corniche, though in fact it is the same length but 3.9 inches wider. The deep, steeply raked windscreen and rear window and curved side windows helped give the Camargue a strikingly rakish appearance. The traditional Rolls-Royce radiator shape was, of course, retained, though as a concession to the styling this feature was much squatter and wider than hitherto,

had a more pronounced curve in plan view and was arranged to lean forward at an angle of four degrees.

Ease of entry and exit was assured for rear seat passengers by the unusually wide doors, a second door opening handle at the rear of the door armrest and an electrically operated front seat squab release. Inside, the immediate impression was an awareness that there was little in common with previous Rolls-Royce interior decor. The most obvious departure, and one which does not appeal to all tastes, was the external mounting of the instruments and other fascia equipment, so that each appears to be set in its own little black box, aircraft style. The fascia itself was of impact absorbing aluminium sheet veneered with boldly figured walnut and surrounded by energy absorbing material. The seats, upholstered in high quality vat-died Connolly hide, were prominently pleated and extremely comfortable. The front seats had integral head restraints, adjustable for height. A large knurled knob gave fine adjustment of squab rake while all other seat adjustments (height, tilt, reach) were electrically operated as on the Silver Shadow and Corniche.

The engineering of the Camargue body benefited from all the work that resulted in the Silver Shadow and Corniche meeting and exceeding all international safety standards. Testing to prove compliance with the very stringent United States legislation was carried out with just one prototype Camargue body in the following sequence:

1. Side intrusion test – fully satisfactory. Anti-intrusion beams to the doors were standard for all markets.
2. Door repaired before roof crash test. 0.5in (1.27cm) deflection under 5,100lb (2,313kg) load.
3. All requirements met in 30mph (48km/h) barrier crash test.

4. Damaged front end removed and body shell used to demonstrate integrity of seat and seat belt anchorages for all world markets.

The coachwork of the Camargue was built up from panels sourced from the same outside firms who supplied the panels for the Corniche (and Silver Shadow two-door cars), except for the roof and boot lid which were made on the hydraulic stretch press at Hythe Road, on a modified but otherwise standard Silver Shadow base unit. At first, construction of the Camargue was divided between Crewe and Mulliner Park Ward in London, with the cars being transported backwards and forwards between the two plants for the various operations. However, in 1976, with world demand for the coachbuilt models soaring, a decision was reached to transfer Camargue production to Crewe in order to relieve the pressure from the overloaded Mulliner Park Ward Division, which was then producing the Corniche and Phantom VI as well as the Camargue. Because Crewe lacked the facilities to produce coachbuilt bodies, a new body shell supplier was sought. This work was contracted to Motor Panels of Coventry. Production of the Camargue at Crewe, on a special line, commenced in the summer of 1978.

Mechanically, the initial batch of Camargues shared the same specification as the Corniche, with twin S.U. carburetters, Lucas 35D8 distributor with centrifugal advance and 9:1 standard compression ratio. For production versions, except those for the United States, Japan and Australia, a Solex four-choke downdraught carburetter was fitted and the compression ratio was lowered to 8:1 (7.3:1 for North America and Japan). Ignition was Lucas Opus electronic with centrifugal and vacuum advance distributor. These changes were also applied to the Corniche.

A major innovation in keeping with the established Rolls-Royce Motors policy of using low volume coachbuilt models as the technical leaders of the range was the fully automatic, split-level air conditioning system. This was designed and developed by Rolls-Royce Motors engineers and, as the first and only such system to offer completely independent automatic temperature control at two levels, it was, and remains, the most advanced available. Once the desired temperatures for the upper and lower parts of the interior have been set, the car may be driven from the Arctic circle to the equator without the need to adjust the controls, and the selected temperatures are maintained automatically and unobtrusively. The ultimate 'set and forget' system.

The pricing of the Camargue was, from its inception, set at 50% above that of the Corniche, not because it cost that much more to build – though it did take some 60% longer to build a Camargue – but merely to ensure its exclusivity as the Rolls-Royce flagship, and to make the point that Rolls-Royce Motors Ltd fully intended remaining at the very pinnacle of the luxury car pyramid. A clear indication of just how relatively expensive the Camargue was at the time of its introduction was the fact that at £29,250 it was fully 35% more expensive even than the Phantom VI, which was much larger and, it could be argued, more hand-built.

There is an amusing anecdote that when the Camargue was launched, in January 1975 in Sicily, Chief Engineer John Hollings took along a trophy, inscribed 'Presented to the first man in the world to have an accident in a Camargue.' This was a precaution in the event of the unthinkable happening. It did, when a motoring journalist bounced one of the Camargues off a lorry! Foresight and a sense of humour defused a potentially dif-ficult and embarrassing situation. When news of the award broke, it is said that three European motoring writers claimed to have been its recipient!

The name Camargue is derived from the Ile de la Camargue, in the delta of the Rhone on the Mediterranean coast. One of the strangest, most solitary and unspoiled regions of France, its largest population centre is the village of Saintes Maries de la Mer, with fewer than 2,500 inhabitants. Over half the Camargue was reclaimed from the numerous lagoons and given over to cattle and sheep raising and the production of wheat, rice and wine. The Camargue's chief sport is bullfighting, which unlike that in neighbouring Spain, does not involve either death or injury to the bull. The bull's heads are decorated with rosettes tied between the horns, and it is the task of the 'razeteurs' to remove the rosette. Such events sometimes take place in public streets. The largest remaining lagoon, Etang de Vaccares, is a zoological and botanical reserve populated by some 300 species of birds, including one of the world's largest flamingo colonies.

Silver Shadow II

The most significant changes to the Silver Shadow range of cars occurred in February 1977. These changes to the technical specification and appearance were considered sufficient to justify revised model designations – Silver Shadow II and Bentley T2. The following month saw the policy of bestowing individual model names to body styles rather than to chassis types extended to the long wheelbase version of the standard car, which became the Silver Wraith II, in honour of the first post-war Rolls-Royce.

The changes introduced in a single package for these Series II cars affected the external appearance, interior, mechanical specification and handling characteristics of the car. Dealing with each in turn, the changes most obvious to the observer in the street were the adoption as standard of American-style, wrap-around, black polyurethane-faced bumpers, a deeper (front to back) radiator shell like that of the Corniche and the fitting of an 'air dam' below the front bumper. These Silver Shadow II recognition points did not apply in the United States, partly because the bumpers and deeper radiator shell were already familiar on U.S. export Silver Shadows and partly because the air dam was not fitted to Silver Shadow IIs for that market, so Americans had to rely for identification on the SILVER SHADOW II badge on the bootlid and the revised fascia.

The most immediately noticeable interior change was that the Silver Shadow II range of cars reverted to having a full set of instruments and a suitably impressive fascia in which to mount them. Actually, the new fascia had appeared a year or so earlier, without fanfare, on the Corniche. Very early Silver Shadows had featured a particularly attractive fascia with full instrumentation, but the U.S. Federal Safety Standards had precipitated a change to a shallower, more heavily padded fascia which left room for fewer instruments. The new fascia for the Silver Shadow II had less prominent padding, particularly along the lower edge, a considerably larger area of wood and full instrumentation incorporated in a classic four-in-one instrument, representing a return to the Silver Cloud – and indeed Bentley Mk VI – style of instrument. Either the larger areas of timber and less heavy crash padding reflected an easing of Federal Safety Standards, which is unlikely, or Rolls-Royce had over-reacted in 1968.

More important than the cosmetic changes were the new technical features of the Silver Shadow II range, and perhaps the most significant of these, from the point of view of the enthusiastic driver, was the rack-and-pinion steering. The Silver Shadow had always suffered from rather vague steering. It was smooth, light, progressive and accurate to a nicety, but nevertheless felt vague, even if less so than that of most of its competitors. Even with the benefit of higher gearing and smaller (16in) steering wheel from August 1971, it was anything but sporting. At speed, the new rack-and-pinion steering with its highly refined power assistance, as well as being more precise and sensitive, provided the positive 'feel' that experienced drivers expect. The 'sneeze factor' was now relegated to history. A still smaller (15in) steering wheel went with the new steering system. Modifications to the front suspension geometry, designed to keep the front wheels more upright when cornering, improved responsiveness still further as well as reducing roll angles, with consequent reductions in noise and scrub and beneficial effects on tyre life.

There were also some power-unit changes, mainly in the cooling and carburation areas. A smaller but more efficient seven-bladed plastic fan, driven through a viscous coupling, was assisted by a thermostatically controlled electric fan mounted forward of the radiator. The large S.U. type HD.8 carburetters, which had served on several Rolls-Royce and Bentley models since 1957, were replaced with the much more technically advanced, though slightly smaller, HIF.7s. Their advanced design, featuring linear ball-race dashpots, provided much more efficient maintenance of exhaust emission control standards and, in conjunction with the lower power absorption characteristics of the revised cooling arrangements and a new low-loss twin exhaust system, helped improve fuel economy. The twin exhaust system, of stainless steel construction, also compensated for the slight loss of power incurred by the smaller car-

buretters. The alternator was of increased capacity and the oil filter was now the modern disposable spin-on type in lieu of the earlier separate element type.

The highly sophisticated automatic bi-level air conditioning system, first introduced on the Camargue and adopted for the Corniche for 1976, was standard on all models in the Silver Shadow II range of cars. This was in line with an established Rolls-Royce pattern of introducing such innovations on the top-of-the-line coachbuilt models first, then following up with their incorporation in the standard cars once larger scale production could be reliably achieved. A further manifestation of this policy occurred from May 1979 when some of the technical features of the coming new Silver Spirit range of cars were quietly introduced onto the Corniche and Camargue. Very briefly, these features were: the use of mineral oil in lieu of conventional brake fluid for the hydraulic systems, revised rear suspension incorporating gas springs and, on the Corniche, a digital display in the centre of the fascia for outside ambient temperature, journey elapsed time indicator and clock. However, these changes belong to the later family of cars and are dealt with in more detail in the following chapter, but before passing on to the Silver Spirit and its derivatives, a few words about that most amazing and enduring of Rolls-Royce cars, the Phantom VI, are appropriate.

Phantom VI
By 1967, with the chassisless Silver Shadow firmly established, the last independent coachbuilding firm James Young Ltd were winding down their operations, leaving H. J. Mulliner, Park Ward Ltd, a Rolls-Royce subsidiary, as the only remaining coachbuilder. The Phantom V chassis remained as the only Rolls-Royce chassis on which true coachbuilt bodies in the traditional sense could be built. This meant that the

Phantom was now a purely H. J. Mulliner, Park Ward* motor car. This, together with the decision to use the 6,230cc Silver Shadow engine (with improved cylinder heads which obviated the need for front wheel removal for access to the spark plugs on a Phantom) and fit as standard separate air conditioning systems for front and rear compartments, led to the designation Phantom VI being applied from 1968. The last Phantom V delivery took place in June of that year and the first production Phantom VI, chassis no. PRH4108, was delivered to the Belfast Corporation, with the guarantee dating from 1st January 1969.

It was originally intended that the Phantom VI would be an entirely new model and in 1966 a proposal for a new, lower chassis with revised rear suspension and a wheelbase of no less than 12ft 11in was considered. This new car would have been externally recognisable by an entirely new style of coachwork. In the event, however, the earliest Phantom VIs could be externally distinguished from an H. J. Mulliner, Park Ward Phantom V only by the opening panels of the bonnet being slightly shorter to make room for an air intake grille on the scuttle top and by turn indicator repeaters on the sides of the front wings. Inside, the only obvious difference was the flat fascia with padded capping rail along similar lines to that of the early Silver Shadows. This change was due to the fitting of the efficient Silver Shadow-type air conditioning system with its swivelling outlets on the fascia, which also explains the new grille in the scuttle.

From 1972 Phantom VIs began to appear with front-hinged doors

The coachbuilding firm H. J. Mulliner was purchased by Rolls-Royce Ltd in 1959. In 1961 it was combined with Park Ward – already owned by Rolls-Royce since 1939 – to form H. J. Mulliner, Park Ward Ltd.

to the rear compartment. This was to satisfy new European safety legislation, which also required burst-proof door locks, a collapsible steering column and a more effective handbrake, all of which were incorporated successfully. Compliance with these regulations also required a 30mph crash barrier test, using the 100 ton concrete block at MIRA. The first pre-production Phantom VI, chassis no. PRH1500, was used for this test, which it failed when the rigid centrally-hinged bonnet penetrated the windscreen. A second barrier test, with a suitably modified bonnet, was a complete success. At around the same time, some subtle changes to the external body details began to appear, including the stainless steel sill embellisher being extended over the wheel arches. The Silver Cloud III-pattern tail lights and foglights were replaced by the Corniche type, and a few cars appeared with hooded tail light clusters like those of the Silver Cloud III Park Ward-designed two-door cars. Interestingly, the task of constructing the Phantom VI chassis was transferred in August 1973 (commencing with chassis PRH4780) to Mulliner Park Ward in London. Thus the coachbuilder became the builder of the complete car, though of course the mechanical units still came from Crewe.

The basically Phantom V mechanical specification, including the four-speed fluid coupling automatic gearbox and mechanical friction-disc servo for the brakes, remained intact on the Phantom VI for ten years. Then, in the Spring of 1978, a number of significant changes were introduced, starting with a very special limousine, chassis no. PGH101, code-named 'Oil Barrel', presented by the Society of Motor Manufacturers to Her Majesty the Queen on the occasion of her Silver Jubilee. These changes brought the Phantom more into line with the Silver Shadow range

in that the 6,750cc engine, GM400 three-speed automatic transmission and high pressure hydraulics for the braking system were all adopted. The change to the brake system was made necessary by the fact that the gearbox rear extension that carried the cross-shaft for the mechanical servo was incompatible with the three-speed transmission. Thus the friction-disc servo that in one form or another served in Rolls-Royce cars so well since 1924 at last gave way to the thoroughly modern system of the Silver Shadow, though an ingenious adaptation was necessary to suit the Phantom's drum brakes. For various technical reasons it was not practical to fit the Phantom with disc brakes and the high pressure hydraulic system was not compatible with drum brakes. The solution adopted was to use the Silver Shadow hydraulics to operate rams connected to the Phantom's twin master cylinders. The drums had heavier heat-dissipation ribbing and an improved lining material was used.

Despite these changes and the fitting of centralised door and boot locking and the like, the Phantom VI remained very much a 1950s design. It is therefore all the more remarkable that there was still a sufficiently healthy demand to justify keeping it in production much longer than the most optimistic forecast. Its longevity is a tribute to the original design.

When it was first announced, in October 1968, the U.K. listed price of the Phantom VI, inclusive of all applicable taxes, was £13,123. Remarkably, that price remained unchanged for three years after which it increased in three stages to £16,058 by October 1973. In 1975 the price was £21,553. After that it was not listed and was available only on an individual order basis with a price quoted on receipt of the order. As production fell from a healthy 45 cars in 1971 to around a dozen per year by 1980, then to three per year, the price quickly passed the

six figure threshold and reached an incredible £350,000 in 1988 – and that for the "basic" specification' without special features or 'production deviations'.

'Alpha' Phantom

In 1965, in response to increasing interest from foreign Heads of State and governments, design and development work began on an armoured version of the Phantom V. This project was dubbed 'Alpha', a specification for which had been completed by October 1966. The first car was scheduled for completion by December 1967 but the chassis was not ready until May 1968 by which time it had become a Phantom VI. The customer for the first 'Alpha' Phantom was 'Darius P. Browne'. As is usually the case when royalty and Heads of State were involved, this was a code-name, in this instance for the Shah of Iran. The chassis number was PRX4182.

The 'Alpha' Phantoms were built around a 1,575 lb. protected 'cupola' of 7mm steel armour plate with 50mm thick glass. All rear compartment windows were fixed – i.e., non-opening. The H. J. Mulliner, Park Ward coachwork, design number 2053, was externally similar to the 'standard' limousine except that the chrome frames around the rear compartment side windows were noticeably thicker and the rear compartment doors were hinged on their leading edges – as became standard after 1972. The curved rear window was of composite glass/acrylic laminate of similar thickness to the side window glass.

The 'Alpha' chassis departed from standard in having specially strengthened 16 inch wheels mounted on ten studs, carrying 7.50 x 16 steel radial ply Dunlop tyres (front) and 8.25 x 16 (rear). Tyre pressures were 60 lb. per sq. in. (front) and 70 lb. per sq. in. (rear). The spare was a 7.50 x 16 inflated to 70 lb. per sq. in. Because a clip-on wheel trim cover was not made for 16 inch wheels the screw-on type, as fitted to the Silver Wraith and other early post-war models, was fitted. The large spanner to fit the centre hub nut for these was carried in the boot with the other road tools.

TECHNICAL SPECIFICATION

Rolls-Royce Silver Shadow, Bentley T Series and derivatives

Engine

Dimensions
As introduced: Eight cylinders in 90 degree vee formation. Bore 4.1 inches (104.14mm), stroke 3.6 inches (91.44mm), cubic capacity 380 cu. in. (6,230cc) Compression ratio 9:1 (8:1 for countries where 100 octane fuel not available).
From serial no. 8742, July 1970: Stroke 3.9 inches (99.1mm), cubic capacity 412 cu. in. (6,750cc).
From October 1975: compression ratio 8:1 (7.3:1 for Australia, Japan and U.S.A.).

Cylinder block/Crankcase
High silicon content aluminium alloy block with cast iron wet cylinder liners.

Crankshaft
Nitride hardened chrome molybdenum steel, with integral balance weights, running in five main bearings.

Pistons
Aluminium alloy. Three compression rings and one oil control ring.

Cylinder heads
Aluminium alloy with austenitic steel valve seats.

Valve gear
Overhead valves. Monikrom cast iron camshaft driven by helical gears, four bearings. Hydraulic tappets.

Carburetters
Two S.U. type HD.8 (2 inch) carburetters with paper air filter element.

From serial no. 19741 (home market Camargue and Corniche): Solex type 4A1 four barrel downdraught.
From serial no. 30001 (Silver Shadow II range): two S.U. type HIF.7 ($1\frac{7}{8}$ inch) carburetters.
From serial no. 40194 (California): Lucas K-Jetronic fuel injection.

Ignition system
Ignition by high tension coil and Lucas distributor with vacuum retard.
From serial no. 22572 (22600 four-door, 23059 Corniche, for Australia, Japan and U.S.A.): vacuum advance distributor.
From serial no. 22118: Lucas 'Opus' electronic ignition.
Firing order A1, B1, A4, B4, B2, A3, B3, A2.

Lubrication system
Helical gear oil pump in crankcase driven by skew gear from crankshaft. Oil pick-up in sump incorporating gauze strainer. Full-flow filter on side of crankcase. Pressure relief valve regulates oil pressure at approximately 40 lb/sq. in. Sump capacity 12.5 pints (15 U.S. gallons, 7.1 litres).

Cooling system
Pressurised system operating at 7 lb/sq. in. Temperature control by thermostat at the front of engine. Belt driven centrifugal coolant pump and fan.
From serial no. 6300: viscous coupling fan drive.
From serial no. 30001 (Silver Shadow II range): plastic fan and supplementary thermostatic electric fan.

Chassis

Monocoque construction with separate front and rear sub-frames:
Front – steel box-section construction mounted to car underframe by resilient metal mounts.
Rear – comprises the final drive cross-member mounted to the underframe by two resilient metal mounts and connected by a torque reaction arm to the rear sub-frame. Short telescopic damper fitted to each front mount to dampen fore and aft movement.

Dimensions
Overall length, standard 16' $11\frac{1}{2}$" (5,169mm)
Overall length, long wheelbase 17' $3\frac{1}{2}$" (5,270mm)
Overall length, Silver Shadow II 17' $0\frac{1}{2}$" (5,194mm)
Overall length, Silver Wraith II 17' $4\frac{1}{2}$" (5,296mm)
Wheelbase, standard 9' $11\frac{1}{2}$" (3,035mm)
Wheelbase, long 10' $3\frac{1}{2}$" (3,137mm)
Track, front and rear 4' $9\frac{1}{2}$" (1,460mm)

Suspension
Front: independent by coil springs and rubber bushed wishbones, double acting hydraulic telescopic dampers and anti-roll bar.
Rear: independent by coil springs and trailing arms, hydraulic telescopic dampers.
From serial no. 12734 (Corniche) and 13485 (all cars): compliant front suspension.

Hydraulic system
Two camshaft-driven hydraulic pumps delivering brake fluid under pressure (up to 2,500 p.s.i.) to a pair of hydraulic accumulators mounted on the side of the crankcase. Hydraulic pressure stored in the accumulators is used for the braking and height control systems. Two low pressure warning lights on the fascia, one for each hydraulic circuit.

Brakes
11 inch disc brakes on all four wheels. Each front wheel fitted with two twin cylinder calipers and each rear wheel with one four cylinder caliper. Three separate and independent hydraulic circuits, two from the high pressure hydraulic system operated by distribution valves connected to the brake pedal and a direct master cylinder circuit. Deceleration-conscious, pressure limiting valve ('G' valve) incorporated in master cylinder circuit on very early cars (later moved to one of the power circuits) to prevent premature rear wheel locking. Separate brake pads for handbrake.
From serial number 22118: master cylinder circuit deleted.

Height control system
Fully automatic hydraulic height control system to maintain the standing height of the car under all load conditions, by means of height control valves and hydraulic rams over the coil spring of each wheel. This system was designed to operate at two speeds – slow levelling when driving and fast levelling with the gear selector lever in neutral or a door opened.
From serial no. 7404: front height control deleted.

Steering
Power assisted recirculating ball, Hobourn Eaton belt driven pump. Three-piece track linkage. Turns lock to lock, 4.
From serial no. 3000: Saginaw pump.
From serial no. 6429: higher steering ratio.
From serial no. 11501: steering ratio increased further.
From serial no. 30001 (Silver Shadow II range): power assisted rack-and-pinion steering with centre take-off.

Transmission
Cars for other than North America: Rolls-Royce automatic gearbox and fluid coupling with selector mounted on the right of the steering column. Four forward speeds and reverse. Ratios: Top 1:1, Third 1.45:1, Second 2.63:1, First 3.82:1, Reverse 4.3:1.
Cars for North America: General Motors GM.400 three-speed automatic transmission and torque converter. Ratios: Top 1:1, Third 1.5:1, First 2.5:1, Reverse 2:1.
From serial no. 4483: GM.400 three-speed automatic transmission all cars.

One piece propeller shaft
Final drive: hypoid bevel rigidly mounted on a cross-member which in turn is mounted to the body underframe by resilient metal mounts. Drive transmitted to the rear wheels by two drive shafts. The inner end of each shaft is connected to the final drive by a Detroit-type ball and trunnion joint and the outer end by a Hardy-Spicer type universal joint. Ratio 3.08:1.

Exhaust system
Single system with three expansion boxes, each tuned to absorb a different range of frequencies.

Lubrication system
Long life grease lubrication.

Fuel system
Rear mounted petrol tank, capacity 24 gallons (29 U.S. gallons, 109 litres). Twin S.U. electric fuel pump mounted in the body underframe.

Electrical system
12 volt negative earth system. Lucas special equipment dynamo (early cars without refrigerated air conditioning) or alternator (air conditioned cars) and starter motor with pre-engagement pinion. Pye or Radiomobile Medium wave/Long wave or Medium wave/Short wave Radiomobile radio with push-button tuning and two speakers. An electrically operated wing mounted aerial standard. Electrically operated seat adjustments. Electrically operated windscreen washer. Triplex heated rear window. Electric windows. Refrigerated air conditioning available at extra cost on very early cars, later standard.

Road wheels and tyres
15 inch steel disc wheels on five studs, carrying 8.45 x 15 tyres. Tyre pressures 23 lb/sq. in. front, 25 lb/sq. in. rear.
Compliant front suspension cars: 205 x 15 radial ply tyres, later 235/70 x 15.

Coachwork

Monocoque construction four-door factory saloon, two-door saloon or drophead coupé.

Chassis numbering system – Silver Shadow and derivative models

In October 1965, when the Silver Shadow and Bentley T Series cars were introduced, a changed system of numbering was adopted. Within these Car Serial Numbers, each digit of the three-letter prefix has a specific meaning, explained below. This prefix is followed by a four or five digit number. The Car Serial Number shown is that of the first Silver Shadow series car, which was actually a Bentley T Series. It should be noted that the Silver Shadow numbering system included the derivative Corniche and Camargue models and was also adopted for the Phantom VI.

S	B	H	1	0	0	1
1	2	3	4	5	6	7

1 body type
S Saloon
C Coachbuilt (including Drophead Coupé cars prior to car number 6646)
D Drophead Coupé (or Convertible) from 6646
L Long Wheelbase
J Camargue
P Phantom VI

2 marque
R Rolls-Royce
B Bentley

3 steering position/year
H home (right-hand drive)
X export (left-hand drive)

On North American specification cars, commencing with the 1972 model year, X was replaced by a year code letter as follows:

A 1972
B 1973
C 1974
D 1975
E 1976
F 1977
G 1978
K 1979
L 1980

4-7 sequential identification number (later five digits)

Cars for California with fuel injection (from 1980) had a 'C' suffix.

The numbers used for Silver Shadow series cars were as follows:

1001-4548
 (except 1500, 4108, 4180, 4181, 4182, 4295, 4296, 4297, 4503, 4504, 4536 – allocated to Phantom VI)
5001-5603
6001-8861
9001-26708
30001-41686 (Silver Shadow II range)
50001-50776 (Corniche and Camargue with mineral oil hydraulic system)

Numbers allocated to the Phantom VI:
1500 (prototype Phantom VI)
4108, 4180, 4181, 4182, 4295, 4296, 4297, 4503, 4504, 4536
4549-4669
4700-4874

Numbers never used:
 1-1000
 4670-4699
 4875-5000
 5604-6000
 8862-9000
26709-30000
41687-50000

Engine numbers
Except in the case of an engine change prior to a car leaving the factory, the engine number was the same as the car serial number, without the prefix.

First and last Car Serial Numbers, Silver Shadow range

Firsts	Chassis No: (prefix omitted)	Date
Silver Shadow Saloon	1002	Oct 1965
Bentley T Series	1001	Oct 1965
James Young two-door Saloon	1067	Jan 1966
Silver Shadow H. J. Mulliner, Park Ward two-door Saloon	1148	March 1966
Bentley T H. J. Mulliner, Park Ward two-door Saloon	1149	March 1966
Silver Shadow H. J. Mulliner, Park Ward Drophead Coupé	1698	Sept 1967
Bentley T H. J. Mulliner, Park Ward Drophead Coupé	3049	
Long Wheelbase Saloon	6599	May 1969
Rolls-Royce Corniche two-door saloon	9770	March 1971
Bentley Corniche two-door Saloon	10420	
Rolls-Royce Corniche Convertible	9919	March 1971
Bentley Corniche Convertible	10122	
Camargue	14674	March 1975
Phantom VI (prototype)	1500	
Phantom VI (production)	4108	Dec 1968
Phantom VI (Armoured)	4182	Feb 1969
Phantom VI (Willesden-built chassis)	4780	Aug 1973*
Silver Shadow II	30001	Feb 1977
Bentley T2	30046	Feb 1977
Silver Wraith II (non-division)	30083	March 1977
Silver Wraith II (division)	30886	May 1977

Lasts:		
Silver Shadow range	26708	
Phantom VI (Crewe-built chassis)	4779	
Bentley T2	41573	
Silver Wraith II	41648	
Silver Shadow II range	41686	

* Date chassis laid down at Mulliner Park Ward, Willesden. Prior to that date the Phantom VI chassis had been built at Crewe.
Car Serial Numbers commencing 50001 were used for Corniche and Camargue with HSMO (Hydraulic Systems Mineral Oil) hydraulic system and Silver Spirit-type rear suspension package. Within the factory these cars were code-named CYZ (Corniche) and DYZ (Camargue). The last numbers in this 'half-way house' series, prior to the introduction of the 17-digit Vehicle Identification Number (VIN) system, were:

Corniche 2-door Saloon	50614 (then discontinued)
Corniche Convertible	50756 (then to 17-digit V.I.N. system – see Chapter 9)
Camargue	50776 (then to 17-digit V.I.N. system – see Chapter 9)

Note: These Corniche and Camargue production figures include only those built up to the end of the 50,001 series Car Serial Numbers. These models then continued in production and were integrated with the Silver Spirit range 17-digit Vehicle Identification Number system from 1981, with the exception of the Corniche 2-door Saloon which was discontinued after Car Serial Number CRH50614. For total Corniche and Camargue production figures see Appendix Four.

Numbers of Silver Shadow and derivative cars built:

Silver Shadow Saloon	16,717
Silver Shadow two-door Saloon -	
James Young	35
H. J. Mulliner, Park Ward	571
Silver Shadow Drophead Coupé,	
H. J. Mulliner, Park Ward	504
Silver Shadow Long Wheelbase Saloon	2,776
Rolls-Royce Corniche two-door Saloon	1,108*
Rolls-Royce Corniche Convertible	1,938*
Camargue	402*
Bentley T Series Saloon	1,703
Bentley T Series Long Wheelbase Saloon	9
Bentley T Series two-door Saloon -	
James Young	15
Pininfarina	1
H. J. Mulliner, Park Ward	98
Bentley T Series Drophead Coupé,	
H. J. Mulliner, Park Ward	41
Bentley Corniche two-door Saloon	63*
Bentley Corniche Convertible	65*
Silver Shadow II Saloon	8,425
Silver Wraith II (long wheelbase)	2,135
Bentley T2 Saloon	558
Bentley T2 Long Wheelbase Saloon	10
Total	37,174

Below *The Silver Shadow was the first Rolls-Royce car to employ unitary, or monocoque, construction. This mode of construction is chassis-less and relies upon the stiffness of the actual body shell for its rigidity, which is superior to that of the best separate-chassis construction. The Silver Shadow had separate front and rear sub-frames of closed box-section construction similar to that of the Silver Cloud chassis frame. The front subframe carried the engine/gearbox unit and front suspension while the rear one supported the final drive and independent rear suspension components.*

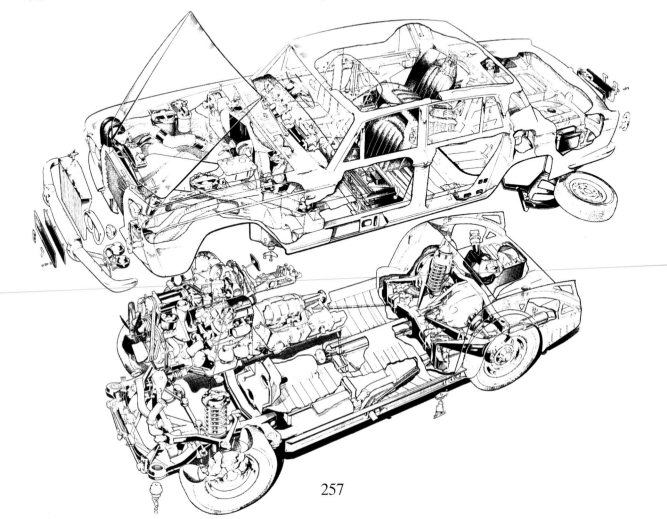

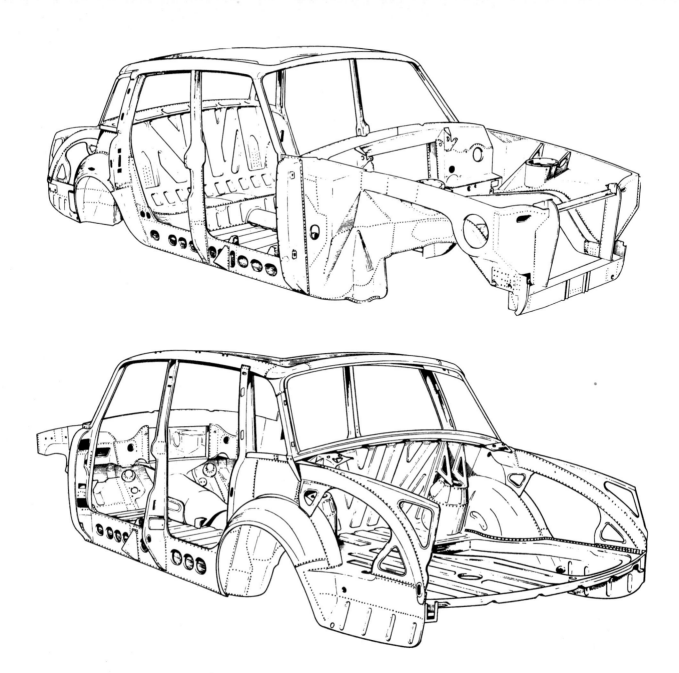

Above top & below *Front (top) and rear (below) Three-quarter views of the Silver Shadow/Bentley T Series body base unit. This was supplied by Pressed Steel Fisher. The panels, from the same supplier, were welded to this structure to form an immensely strong and rigid body. A modified version of this base unit formed the basis of the H. J. Mulliner, Park Ward two-door coachbuilt cars.*

Above & left *The Silver Shadow (above) and Bentley T Series (left) Standard Saloons, though having some subtle styling features in common with their predecessors the Silver Cloud and S Series, they were a vast departure from those tall, elegantly sculptured cars. One thing that did not change was the quality of build, materials, fittings and finish, all of which were of a high order. They were a runaway success and a quarter of a century later they remain extremely impressive cars to drive.*

Above *A Silver Shadow in the snow, in a medieval setting. '1850 TU' is one of the factory's cherished Cheshire registration numbers, retained for demonstrator cars.*

Right *Like the moated Little Moreton Hall in the background, which has remained virtually unchanged since 1580 and is one of the architectural treasures of Cheshire, this Silver Shadow has been given the two-tone treatment. Like the Silver Clouds, the styling of these cars was the work of John Blatchley.*

Top right *The Silver Shadow won instant acclaim from the motoring press after its October 1965 announcement. The car was smaller overall, roomier inside and had considerably greater luggage space in a boot of more practical shape. The hinged front quarter windows were deleted as the (at first optional) refrigerated air conditioning became standard.*

Right *It was March 1966 before deliveries of left-hand drive Silver Shadows commenced. The new cars were highly regarded by American buyers, who regarded them as 'compacts'. Unlike their home market counterparts, cars for the North American market were fitted from the outset with the General Motors type 400 three-speed automatic transmission that was later adopted as standard and was still used by Rolls-Royce until the end of the 1991 model year.*

Bottom right *Export sales were extremely important and the eleventh Silver Shadow-series car built, SRH1011, was sent to Australia for exhibition at the Sydney and Melbourne Motor Shows. Seen here with the car are, from left to right: the late A. E. Ward, then York Motors Service Manager; the late Eric C. Webb, then Chairman and Managing Director of York Motors; Ken Wright, Manager, Rolls-Royce of Australia Ltd, and the late E. J. (Jack) Vidler (Vlr), Australian Representative of Rolls-Royce Ltd.*

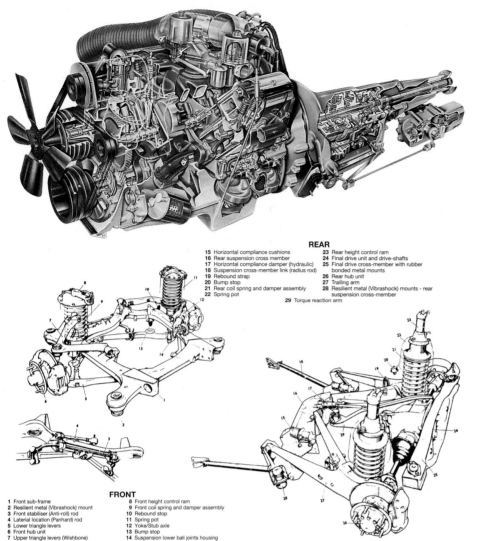

REAR

15 Horizontal compliance cushions	23 Rear height control ram
16 Rear suspension cross member	24 Final drive unit and drive-shafts
17 Horizontal compliance damper (hydraulic)	25 Final drive cross-member with rubber
18 Suspension cross-member link (radius rod)	bonded metal mounts
19 Rebound strap	26 Rear hub unit
20 Bump stop	27 Trailing arm
21 Rear coil spring and damper assembly	28 Resilient metal (Vibrashock) mounts - rear
22 Spring pot	suspension cross-member
	29 Torque reaction arm

FRONT

1 Front sub-frame
2 Resilient metal (Vibrashock) mount
3 Front stabiliser (Anti-roll) rod
4 Lateral location (Panhard) rod
5 Lower triangle levers
6 Front hub unit
7 Upper triangle levers (Wishbone)
8 Front height control ram
9 Front coil spring and damper assembly
10 Rebound stop
11 Spring pot
12 Yoke/Stub axle
13 Bump stop
14 Suspension lower ball joints housing

Above *The body was mounted onto the front and rear sub-frames by means of 'Vibrashock' mountings, colloquially called 'pan scrubbers' due to their compressed steel wire construction. Note the hydraulic levelling ram above each spring, the front ones of which were later deleted. These were the first Rolls-Royce and Bentley cars with independent rear suspension. The final drive unit was carried on its own Vibrashock-mounted cross-member and linked to the main sub-frame by a fore-and-aft torque reaction arm, shown in greater detail in the drawing below, which also shows the inner Detroit-type ball-and-trunnion and outer Hardy-Spicer universal joints for the short axle-drive shafts.*

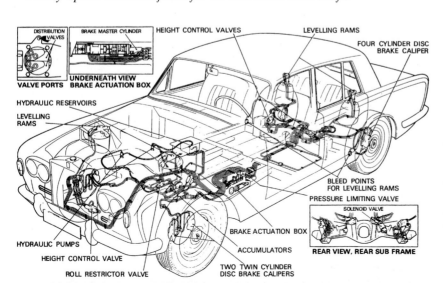

Top left *The 6,230cc V-8 engine received new cylinder heads for the Silver Shadow and Bentley T Series, providing improved gas flow and spark plug access above the exhaust manifolds. The lower body lines prevented the mounting of a large air filter and silencer above the engine where it had been on the Silver Clouds. Instead, an air filter was fitted under the off-side front wing and connected to the air intake via large diameter flexible trunking as shown in the drawing. The refrigerant compressor, on air conditioned cars, took the position otherwise occupied by the generator, which was replaced by an alternator mounted lower on the off-side of the engine. The Hobourn-Eaton power-steering pump was a short-lived feature carried over from the Silver Clouds. The later Saginaw (American) pump went to the off-side of the engine, the alternator then going to the space vacated by the old Hobourn-Eaton pump. Note the nitrogen charged hydraulic accumulators mounted on the nearside of the crankcase. The gearbox shown, with its electric actuator, is the four-speed type fitted to early right-hand drive cars.*

Bottom left *One of the many revolutionary features of the Silver Shadow and Bentley T Series was their hydraulic system. Two camshaft-driven pumps in the vee of the engine supplied fluid under pressure to a pair of spherical accumulators mounted on the near-side of the crankcase. From these, fluid pressurised at up to 2,500 psi was drawn for use in the two power brake circuits and for the self-levelling system, which operated on all four springs on the early cars. A third brake circuit, worked from a conventional master cylinder connected directly to the brake pedal, was incorporated to provide 'feel' in what would otherwise have been a soft, 'dead' feeling pedal. The master cylinder was later deleted and its braking function re-assigned to one of the power circuits after a simpler way was found of providing good pedal feel.*

Top right & below *For the seasoned Rolls-Royce or Bentley driver and passenger there was much that was familiar in the Silver Shadow and T Series. Acres of fine Connolly hide (Rolls-Royce get the best, others get the rest), including at first the black padding around the fascia, beautiful burr walnut veneers and deep pile Wilton carpet with hide edge binding. Many of the switches and fittings, too, were unchanged from the Silver Cloud III and the steering wheel was of the same size and rim section, though now with two spokes instead of three. The view of the right-hand drive fascia (below) shows that the electrically-operated gear range selector lever on the right of the steering column was identical in appearance to the turn indicator stalk on the left. This applied only to a very small number of the very earliest cars. The potential hazard is obvious, particularly given the extreme lightness of the gear selector, which was very quickly changed to a larger lever, cranked upwards to distinguish it from the turn signal stalk.*

Left *The separate front seats were electrically operated for reach and height/cushion tilt adjustments, by means of two eight-way switches mounted between the seat cushions. The squab rake adjustment was by a chrome-plated handle on the outside of the seat, as before.*

Above *James Young Ltd, whose coachbuilding activities ceased in 1968 when the last of their magnificent Phantom Vs was delivered, also turned their hand to the Silver Shadow and Bentley T Series with a series of two-door saloons adapted from Standard Saloon body shells. The rebuilding as two-door cars included the elimination of the chromium waist embellisher and the fitting of the distinctive James Young door handles, seating and interior woodwork. The overall effect, though, it must be said, was rather plain and easily outdone by the graceful styling of the fully coachbuilt H. J. Mulliner, Park Ward two-door saloon which followed within two months. Fifty of these cars emerged from the James Young works, of which fifteen were Bentleys. Our photograph shows the first, CRH1067, which was finished in Brewster Green and delivered in January 1966.*

Above *At first there was no long wheelbase variant of the Silver Shadow. However, this special saloon, four inches longer than standard, was delivered on 19th July, 1967 through Messrs Kenning Car Mart Ltd to HRH Princess Margaret and the Earl of Snowden. The coachwork was finished in dark green and the interior design incorporated many features suggested by Her Royal Highness and Lord Snowden. The upholstery was of special green leather with pale grey-green carpets. The normal timber door capping rails were replaced by leather the same colour as the upholstery and the fascia was of oiled teak. Stainless steel and chromium fittings had a satin finish in place of the normal brightwork. For maximum visibility for ceremonial occasions, the rear seat was adjustable for height and forward movement and extra night illumination was installed. This car, LRH2542, was the forerunner of the Silver Shadow Long Wheelbase Saloon introduced in mid-1969. Note the 'police light' above the windscreen, a standard Royal car fitment.*

Left *The only coachbuilder other than James Young and H. J. Mulliner, Park Ward to construct a body for a Silver Shadow series car was Pininfarina, who built this distinctive and stylish Bentley T Series two-door coupé. This car is believed to have inspired the commissioning of Pininfarina to style the Camargue. It was built in 1968 for James (later Lord) Hanson.*

Above *This photograph shows to advantage how much more visually appealing the H. J. Mulliner, Park Ward two door Saloon was than the James Young version. While the latter was basically a converted Standard Saloon, the styling of the H. J. Mulliner, Park Ward two-door saloon, design number 3010, owes little to that of the four-door car. The steeply raked windscreen, the traditional but sleek wingline and details like the H. J. Mulliner-pattern door handles all add flair to this graceful and enduring design. Just how enduring is amply demonstrated by the fact that the drophead coupé version (design number 3020, introduced in 1967) is still made, having been marketed as the Corniche since 1971 and called Corniche IV in its technically highly sophisticated current form.*

Above & below, left & right *The interior views show the distinctive seating and other details. The fascia shared the Standard Saloon layout but the centre panel stood out slightly from the surrounding areas and flame-pattern veneers with pale crossbanding added an extra air of quality to these coachbuilt cars.*

This page *September 1967 saw the introduction of this drophead coupé variant of the H. J. Mulliner, Park Ward coachbuilt car. Apart from the smaller rear quarter-light, the lines are identical to those of the two-door Saloon. The hood was power-operated by means of an electric motor driving a hydraulic pump, with hydraulic rams. The stowed hood and its operating mechanism infringed on luggage space to a considerable degree and the rear seat was of necessity narrower and mounted further forward than that of the two-door Saloon, none of which detracted seriously from the extreme desirability of this fine convertible. The lower picture shows the later interior redesign with safety features for the American market (1968) and elsewhere (1969). Note particularly the more heavily-padded fascia with fewer instruments, relocated ignition/lighting 'switchbox', flush door handles, round-edged door cappings and centre console. The coachbuilder's design number was 3020.*

Above, left & right *In May 1969 the Silver Shadow Long Wheelbase Saloon, with or without division, was introduced. This variant, marketed in the United States as the 'Formal Sedan', was four inches longer than the Standard Saloon aft of the centre pillars. The backlight was smaller, though the standard rear glass was sometimes specified, particularly on cars without division, and an Everflex-covered roof often distinguished these cars.*

Right & below *Heavy padding and lots of leather replaced the cabinetwork previously associated with division-equipped cars. This was at the height of a flurry of passive safety legislation in the United States, which also gave rise to the revised fascia, recessed door handles and other interior details shown, which applied to all models in the range.*

Below *The Long Wheelbase Saloon with division was equipped with separate front and rear air conditioning systems. Cars so fitted had an additional air intake grille between the rear window and the bootlid.*

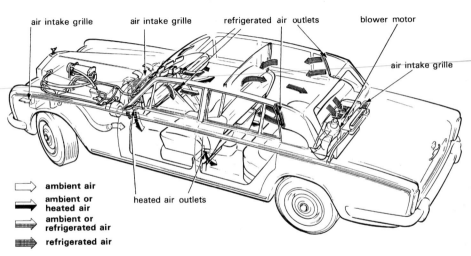

air intake grille · air intake grille · refrigerated air outlets · blower motor · air intake grille · heated air outlets

⇨ ambient air
⇒ ambient or heated air
⇛ ambient or refrigerated air
⇛ refrigerated air

267

Above *To have announced a new model just after the Company had been placed in the hands of the official receiver over financial problems associated with the RB.211 jet engine project demonstrated just how confident and forward-looking the Car Division remained. This confidence was well founded. The Division was completely solvent, profitable and, furthermore, their instructions from the receiver were quite specific – business as usual. So, early in March 1971, the Corniche was unveiled. It was not so much a new model as a significantly revised existing one. With a new low-loss exhaust system, bolder radiator shell (half an inch deeper, measured front to back), new fascia, new spun stainless steel wheel trims and 'Corniche' badging, the H. J. Mulliner, Park Ward two-door cars had a new lease of life that has yet to come to an end. Note the optional Everflex-covered roof on this two-door saloon.*

Inset *The Company announced at the time that 'the name Corniche has been chosen for the latest coachbuilt models because it symbolizes their high cruising speeds and their ability to cover great distances with the minimum of fatigue for driver and passengers'. An elegant badge on the bootlid proclaimed the pedigree.*

Right *The Corniche radiator shell was noticeably more massive than that of the Silver Shadow, being some 15 percent deeper front to back. The Rolls-Royce radiator shell was, and remains, completely hand made in stainless steel.*

268

This page *The Corniche Convertible is a highly desirable modern Rolls-Royce. In its latest form it continued to find ready buyers from London to Los Angeles and Monte Carlo to Melbourne, though it is now only available to special order. In its original form, shown here, it was so in demand in the early seventies that two-year-old examples were fetching the then current list price plus eighty percent! The waiting list for a new one was longer than the patience of many buyers. As a result, unfortunately, some people wait-listed themselves solely for the assured capital gain.*

Left *The Corniche fascia was all new, with comprehensive instrumentation including a tachometer. The 15-inch wood-rimmed steering wheel with leather covered spokes was a short-lived casualty of the emerging safety consciousness and the standard Silver Shadow wheel was quickly substituted. The controls to the right of the steering column are for the automatic speed control, or cruise control. This was standard on the Corniche, though it was occasionally omitted at the customer's request.*

Above & left *The Bentley Corniche is a rare variant in both its open and closed guises. The lower car, a 1971 Convertible, chassis no. DBH10509, is one of a fine collection of Rolls-Royce and Bentley cars owned by Robert McDermott (RROCA).*

This page *During its fifteen year production run the Silver Shadow and Bentley T Series underwent a continuous programme of changes, both mechanical and coachwork. The cars on these pages have such later features as ventilated wheel covers, more boldly flared wheel arches, three-speed automatic transmission (standard from the outset on left-hand drive cars), compliant front suspension and 6,750cc engine. The interior view shows the 'T.V. screen'-style warning lights introduced in September 1972 as part of a major electrical system revision. The car above right is a Long Wheelbase Saloon, without division. Note the Everflex-covered roof and smaller rear window.*

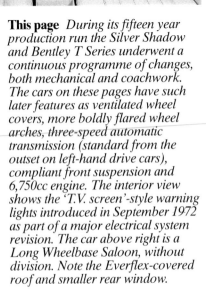

271

This spread *Code-named 'Delta' within the Company, the Camargue was announced in March 1975. Like the Corniche it was built on the Silver Shadow floor pan from welded steel pressings with aluminium doors and boot and bonnet lids. The Camargue's styling, by Sergio Pininfarina, was quite different to that of any Rolls-Royce that had come before it. In detail, too, it was in a class apart, with its special seats upholstered in Connolly 'Nuella' hide, distinctive aircraft-style fascia and the world's first fully automatic split-level air conditioning system. The pricing of the Camargue, at fifty percent higher than the Corniche, exploited a previously untapped premium market that in the early 'seventies had seen Corniche cars changing hands at up to eighty percent above list. Buyers willing to part with £29,250, a new world record price for a production car, were readily found, but exclusivity was assured.*

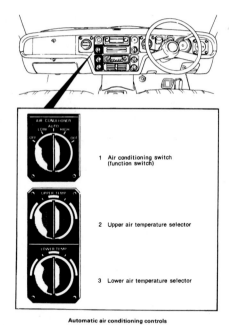

1 Air conditioning switch (function switch)

2 Upper air temperature selector

3 Lower air temperature selector

Automatic air conditioning controls

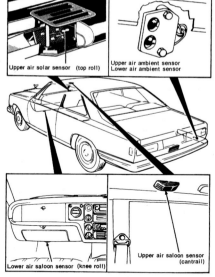

Upper air solar sensor (top roll)

Upper air ambient sensor
Lower air ambient sensor

Lower air saloon sensor (knee roll)

Upper air saloon sensor (cantrail)

Temperature sensors

Left & below *The Camargue's very advanced fully automatic two-level air conditioning system was later adopted, with improved controls, for the Corniche for 1976, then from 1977 for the Silver Shadow II range and all subsequent models. It remains the most sophisticated and technically advanced car air conditioning system in the world. Separate temperature controls for the upper and lower levels in the car are a feature of this unique system, which automatically maintains the temperatures of the two zones regardless of outside temperature. One could drive from Murmansk to Mombasa without adjusting the controls. An outside temperature indicator on the fascia of all models equipped with this system served to reinforce in the minds of the occupants just how effectively the system was working! The photograph shows the upper saloon sensor in the cantrail.*

Above *After the first thirty Camargues had been built with standard twin S.U. carburetters, a change was made to a Solex four-barrel downdraught carburetter for all markets other than North America, Japan and Australia. Together with the Lucas Opus breakerless electronic ignition introduced at the same time and the Camargue's dual exhaust system, this made for considerably enhanced performance, particularly at the higher end of the rev range. The same changes were applied to the Corniche. The Solex installation, with its large circular air filter housing, is shown here in a 50001-series Camargue, with Mineral Oil hydraulic system.*

This page *Sufficient new features were introduced at the same time on the Silver Shadow and T Series cars for deliveries commencing February 1977 that it was felt new model designations were justified. Hence the Silver Shadow II and Bentley T2, and for the first time, a distinctive name for the long wheelbase car, named Silver Wraith II in honour of the first post-war Rolls-Royce. Externally, the obvious changes were black polyurethane-faced bumpers (already seen on U.S. export cars from mid-1973) and an air dam under the front bumper (not fitted to U.S. exports). Also, the radiator was increased in front to back measurement by fifteen percent to present a bolder, more massive appearance, like that of the Corniche. The headlamp wash/wipe facility, seen on the Silver Shadow II (top) was introduced in June 1978, but again this did not apply for the U.S. market. The Silver Wraith II (bottom) was further distinguished from its shorter wheelbase stablemate by the fitting of Corniche/Camargue-pattern wheel trims.*

All interior dimensions shown with front seats in central position.

	cm	in
A	305	120
B	152	59.75
C	91	36
D	34	13.5
E	32	12.5
F	38	15
G	93	36.5
H	122	48
I	41	16
J	57	22.5
K	125	49
L	140	55
M	125	49
N	135	53
O	182	71.8
P	519	204.5

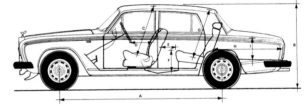

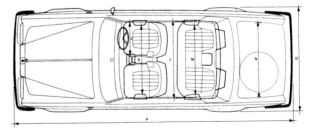

Top left By the time the Silver Shadow II appeared, the Company's efforts at providing a Bentley alternative had become a little half-hearted. The name on the engine rocker covers was Rolls-Royce, the chassis number was stamped on a Rolls-Royce maker's plate and the instruments on the fascia carried the entwined Rs logo. In spite of this, demand for the Bentley would not go away and a remarkable Bentley resurgence was just around the corner. This is the first Bentley T2 built, SBH30046.

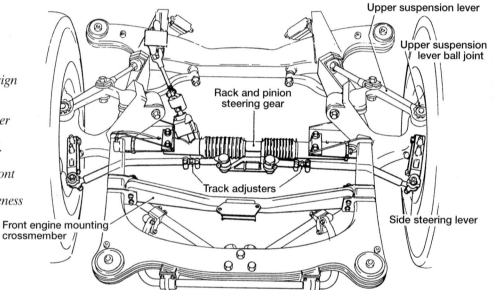

Right The revised front end design for the Silver Shadow II range incorporated rack-and-pinion steering with highly refined power assistance for precise, sensitive steering with more positive 'feel'. Modifications to the front suspension geometry kept the front wheels more upright when cornering, improving responsiveness and reducing roll angles.

Upper suspension lever

Upper suspension lever ball joint

Rack and pinion steering gear

Track adjusters

Side steering lever

Front engine mounting crossmember

Bottom left The under-bonnet installation for the Silver Shadow II range of cars included a change to S.U. type HIF.7 carburetters which, while smaller, were of more efficient design and helped reduce fuel consumption and exhaust emissions. A new spin-on oil filter simplified maintenance (a change actually necessitated by the new rack-and pinion steering) and a new cooling fan with electric booster fan improved cooling efficiency.

Top right *Inside the Silver Shadow II family of cars, the only obvious change was the all new fascia. A four-in-one instrument rather like that of the Silver Clouds and some earlier models was positioned in front of the driver alongside the new electronic speedometer. There was also an outside temperature gauge as an adjunct to the automatic air conditioning system, the controls for which can be seen to the left of the steering wheel. The controls for the electronic speed control were now incorporated in the gear selector stalk.*

Right *The fascia of the left-hand drive Silver Shadow II was a mirror image of its home counterpart. The seating and other interior details other than the fascia remained unchanged from those of earlier Silver Shadows.*

Bottom right *The rear compartment, too, was unchanged. The generous legroom and narrow rear window seen here indicate a Silver Wraith II, the long wheelbase variant.*

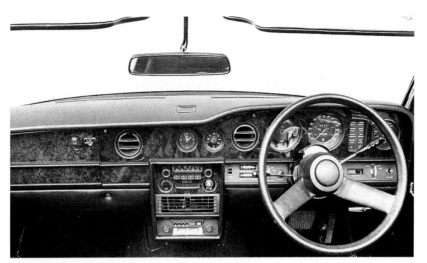

Left & below *The Silver Shadow II style of fascia and automatic air conditioning had actually been quietly introduced for 1976 on the Corniche (left). Note also the leather covered steering wheel. In May 1979 the Corniche fascia was again changed (below) to incorporate a central digital display for outside temperature, time of day and elapsed journey time indicator. This change accompanied the introduction of a revised rear suspension arrangement and Mineral Oil hydraulic system. All these features were standard on the Silver Spirit range of cars which followed in October 1980.*

Left *To further improve control of exhaust emissions, Bosch fuel injection was adopted, for California only, commencing with the 1980 model year cars. This engine was the forerunner of that in today's fuel injected cars, now standard for all markets.*

278

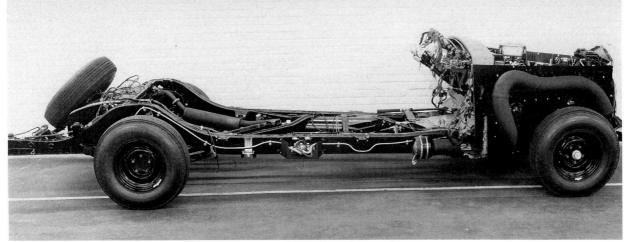

Above *The Phantom VI was the last Rolls-Royce built with a separate chassis, non-independent rear suspension with leaf springs, conventional brake fluid (as opposed to Mineral Oil) for the hydraulic system and carburetters. It was also the last car of any make to be coachbuilt in the old, traditional sense in that the body was built from scratch entirely by hand. Construction of the chassis, which was basically unchanged from that of the 1959 Phantom V, was transferred from Crewe to Hythe Road, Willesden in 1973. At the same time, coachwork construction was moved there from the old Park Ward coachworks in Willesden. This chassis is a PVI-40 specification Phantom VI with three-speed automatic transmission and Silver Shadow-type high-pressure hydraulics. The first of these was on the road by 1974 and went into 'production' in time for chassis PGH101 to be delivered to H.M. The Queen in March, 1978.*

Above *The Phantom VI engine was the last to be fitted with carburetters. Engines were built at Crewe and transported to Hythe Road for installation in the chassis.*

Right *One detail that did change, with the introduction of the PVI-40 specification chassis, was the passing of the four-speed automatic gearbox and fluid coupling in favour of the three-speed GM400 automatic transmission used for all other models. Because there was no practical way of driving the old mechanical brake servo from this transmission the drum brake system had to be adapted to work with the Silver Shadow-type power hydraulic system. The power system was unsuitable for piping direct to the brake cylinders, so special rams worked from the power hydraulics were rather cleverly contrived to operate the twin master cylinders of the old system.*

Above *The Phantom VI, in its earliest form, was basically a Phantom V fitted with separate front and rear air conditioning units, a revised fascia similar to that of the early Silver Shadows and the Silver Shadow-type 6,230cc engine. The first Phantom VI was delivered on 1st January, 1969. The only external recognition feature of the earliest cars was that the bonnet lids were shorter than those of a Phantom V, to allow the fitting of a Silver Shadow-type air conditioning intake grille in the scuttle top.*

Below *However, from 1972 more changes began to appear, starting with the rear compartment door being hinged at the front instead of at the rear. This and other changes such as burst-proof locks and collapsible steering column were incorporated to comply with European safety legislation. The car in this photograph is the Company Trials car, chassis PRH4700 – the first to have the front-hung rear compartment doors. U.S. Federal Safety Standards, incredibly enough, prevented sale of the Phantom VI in that market, although in 1972 one was supplied to the British Ambassador to the U.N. in New York and in 1977 dispensation was granted to Bill Harrah to import one for his famous motor museum. The H. J. Mulliner, Park Ward coachwork design number was 2003/1.*

Left & below. Next page, top *The rear compartment of the Phantom VI remained unchanged in all but detail from that of the design number 2003 H. J. Mulliner, Park Ward limousine on the Phantom V chassis. The twill upholstery shown here could be specified in lieu of the more usual West of England cloth or leather. In fact, virtually any material could be chosen and bespoke changes to the standard interior design and fittings could be accommodated. The front compartment was usually upholstered in leather regardless of rear compartment material. The fascia, on the other hand, was all new for the Phantom VI and bore a distinct family resemblance to that of the early Silver Shadow and changed only in detail during the nearly twenty-five year production run of the Phantom VI.*

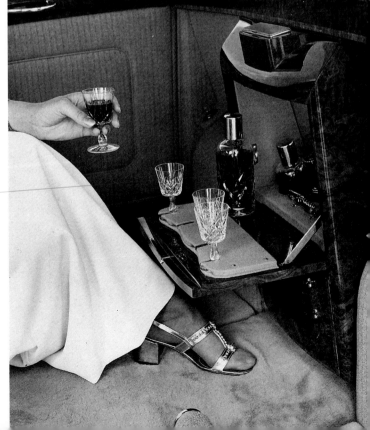

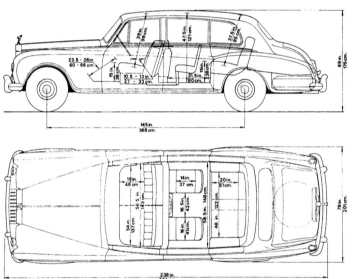

Below *Not all Phantom VIs were design number 2003/1 limousines. The State Landaulette, design number 2052, of which four were built on Phantom V chassis, was also made available as a Phantom VI. It is worth noting again that the very early Park Ward design number 980 style of boot was retained for this design, as opposed to the razor-edged boot of design numbers 2003 and 2003/1. This is a 1972 or later Phantom VI, with front hinged doors to the rear compartment and stainless steel trim along the lower edge of the body, including the wheel arches. Note also the Corniche-type rear lights, which were fitted to most of the later Phantom VIs in lieu of the Silver Cloud III pattern of the early examples.*

Above *This special Phantom VI, to HM The Queen's 'Canberra' style, was ordered by the Society of Motor Manufacturers and Traders as a gift to Her Majesty on behalf of the motor trade on the occasion of the 1977 Royal Jubilee. Construction of this car, code-named 'Oil Barrel', began early in 1976, but an industrial dispute at Mulliner Park Ward and a decision by Rolls-Royce Motors to incorporate new technical features planned for production, delayed delivery until 29th March, 1978. This was the first of the 'PVI-40' specification Phantom VIs, chassis no. PGH101.*

Below *This must surely be the biggest drophead coupé ever built in modern times. The Italian coachbuilder Frua bodied this Phantom VI for a Swiss customer. It was exhibited at the 1973 Frankfurt Motor Show. Chassis PRX4705.*

This page *The 'protected' Phantom VI, code-named 'Alpha' and marketed as the 'Special Limousine'. Note the bolder than usual chromium frames around the 2 inch thick glass, the deeply recessed rear window and the Silver Wraith-type wheel covers fitted to the 10-stud, 16 inch wheels. The Mulliner Park Ward design number was 2053.*

Chapter Nine

Spirit of the Eighties and Beyond

The Silver Spirit, Bentley Mulsanne and derivatives

'We will have succeeded in our task if, late on a winter's evening, in a dimly lit street, someone looks out of a window and catches a glimpse of a dark and travel-stained Silver Spirit and says "a Rolls-Royce has just gone by."'

Fritz Feller, Chief Engineer for Styling and Future Projects, Rolls-Royce Motors Ltd, 1980, on the task that confronted him and his team in styling a new generation of Rolls-Royce cars.

The Silver Shadow and its derivatives, in terms of sales, particularly in export markets, represented by far the most successful range of cars in the Company's history. Although their fifteen year production run was well short of that of the Silver Ghost, the car that unquestionably made the Rolls-Royce name, the total number of that model produced, including the U.S.-built cars, was under 8,000, compared with many times that number of Silver Shadow series cars, with a record 3,347 cars being built in 1978 alone. Indeed, one Silver Shadow-derived model, the Corniche, remains part of the current range, albeit now with a rather more sophisticated technical specification and the name Corniche IV.

The new cars, introduced in October 1980, were based on the Silver Shadow II base unit, using the same engine and drive train, but with revised rear suspension and Mineral Oil hydraulics first seen from March 1979 on the coachbuilt Corniche and Camargue. The Silver Shadow II was replaced by the Silver Spirit, the Silver Wraith II by the Silver Spur and the Bentley T2 by the superbly-named Mulsanne. At this time Rolls-Royce Motors was merged with Vickers to become the largest member of that Group.

The objectives that were kept in mind in designing the Silver Spirit range of cars fell into two categories, viz., (a) appearance and (b) technical. The new saloon coachwork, with its modern, more angular styling incorporating a lower waistline and one third greater glass area than its predecessor, has a more eye-catching 'presence' and looks appreciably larger, being in fact three inches longer and a little over two inches wider.

In order to accentuate width, the accent is on the horizontal design features. For the first time, Rolls-Royce plumped for large rectangular headlamp units (smaller paired ones for U.S. exports) and large wrap-around rear light clusters, extending onto the bootlid, which

can be wired in a variety of combinations to suit various countries' legislated requirements.

The familiar Rolls-Royce radiator shape was, of course, retained, though in a wider, squatter form than that of the earlier cars and rather like that of the Camargue. A special radiator shell with rounded edges had been fitted to Silver Shadow II models for the German market and this feature was adopted as standard for the new cars. Although it could be argued that this effectively renders obsolete any need to make the radiator shell by hand, the Company has not seen fit to change that time honoured work practice at Crewe. It may be recalled that the earliest examples of the 20 h.p. model, introduced in 1922, sported a radiator with distinctly rounded edges, but this soon gave way to the traditional sharp-edged structure. Problems posed by certain countries' laws regarding bonnet mascots, or 'hood ornaments' in American terminology, were overcome by the development of an ingeniously designed retracting Spirit of Ecstasy, which withdraws into the radiator shell if struck. Having done so it can be pulled back into position against spring pressure until it latches into place. This version of the mascot, for the first time, dispenses with the dummy filler cap on which she has been mounted since the filler cap really was a filler cap. For countries with less stringent mascot laws, the Spirit of Ecstasy remained as she was – spring-mounted on a dummy filler cap with an anti-tamper alarm switch wired to the car's horns. Nowadays, the safety mascot is standard for all markets except the United States.

The principal technical objectives of further improved handling and road-holding with even less intrusion of road noise into the car were met by the revised rear suspension arrangement which, as mentioned in the previous chapter, had been quietly introduced on the Corniche and Camargue some eighteen months earlier. Compliant front

suspension had been introduced on the Silver Shadow in 1972 and rack-and-pinion steering and further front suspension changes on the Silver Shadow II of 1977, so the new rear suspension enabled the rear to catch up, technologically, with the front. The new design retained the semi-trailing arms of the previous layout, but the pivots are more inclined in order to induce a more pronounced change of camber as the wheels rise and fall. Also, the wheels remain more upright as the car rolls and consequently it rolls less, giving the tyres more cornering power, improving handling and reducing tyre wear. The levelling rams of the earlier rear suspension were replaced by a Girling self-levelling system which uses each of the rear dampers as a strut, by connecting them via columns of hydraulic fluid (actually Mineral Oil) to gas springs. The levelling valves adjust the level of oil in the dampers to keep the car's attitude constant regardless of load or load distribution. The car is still suspended on coil springs, but these refinements allow the use of much smaller rear springs which do not intrude into the boot, and the Girling gas struts are mounted aft of the springs rather than concentric with them as the earlier dampers and levelling rams had been.

The trailing arms are mounted on a sub-frame comprising two crossmembers, one for the suspension pivots and one for the final drive – differing from the Silver Shadow design by the two crossmembers being linked by six diagonal tie-bars to form a single unit, rather than by a single rubber bushed torque arm. The corners of this assembly are attached to the car by means of cylindrical rubber mountings which have a horizontal fore-and-aft axis to give good lateral control of the suspension, contributing further to improved handling, ride and noise suppression.

A major change that accompanied the incorporation of the new rear suspension layout, firstly on the coachbuilt Corniche and Camargue and subsequently on the Silver Spirit range, was the adoption of Hydraulic Systems Mineral Oil for the hydraulic system in place of RR363, the brake fluid previously employed. As its name implies, HSMO is derived from mineral (i.e. petroleum) sources as opposed to the vegetable by-products and synthetic substances used in the manufacture of conventional brake fluids. The practically universal use by other manufacturers of brake fluids of the conventional type is attributable solely to the fact that the seals in automotive braking systems were originally of natural rubber, which deteriorated rapidly if exposed to mineral oils. In other industries – aviation, machine tools, etc. – mineral oils have been used for many years because compatible materials had been developed for seals in these applications. Now these improved seals, made from synthetic rubbers and plastics, have been adopted in the motor industry – at least by Rolls-Royce.

The benefits inherent in the use of HSMO for motor car hydraulic systems are many. It is much less corrosive and does not have the notoriously effective paint stripping properties of brake fluid when accidentally (or deliberately) spilt onto bodywork. It is non-hydroscopic – i.e. it does not absorb water, and so eliminates the risk of internal corrosion. In the levelling system its superior vibration damping qualities improve ride and noise suppression. Lastly, but not least, HSMO is a superior lubricant to conventional brake fluid, which has the effect of reducing friction in the braking and levelling systems, thereby prolonging component life. These advantages bring with them one very real and serious risk – that of contamination of the hydraulic system with brake fluid, and indeed of the inadvertent introduction of Mineral Oil into an earlier car with a system designed for conventional brake fluid. Either way it is very expensive to rectify and potentially

dangerous. Naturally, everyone within the Company and the Dealer Network who is directly or indirectly concerned with hydraulic systems is totally aware of the vital importance of using the correct fluid when topping up or carrying out hydraulic system fluid changes. Owners are warned by means of prominent multi-lingual labels on fluid reservoirs of HSMO cars as well as by clear instructions in the car handbook. More recently, lead seals have been fitted to the reservoir filler caps as an additional precaution.

The Bentley Revival
One particularly positive aspect that manifested itself with the introduction of the Silver Spirit range was a resurgence of enthusiasm within the Company for the Bentley name. It was difficult to escape the conclusion that the marque was being allowed to die out, but the adoption of a distinctive model name – Mulsanne – for the Silver Spirit's Bentley counterpart may be seen as the start of a Bentley revival that has gathered such momentum that there are now no fewer than five distinct models in the range, not including long wheelbase variants. In the first few years of motor car production at Crewe after World War II, Bentleys accounted for around 65% of total production. By 1980 this had fallen to a derisory 5% or so and the Company seriously considered shelving the famous name. Instead, however, the planned revival in the marque's fortunes saw a target figure of 40% set. This target was more than half way met by 1984 and was fully realised in the home market by 1987. Subsequently, Bentley production exceeded 50% of total output and rose still further following the 1991 introduction of the Continental R, of which more anon. How was this achieved? Firstly by offering an attractive range of Bentley cars with a character increasingly distinct from that of their Rolls-Royce counterparts and secondly

by marketing them effectively. The old axiom that 'Rolls-Royce do not sell cars – people buy them' has long since been abandoned in favour of effective, modern marketing strategies.

The Mulsanne, which could be termed the base model of the Bentley range, appeared concurrently with the Silver Spirit in October 1980 and was identical to that model except for radiator shell and badging. The Bentley radiator shape is perhaps less tolerant of alterations to its proportions than the more resilient Rolls-Royce Palladian radiator. However, the current lower, wider Bentley radiator is still an impressive feature in all its forms and the author is not alone in hoping that changes in its proportions never progress to the rather absurd extreme seen on such cars as the modern Lagonda, which carries a radiator grille of such diminutive height that considerable elasticity of imagination is called upon if it is to be seen as any more than a vestigial parody of the formerly impressive Lagonda radiator which it supposedly represents. Since 1980 there have been five distinct versions of the Bentley radiator.

The EEC regulations that necessitated the development of a retractable Spirit of Ecstasy also resulted in the disappearance of the winged 'B' mascot from the current crop of Bentleys. The mascot is still sold as an accessory and provision was made for its fitment to its traditional position on all models (except the Continental R) until 1993, but the Company warns, on a special notice packaged with this item, that fitting it to the car would contravene Type Approval legislation and that any such contravention is the owner's responsibility.

The most remarkable Bentley development of all, and the one that undoubtedly contributed most to rescuing the marque from oblivion, was the announcement at the 1982 Geneva Motor Show of a turbocharged version of the Mulsanne. The Mulsanne Turbo employed a

Garrett AiResearch turbocharger to pressurise the air supply to the Solex four-barrel downdraught carburetter. This was the same carburetter that was fitted to later Corniche and Camargue models (mainly for the home market) with the difference that on the Turbo it was sealed within a cast aluminium alloy air-box, or 'plenum chamber' with 'TURBO' boldly cast on its top cover. Whereas the power output of Rolls-Royce and Bentley car engines had traditionally been described as 'adequate' or 'sufficient', that of the Mulsanne Turbo was said to be 'sufficient – plus fifty percent'!

Like the Continentals of the 1950s and early '60s, the Mulsanne Turbo had a higher final drive ratio than the standard car – 2.69:1 instead of 3.08:1. Maximum speed was deliberately limited to 135 mph (217 km/h) in order to limit engine rpm to the same as that of the standard car at its rather lower top speed. This was achieved by means of a signal sent by the electronic speedometer to a wastegate, the principal function of which was to limit boost pressure to 7 psi at any speed.

Externally, the Mulsanne Turbo could be distinguished from its normally aspirated stablemate by discrete 'TURBO' badging, dual exhaust tailpipes and, more obviously, by its radiator cowl being painted in body colour rather than chrome plated. In the 'fifties and earlier more than one coachbuilder experimented with painted Bentley radiator shells and there is considerable doubt that the practice really enjoyed Company approval at the time. However, times change!

The next shot fired in the campaign to increase Bentley sales was the advent of the Bentley Eight, introduced in mid-1984. At just under £50,000 the Eight was intended to be the lowest priced car in the Rolls-Royce range in order to bring Bentley ownership within range of many more potential new customers, who might not otherwise have considered a Rolls-Royce or Bentley motor car, to build on the revival of interest in the marque created by the Turbo. The external appearance of the Eight represented a further variation on the standard Mulsanne, with a chrome wire mesh grille reminiscent of the famous race-bred Bentleys of the 1920s. In order to further increase the appeal of the car to 'young entrepreneurs' the front suspension was stiffer than that of the other models. The interior furnishings, though slightly reduced in detail, were nevertheless of an extremely high order. The Company announced an intention to build around 100 Bentley Eights per year.

Concurrently with the launch of the Eight, the name Continental – long associated with sporting coach-built Bentleys – was revived after an absence of eighteen years for the drophead coupé formerly marketed as the Bentley Corniche Convertible. This latter day Continental featured colour-keyed bumpers, external mirrors and radiator grille vanes, redesigned front seats incorporating adjustable lumbar support and a restyled fascia.

A further major step in a remarkable Bentley revival came in 1985 when the stiffer front suspension was incorporated, logically enough, into a new turbocharged Bentley, the Turbo R ('R' for roadholding). This new model featured a revised fascia with centre console, new body-hugging seats with lateral pleating, a leather covered steering wheel of completely new design and Continental-style instrumentation including a revolution counter and was externally distinguished by new alloy wheels carrying very wide low profile (275VR55VR15) tyres. The Mulsanne Turbo was discontinued a short time after the introduction of the Turbo R. The amazing growth in Bentley sales, from around 5% of total production in 1980 to well over 50% today, is in no small measure attributable to the Turbo R, which has been further developed over the ensuing years in order to remain at the very pinnacle of the very high performance four-door saloon market. The other Bentley models did not rest on their laurels either. From 1987 the Mulsanne gave way to the Mulsanne S, with Turbo R suspension and interior features. A variant of the Turbo R alloy wheels appeared on this and all other models in the Bentley range.

Developments for 1987

The Silver Spirit range of cars was continuously developed from its introduction, but the 1987 model year saw a range of significant improvements introduced as a single package.

From the introduction of the range, cars for the U.S. and Japan had fuel-injected engines. For 1986 the Australian market followed suit and from the 1987 model year fuel injection became standard for all markets. The 1987 engine complied with all European emission control standards and when unencumbered by additional emission control devices produced 22 per cent more power than the twin S.U. carburetter version it replaced (14 per cent more than the Corniche four-choke Solex version) as well as delivering better fuel economy, quoted as a 16 per cent improvement at a constant 55 mph (90 km/h). Amazingly, the number of engine components was reduced by 40 per cent. Lower friction pistons helped improve fuel economy and cylinder heads of revised design were fitted.

Electrical equipment changes included a higher capacity alternator and a new smaller, quieter but more powerful (Japanese) starter motor.

Anti-locking (ABS) brakes were fitted to all cars for markets other than North America. The electronically-controlled system measures wheel speed and modulates braking pressure when wheel slip exceeds a determined limit.

Interior changes included slimmer front seats with increased lateral support and comfort, with fully-adjustable head restraints and the addition of power squab rake

SPIRIT OF THE EIGHTIES AND BEYOND

control and four position memory switches to the power operated seats.

Developments for 1989

On June 14th, 1988 a number of significant changes were announced for the 1989 model year, the most externally obvious being a change of frontal appearance for the Bentley saloon models, part of a longer term plan to move Bentley models away from their Rolls-Royce counterparts and give the Bentley range a character and appeal of its own.

Twin seven inch round headlights gave the Bentley Eight, Mulsanne S and Turbo R saloons a more purposeful and distinctive frontal appearance, while the Turbo R also received a striking new, deeper front air dam, steel sill extensions and a rear skirt – all colour-keyed. Other visual clues on the 1989 Bentleys were a new 'winged B' boot centre badge (incorporating the boot lock), in red for the Turbo R and black for the Eight and Mulsanne S, and colour-keyed door mirrors. Twin seven inch round headlights are not allowed in the United States, so for that market the inner pair are actually separately switched 35 watt foglamps, preserving uniformity of appearance for Bentleys world-wide.

The visual changes to the Bentley saloon models were matched by power train developments designed to provide all models in the range, both Rolls-Royce and Bentley, with increased refinement and even more power. The engine crankcase was ribbed and cross-bolted and the stiffened, heavy duty type THM400 transmission was fitted.

The Bentley Turbo R further benefited from an intercooler, MK Motronic digital fuel injection and ignition system and a fuel cooler. The Bentley Turbo R had not been available in the United States and other countries with strict emission control requirements due to the inherent incompatibility of turbochargers and catalytic converters.

Since it was, for obvious reasons, regarded as vital to gain entry to the lucrative U.S. market for the Turbo R, the Company's engineers worked very hard to resolve the problem. The solution adopted was the fitting of a pre-catalyst between the engine and the normal catalytic converter. At full turbo boost a modified wastegate was arranged to divert part of the exhaust flow past the turbocharger and pre-catalyst. Very accurate control of fuel injection and ignition timing are essential requirements of an efficient emission control system, so the Bosch K-Motronic engine management system was adopted for the 1989 model year Turbo R. As a result, the Bentley Turbo R was offered for the first time in the United States and even satisfied the ever more stringent emission control requirements of the State of California. A reduction in power output and torque of around five percent for the catalyst-equipped Turbo R had the perfectly acceptable effect of increasing the 0–60 mph acceleration time by around one second.

The Silver Spirit and Silver Spur saloons received a new front air dam while all saloon models, both Rolls-Royce and Bentley, received a more powerful in-car entertainment system and bright cantrail finishers.

The Corniche II and Bentley Continental convertibles for 1989 had redesigned seat trim with horizontal pleating, a fixed centre armrest between the front seats incorporating a storage compartment, an illuminated cassette storage drawer, all-analogue instruments and a more powerful in-car entertainment system.

Silver Spirit II

If precedents are any guide to the pattern of Rolls-Royce model names, the Silver Spirit II was probably not unexpected. The Silver Spirit II, the long wheelbase Silver Spur II and the revised Bentleys (which were not renamed) made their debut in October 1989 at the

Frankfurt Motor Show. Again, a number of significant improvements were introduced as a single package.

These series II cars set new standards of ride comfort, even for Rolls-Royce, with the introduction of a computer activated automatic ride control system developed over a four year period in the Experimental Department at Crewe. This continues the evolution of the self-levelling system which in one form or another has been a feature of Rolls-Royce and Bentley cars since 1965, as well as recalling the 'Ride Control' fitted to all models before 1966, right back to the 1930s.

If good handling is to be achieved in any motor car, conventional single setting damper systems must inevitably represent a compromise between the stiffness needed to limit roll when cornering and softness required for good ride quality. With the introduction of this new Rolls-Royce suspension system the self-levelling feature remained as before but the need to compromise damper settings was eliminated by adapting in 1/100th of a second to changes in road conditions and automatically selecting the appropriate 'comfort', 'normal' or 'firm' ride mode. This is achieved by means of an electronically controlled system comprising a micro-processor and vertical, longitudinal and lateral accelerometers which monitor acceleration, deceleration, road surface condition and steering changes. The mode changes occur so quickly and unobtrusively that the driver and passengers are unaware on entering a tight corner that the suspension has moved imperceptibly from 'comfort' to 'firm'. Unlike the pre-1966 ride control systems, the driver has no manual control over the settings.

New alloy wheels, quite unlike those of the Bentley models, distinguish the Silver Spirit II and its derivatives externally. Alloy wheels have a practical function in addition to their aesthetic value. They improve a car's ride and handling characteristics by relieving the suspension of part of the load it has to bear – i.e., less unsprung weight. The light alloy imposes less 'drag' on the system than steel, allowing the suspension to react more readily to changing road conditions. The resultant heightened responsiveness, particularly in combination with the automatic ride control, produces a smoother, more subtle motoring experience.

Inside, a new fascia with improved ergonomics and a new leather covered steering wheel left no doubt that this was a new model, or at least a significantly revised one. The traditional burr walnut on the fascia is now surrounded by striped walnut 'crossbanding', the two timbers being separated by a light coloured boxwood inlay or 'stringing'. This theme is repeated throughout the car's woodwork and is very appealing to the eye. Crossbanding has been a feature of the woodwork in all post-war standard saloon models (though in the earliest Silver Spirits it was confined to the mirrors in the rear quarters) and the inlaid stringing is not new, having been applied (in silver) to the 'Centenary' Silver Spurs, as well as being a traditional device in coachbuilding, using such materials as silver, brass and pewter as well as boxwood.

With the exception of the inlaid woodwork the new features applied also to the concurrent Bentley saloon models, which also retained their own distinctive styles of alloy wheels and do not carry the series II tag. The Corniche Convertible remained in the range and was dubbed 'Corniche III', having been called 'Corniche II' since 1987 (U.S.A. only) and 1988 (elsewhere). Again, the new interior features applied to this model with the exception of the automatic ride control, which was not fitted to either the Corniche III or the equivalent Bentley Continental Convertible until the 1992 model year.

New features introduced for the Silver Spirit II, Silver Spur II, Corniche III and the equivalent Bentley range may be summarised as follows. Exceptions are given in parenthesised italics.

- Automatic ride control system *(Except Convertible models, which did not receive this system until the 1992 model year)*
- New appearance of wood veneers incorporating boxwood stringing and crossbanding *(Bentleys retain their previous veneers)*
- Redesigned fascia with improved ergonomics, a new warning light panel incorporating the gear range selector indicator and digital odometer, new ignition/lighting 'switchbox' and two additional air conditioning outlets
- One of the best available sound systems with ten speakers to provide a richer, fuller sound. There are two tweeter speakers in the demister panel, mid-range and bass units in the front doors and mid-range bass/tweeter units in the rear doors
- New leather trimmed steering wheel *(All Bentley models now have the Turbo R style leather trimmed wheel)*
- New 6½ inch wide alloy wheels with stainless steel trims to enhance appearance, ride and handling
  (Bentleys retained their previous alloy wheel designs)
- K-Motronic engine management system and improved exhaust system as previously fitted to the Bentley Turbo R
- Driving convenience further enhanced by an automatic parking brake release electrically linked to the gear range selector and a new single action window lift to the driver's door
- Electrically adjustable front seat lumbar supports combined with upper and lower inbuilt front seat heaters
- The long wheelbase Silver Spur II has electrically adjustable rear seats and the rear armrest incorporates a telephone socket to enable the standard cellular telephone to be used in either the front or the back
- A pocket arrangement for the rear seat belt buckles
- Vanity mirrors in both sun visors, each with its own burr walnut sliding cover
- Security benefits from a remotely operated anti-theft alarm.

Corniche

The Corniche Convertible remained in the range and is now dubbed 'Corniche IV', having been called 'Corniche II' since 1987 (U.S.A. only) and 1988 (elsewhere), 'Corniche III' since 1990 (with Silver Spirit II features, except Automatic Ride Control) and 'Corniche IV' (with Automatic Ride Control) since 1992. The Bentley version, which was renamed Continental in 1984, developed similarly, though without the series II, III and IV designations.

The styling of these magnificent convertibles remains essentially unchanged since 1967, when John Blatchley's fine design was first introduced as the Silver Shadow and Bentley T Series drophead coupés. Consideration was given to re-styling the Corniche to give it a close family resemblance to the Silver Spirit range of cars, possibly using the four-door saloons' front wings and bonnet. Former Park Ward draughtsman Peter Wharton prepared drawings and a colour wash painting of the proposed car and a full-size mock-up was built. However, a decision was reached to continue with the more traditional styling for the convertible models. In retrospect, this was undoubtedly the commercially correct decision given the subsequent strong demand for the convertibles.

The Corniche two-door saloon was discontinued at the end of 1980. A 1986 proposal, dubbed 'CZS', for a revival of this model was not proceeded with. This would have used a fixed fibre-glass 'hard-top' turret. Four years earlier, a four-door long wheelbase saloon with Corniche styling reached the drawing stage but was also not proceeded with.

Camargue

This model continued in production alongside the Silver Spirit range but, unlike the Corniche, never received the full Silver Spirit type underframe, though all the Silver Spirit mechanical features were incorporated. Indeed, this had occurred some 18 months before the Silver Spirit range was introduced, on the 50,001 series cars.

Bentley Continental R

On Tuesday March 5th, 1991, Rolls-Royce Motor Cars Ltd launched the Bentley Continental R, describing it as 'the first new style Bentley since 1952'. The obvious inaccuracy aside, this is an exciting development. As a sleek and stylish two-door car it fills a space in the range left by the 1986 departure of the Camargue. The pricing of this new model, too, recalls the Camargue, which upon its introduction was priced at a staggering 50% higher than the Corniche. Not because it was that much more expensive to build, but because that was what the market would bear, because it was intended to keep the model ultra-exclusive and to make the point that in the troubled times of 1975 (shades of 1991!) Rolls-Royce were moving forward and intended to remain at the very pinnacle of the luxury car pyramid. In an initial press release the Continental R was priced at £160,000 in the U.K., inclusive of all applicable taxes. However, this was revised in a slightly later release to £175,000, possibly as a result of an increase in the VAT rate announced in the U.K. budget.

With the resurgent interest in the Bentley marque from the early 1980s came thoughts of an exclusive Bentley body style, and Chief Executive Peter Ward is known to favour this approach to the marque's future. The 1985 'Project 90', a full size glass fibre mock-up exhibited at the 1985 Geneva Motor Show, was a step in this direction and the Continental R is an obvious derivation of that concept. The subtleties of the body styling are, however, quite different. The number of people seeking to place orders for a 'Project 90' type car, following the 1985 Geneva showing, together with acclaim in the press, left no doubt about the strength of appeal of such an individual Bentley, and the decision to proceed with an exclusive Bentley model that would further enhance the marque's sporting image was taken.

By 1986 the design team had advanced a number of proposals, all benefiting from Turbo R developments and other exclusively Bentley features such as the 7 inch round headlamps. After considering – and rejecting – the idea of a two-door version of the standard saloon, a dedicated body style, designed with the aid of John Heffernan and Ken Greenley of International Automotive Design, was settled on. Radical departures from tradition were incorporated into the design, including cut-into-roof doors and sophisticated use of new composite materials for the integrated bumper system. The traditional skills of the coachbuilder were complemented by the latest computer technology to create a shape appropriate to the marque, of distinctive appearance and with good high speed stability and low wind noise.

The Continental R, which was code-named 'Nepal' in a long standing Experimental Department tradition of using Far Eastern names for new projects, was designed to be built entirely at Crewe. However, Mulliner Park Ward had a hand in the design and development work and Heffernan and Greenley worked from a design studio adjacent to the Mulliner Park Ward Hythe Road, Willesden works in a building that later became the Metrology Department. The pressed steel body panels are supplied by Park Sheet Metal, who also supplied the pressings for the Camargue body.

As had been the case with the original Bentley Continental forty years ago, the Continental R body shape was wind-tunnel proven, the well contoured form and carefully raked windscreen proving their worth with notably lower Cd (drag coefficient) than the current cars. This also brings benefits in reduced fuel consumption and enhanced performance. It is worth recording that when Continental R was unveiled at Geneva it was one of the few occasions on which the assembled throng has broken into a spontaneous round of applause at the first sight of a new car.

Although all Rolls-Royce and Bentley models since 1955 have had 15 inch wheels, the Continental R had 16 inch wheels carrying low profile Avon tyres, and now has 17 inch wheels. The styling of the alloy wheels was at first similar to that of the other Bentley models, but entirely new wheels appeared in 1994.

Although Heffernan and Greenley's design drawings show that they had something rather more radical in mind, the interior styling is reassuringly familiar, with similar seating to that of the Turbo R and a basically similar layout to the instruments and controls, except that the centre console extends into the rear compartment. The electric gear range selector is mounted in the centre console – the first time this had been anywhere other than on the steering column on an automatic Bentley. The automatic transmission itself is also new, having four forward speeds with the direct drive in third and an overdrive fourth speed for even more effortless low-rpm cruising and improved fuel economy. (For the 1992 model year this new automatic gearbox was standardised for all Rolls-Royce and Bentley models).

The Continental R is fitted with the turbocharged engine as in the Turbo R, providing scorching performance. Top speed is turbo-boost regulated to 145mph (233km/h) and acceleration 0–60mph takes a mere 6.6 seconds. A very fast flying B to take the Bentley marque into a challenging new era.

Touring Limousine

The Silver Spur II Touring Limousine was launched at the Frankfurt Motor Show in September 1990. Whilst it could scarcely be regarded as a replacement for the Phantom VI it nevertheless offers unrivalled features and passenger luxury. It also means that Rolls-Royce Motor Cars Ltd is still very much in the carriage trade, despite the Phantom's passing.

A fairer comparison would be against previous 'stretch' limousine designs which were invariably produced by adding extra length between the front and rear doors. This time, however, a much more satisfactory and visually pleasing approach has been taken. All the extra length – an additional 24 inches (610 mm) – is aft of the rear doors, giving a traditional six-light window configuration.

The Touring Limousine project began in August 1989 at Mulliner Park Ward in London, where a full size mock-up was built, followed by a prototype car. The modifications to the standard body shell required to produce the Touring Limousine body are still carried out by the present scaled down Mulliner Park Ward operation, but the finishing of the cars, including the complete interior, is carried out at Crewe.

The Touring Limousine starts out as a standard Silver Spur II body shell with no rear doors or roof. The extra length is added to the floor pan and a new roof is fitted. The roof is just over 2 inches (55mm) higher than the standard roof, which provides more interior headroom and nicely restores some of the exterior proportions that would otherwise be lost in the 'stretching' process. The rear doors have no cut-aways for the wheel arches, which are well back behind the rear quarter-lights. The rear window is smaller than standard to provide a distinctive limousine look and greater privacy. The standard Silver Spur II front doors are used, but fitted with taller stainless steel window frames to suit the higher roofline.

In all but detail the front compartment interior is unchanged from that of the standard car. Behind the electrically operated division, however, is where the coachbuilder's crafts are given free rein. A central cabinet houses a 10 inch colour television, a video player and a radio/cassette player which also controls the multi-play compact disc unit fitted in the boot. All 1990 model year and later cars have a ten-speaker in-car entertainment system, but the Touring Limousine has ten speakers in the rear compartment alone, through which the audio output of the radio, tape player, CD player, video and television are all channelled. A fold-down, rearward-facing occasional seat is fitted to the right-hand side behind the division and a cocktail cabinet on the left (these positions are reversed on left-hand drive cars). There is a folding picnic table on each side which can be used when the occasional seat is stowed and the drop-down cocktail cabinet door is closed. The cocktail cabinet is mirrored inside and fitted with three crystal decanters with silver tops and four crystal tumblers and there is storage space for four mixer bottles.

Each of the individual rear seats is adjustable, as in the standard Silver Spur II, with controls for this adjustment and the in-built seat heaters fitted into the side armrests, which are recessed into the body-side rather than projecting into the passenger space. Also in the armrests are controls for the division glass, division privacy blind, moon-roof blind, door window and, on one side only, the separate rear compartment heating and air conditioning system. These controls are of the traditional chrome-plated 'violin key' type. There is also a pneumatic lumbar support adjustment for the rear seat, like that fitted to front seats of 1990 model year and later standard cars. Between the rear seat cushions is a compartment fitted with a cellular telephone, a cordless remote control for the television, a leather-bound notepad and a silver pencil. Between the squabs is a fold-down veneered tray revealing a small refrigerator with space for two one-litre wine bottles.

The three-position electronically controlled automatic ride control system, standard on all four-door models since the 1990 model year, gives the Touring Limousine handling characteristics that would otherwise be impossible in a large, softly sprung limousine, and the long wheelbase means that rear seat passengers benefit from an even smoother ride.

The Touring Limousine is 19ft 7.4in (5,980 mm) long, weighs 5,820lb (2.64 tonnes) and in the overdrive (0.75:1) fourth gear a catalytic converter-fitted car returns a quite creditable 17.2mpg (16.4 litres/100Km) at 75mph (120km/h).

About 25 Touring Limousines will be built each year. The interior configuration described in this article is variable and can be tailored to the requirements of individual customers. For example, you may prefer cloth upholstery for the rear compartment instead of Connolly hide, or special veneers such as birdseye maple or mahogany, perhaps a silver inlay to the woodwork instead of boxwood, or you may want curtains to the rear compartment windows or a fax machine, all of which can be provided.

Bentley Brooklands

October 1992 saw the introduction of the Bentley Brooklands, a new 'entry level' saloon which replaced the Eight and the Mulsanne S, both of which were discontinued. The specification of the Brooklands was similar to that of the last of the Mulsanne S model, with the following changes:

- The radiator shell is painted in the body colour, as on the Turbo models;
- There is no chrome moulding along the centre-line of the bonnet;

- The enamel in the winged 'B' badges on the radiator shell and boot lid is green for the 1993 Model Year only;
- The selector for the four-speed automatic transmission is a short lever with a hand-stitched leather covering located in the centre console, as on the Continental R;
- The leather door trims have vertical pleated inserts, rather in the fashion of the 1930s;
- A new 'electrochromatic' rear-view mirror is fitted;
- The alloy wheels, though not dissimilar to those of the discontinued Mulsanne S and Eight, are of a subtly new design;
- There is a new front air dam with small, integral foglamps.

Phantom VI

Before concluding this final chapter some mention should be made of the largest and most expensive Rolls-Royce ever, the Phantom VI. The Company had entertained thoughts of halting production of this incredible motor car by the end of 1985. However, the U.K. Government allowed an easement of Type Approval regulations for the Phantom VI which allowed it to remain in production until the end of 1990. The word 'production' should be read here in the context of around three cars per year in these final years of the model!

Although the last of the Phantom VIs were still very much the same Silver Cloud-based cars that they were when first introduced (as the Phantom V) in 1959, the design had incorporated, since 1978, a number of changes which brought it more into line with other cars in the range. These changes included adoption of the 6.75 litre engine and GM400 three-speed transmission and are detailed in the Phantom VI Technical Specification.

The final two Phantom VIs were delivered in late 1991. The second last car was a limousine delivered to Mr George Moore CBE of Yorkshire, a Rolls-Royce customer of long standing and a previous Phantom VI customer. At a handing over ceremony at the Berkeley Square, London showrooms of Jack Barclay Ltd, Mr Moore was handed the keys by Rolls-Royce Motor Cars Chairman and Chief Executive Peter Ward. Mr Moore reciprocated by presenting the Company with a specially commissioned solid silver model of the car and hosting a dinner for eighty people, mainly the Mulliner Park Ward employees involved with the building of the car.

The final Phantom VI was a landaulette and was built specifically for retention by the Company, though reputed offers of several million pounds early in 1992 must have been tempting to the Company as it weathered the recession, a halving of 1990 sales and the attendant financial losses. Sufficiently tempting, in fact, for the car to have been sold in Mid-1992, to the Sultan of Brunei.

The Phantom VI had run its course. The company that built them, Mulliner Park Ward, is now but a shadow of its former self, its function confined entirely to the building of Corniche and Continental Convertible body shells and the modifications to Silver Spur body shells for the Touring Limousine model for completion and finishing at Crewe. The highly skilled workforce has been largely disbanded and dispersed. It is unlikely that we shall ever see the like of either Mulliner Park Ward's London coachbuilding operations or the Phantom VI again.

The 1991 downturn

The worldwide economic recession which began to bite hard early in 1991 had the almost immediate effect of halving Rolls-Royce and Bentley car sales, with the vital North American markets worst hit. The fact that other luxury car makers suffered similar or worse sales downturns was of no consolation. The break-even point for Rolls-Royce Motor Cars Ltd was an unsustainable 3,000 cars per year. This had been comfortably exceeded throughout most of the prosperous 1980s, with more than 3,300 cars being built and sold in the boom year of 1990, but with sales plummeting to less than half the break-even figure, it was clear that decisive action needed to be taken without delay.

Two years of heavy losses followed, during which time there was considerable press speculation about the possibility of a take-over by a German, or even Japanese, manufacturer. Nothing ever came of this and parent company Vickers made it clear that they had long term plans for Rolls-Royce Motor Cars Ltd. Radical restructuring of the Crewe factory and its manufacturing processes enabled the break-even point to be reduced to a more realistic figure of between 1,300 and 1,400 cars per year. This was achieved at considerable financial and human cost in employee lay-offs, redundancies and early retirements but meant that profitability had been restored. Moreover, today's lean, efficient operations at Crewe have been achieved without in any way compromising the standards of quality for which Rolls-Royce and Bentley cars are justly renowned around the world and which are central to the cars' reputation. Whereas in the 1980s the Company had been able to sustain highly labour-intensive manufacturing methods at Crewe, the 1990s ushered in a new era in which the traditional labour demarcation lines and restrictive work practices were swept aside and a stronger, better equipped Company emerged, allowing a much more difficult marketing environment to be faced squarely.

The London based Mulliner Park Ward coachbuilding division was pruned much more heavily than Crewe. Indeed, the Hythe Road, Willesden, operation has been all but closed. All that remains of a highly skilled and specialised workforce of well over 500 is a total of 40 craftsmen and staff occupying the ground floor of what is now termed 'H. J. Mulliner Coachworks', building the 'bodies-in-white' for the

Corniche/Continental convertibles and the Touring Limousine. The completed body shells are despatched to Crewe for mounting on their front and rear drive-train subframes, wiring, painting, interior trimming and finishing. Formerly, the cars had been returned to London for the last three operations but all the toing and froing was deemed too inefficient to continue.

Silver Spirit III

In August 1993 a significantly revised range of cars was announced. The standard and long wheelbase Rolls-Royce saloons became the Silver Spirit III and Silver Spur III respectively, all other model designations remaining unchanged.

Introducing the most refined model range ever, the Company's Commercial Managing Director Michael Donovan stated: 'In introducing a new engine which meets world-wide emission standards through to the year 2000 we have used the most advanced technology in the world to help us exceed the expectations of our owners. The new higher powered and more refined engine, improved ride characteristics, front passengers' airbags as standard and a number of other significant improvements have moved even the world of Rolls-Royce to a new level of excellence.

'The action that we have taken over the last two years has created a new dynamic company. We have focused and improved on the core activities that have made this company a byword for motoring excellence and we will not stop there.

'We now have the widest range ever of beautifully engineered motor cars. The new engine, transmission and suspension technology work together in total harmony, delivering the company's most highly refined driving experience yet.'

More than 70 engineering changes have been made, requiring the greatest ever investment by the Company in the improvement of an existing model range. At the heart of the package of improvements is a new version of the 6.75 litre V-8 engine, which blends state-of-the-art technology with a proven layout to create an engine that produces dramatically more power across the speed range while improving refinement still further. Redesigned cylinder heads and manifolding are largely responsible for the increased power output. The Rolls-Royce four-door saloon models now have a top speed well in excess of 130 mph (210 km/h), while the turbocharged Bentley models are, of course, significantly faster still.

Rolls-Royce and Bentley owners have become accustomed to the sight of a bewildering array of plumbing, trunking, wiring and electronic equipment largely obscuring the view of the engine when they open their bonnets. The under-bonnet view has now been improved by the fitting of a new engine cover featuring a machined aluminium cooling grille. Additional covers are fitted to the inner wing valances on all but the convertible models.

Occupant safety and comfort have been still further improved. Airbags are now standard for both driver and front seat passenger, the Bentley Continental R has a new hide-trimmed automatic seat belt presenter and the non-turbo four-door models benefit from new, even more comfortable front and rear seats. The steering column cowl is now trimmed in hide, colour-keyed to the upholstery on the Rolls-Royce models and black on the Bentleys. The picnic tables fitted to some models have been re-styled and are now illuminated for night use.

The long wheelbase Silver Spur III for the North American market is fitted with a video cassette player and a small television in the back of each front seat head restraint. At the time of writing this feature was expected to soon become available for the PAL television system used in the United Kingdom and many other countries.

Further environmental benefits accrue from the use of a CFC-free refrigerant in the air conditioning system.

The responsiveness and performance of the Bentley Turbo R and Continental R models, which were already remarkable by any standards, are further improved by the development of Electronic Transient Boost Control. This temporarily overrides the turbocharger's normal maximum boost when full load acceleration is required, effectively over-boosting the engine during the initial stages of heavy acceleration, such as when overtaking.

Both turbo Bentley models also benefit from new alloy wheel designs. The Continental R now has heavily-spoked 17 inch wheels with specially developed low profile tyres, while the Turbo R has more subtly redesigned 16 inch wheels with a wider rim section.

The external appearance of all models is improved by the introduction of mica paint technology. Mica, a naturally occurring substance, has the ability both to reflect and transmit light. Depending on how the car is viewed, subtle changes in colour enhance the appearance.

Concept Java

Every now and again the Company gives us a tantalising glimpse of what the future holds. An example of this was the 'Project 90' Bentley coupé concept car which was exhibited at Geneva in 1985. This time, with Concept Java, the Company has been much more forthright and revealed many more details including projected performance figures. The impression this forms is that this new car is closer to becoming a reality on the showroom floor than Project 90 was in 1985. At that time considerable numbers of customers sought to place orders for a car that in the event was six years away and which in any case evolved into a very different car by the time it eventually emerged as the now legendary Bentley Continental R.

For some years the Company has been moving towards a divergence of the Rolls-Royce and Bentley marques, with the attributes of each being fully developed and emphasised. The mindset that produced the Rolls-Royce Silver Spirit and Bentley Mulsanne as identical cars but for radiator shells and badging is giving way to a spirit of allowing free rein to the essence and vitality of both marques, each complementing the other but neither trespassing on the other's personality. In other words, in the future the Bentley will not, by and large, be a limousine while the Rolls-Royce will have no sporting pretensions. The Bentley of the future will very probably also be a smaller car both than it is now and relative to the future Rolls-Royce car. This process of change has already begun and Concept Java points to further change along these lines in the future.

What of the name 'Java'? There is a long established tradition at Rolls-Royce of using far eastern place names as code-names for experimental and prototype cars. The experimental Silver Cloud/S Series cars, for example, were called 'Siam', the Silver Shadow was 'Tibet' and the Bentley Continental R was, and still is within the factory, called 'Nepal'. There has been a 'Java' before, in the early 1960s when Rolls-Royce and the British Motor Corporation were co-operating with each other on projected lower priced Rolls-Royce and Bentley cars using BMC body shells. One of these projects, code-named Java, was eventually produced by BMC as the Vanden Plas Princess 4-Litre R.

The Concept Java which was unveiled at the Geneva Motor Show in March 1994 promises to further enhance the sporting image of the Bentley marque. It is more compact and is powered by a much smaller engine than any current or recent Bentley car.

Java, at this stage, is only a concept vehicle designed to gauge market reaction. However, work on the design has progressed to the extent that a suitable new engine has been identified and performance figures calculated. These are impressive in anybody's language – 0–60 mph (0–96 km/h) in 5.6 seconds, 0–100 mph (0–160 km/h) in 14.2 seconds and a top speed of 170 mph (273 km/h) electronically governed to 155 mph (249 km/h), while being capable of achieving around 30 mpg fuel economy at a constant 75 mph (120 km/h).

The engine, which has been conceived in conjunction with Cosworth Engineering, is a 3.5 litre, twin overhead camshaft, 32-valve, twin turbo V-8. If all that sounds impressive, there is little doubt that it will be! Cosworth Engineering is a member of the Vickers group of companies, of which Rolls-Royce Motor Cars Ltd is the biggest member. This partnership enables Rolls-Royce to draw on the considerable Formula One, Indycar and other motor racing experience and successes of Cosworth. It will be the first completely new engine for a Bentley car since the earliest phase of the current V-8 was introduced in 1959.

Concept Java is a full four-seater (as opposed to a 2+2) compact Bentley coupé. With its coupé roof fitted it bears a close family resemblance to the much larger Continental R. With the roof removed it is a stylish convertible with completely disappearing power-operated hood.

The styling is the result of collaboration between the Company's in-house design team, led by Graham Hull, and Design Research Associates Limited of Warwick, whose design work covers all forms of transport – automotive, rail, air and water. DRA is led by Roy Axe who was Director of Automotive Design for Chrysler in the U.S. in the early 1980s. After his success at Chrysler Axe joined Rover in 1982. Which he left in 1991 to form Design Research Associates with former colleagues Les Wharton (Chairman) and Creative Directors Adrian Griffiths and Graham Lewis. The Java project began in mid-1992 when DRA received a brief from Rolls-Royce Motor Cars.

The initial ideas of Axe and his team were accepted by the Company and it was decided to proceed to the next stage – the building of full-size models. Axe recalls: 'At this stage a great deal of discussion took place between the two companies about Bentley product values, and a key player was Chief Stylist Graham Hull, who has been steeped in Rolls-Royce and Bentley 'imagery' for many years. Obviously the Continental R, then recently introduced, was a major influence, as was the customer and public reaction to it. There had never been a 'small' Bentley before, so for this project to sit comfortably beside the Continental R, a full understanding of the values was essential.'

The detachable roof presented its own particular problems. Rolls-Royce wanted to avoid the 'planted on' effect of most detachable hard-tops and meticulous design work by DRA succeeded in giving it an integrated appearance. Carbon fibre was used for lightness coupled with great strength.

The interior is pure Bentley with the traditional ambience of rich leather and wood, exactly as a Bentley buyer would expect and demand. The full four-seater accommodation means just that, with seating for four adults, good headroom and adequate rear seat legroom all successfully provided within the compact size without compromising the feeling of luxury essential in a Bentley car.

Michael Donovan is enthusiastic about the possibilities for Concept Java and the development opportunities it presents for current vehicles: 'Concept Java' is a powerful demonstration of our confidence in, and understanding of, the future of the Bentley marque. It is also a key step in professional test marketing of possible motor cars for the future.

'Part of the development process is also to gauge the reactions of the most important people to us – our customers. We view Concept Java as a logical addition to the Bentley range but we want, nevertheless, to find out what potential owners think at this stage. The input we gain will be invaluable in terms of ultimately providing the best possible motor car from a stable where nothing but the best will do.'

The Company today

After losses exceeding £100 million over the previous two years and production reduced to well under half the 1990 figure, the Company was able to announce, in July 1993, that production was to be increased by 25 per cent. Investment in sophisticated machinery, including the £13 million computerised paint facility, and the more highly motivated, better organised labour force were beginning to pay off. The emerging changed world order is also a significant factor in the Company's ability to sell more cars by tapping new markets in which potential buyers had previously not had the opportunity to buy Rolls-Royce and Bentley cars. A new showroom was opened in Moscow in July 1993 after sales of around 60 Rolls-Royce and Bentley cars to Russian buyers in the first half of the year. Likewise, sales to Hungary are encouraging, with a new showroom opening in Budapest. In China, where capitalism is relentlessly gaining ground despite communism's continued grip on political power, sales of up to 100 cars were expected in 1993.

Today Rolls-Royce Motor Cars Ltd has 2,400 employees. This is only half the workforce of 1990, building approximately half the number of cars. The Company management structure is now much flatter than it had been, with only four levels of management. This has markedly improved communication and accountability. Likewise, on the workshop floor new, more flexible work practices and skills integration have replaced the old, inefficient lines of demarcation. Employees now work in teams in which the individuals and the team as a whole are responsible for the quality of their work. The role of the traditional inspector has changed so that he has become a working member of the team and is accountable for the maintenance of quality standards within the team. Each team's output is constantly monitored for quality by sample audit procedures.

The Company is now building its eight Rolls-Royce and Bentley models more efficiently than ever before. The two marques are both recognised as occupying their own complimentary but separate market niches and are defined by their makers as follows:

'Rolls-Royce motor cars are the most prestigious in the world. They are personalised for their owners who rank among the most successful and discerning people in society. Rolls-Royce is the ultimate in exclusive luxury and elegance, incorporating refined automotive technology to ensure exceptional comfort for driver and passengers alike.'

'Bentley motor cars provide a unique combination of luxury and performance for owners who appreciate an exciting driving experience in luxurious surroundings. Bentley's sporting elegance encompasses proven automotive technology that maximises the owner's driving pleasure.'

Today's Model Range

The 1995 Rolls-Royce and Bentley motor car range comprises the following models:

Rolls-Royce
Silver Spirit III. Standard four-door saloon.
Silver Spur III. Long wheelbase saloon, 4 inches longer than the Silver Spirit III.
Rolls-Royce Limousine. Spacious and luxuriously appointed limousine, 24 inches longer than the Silver Spur II.
Corniche IV. Four-seat convertible with the same wheelbase and mechanical features as the Silver Spirit II. Special order only.

Bentley
Brooklands. Standard four-door sports saloon. Also available with 4 inch longer wheelbase.
Turbo R. Turbocharged, high performance sports saloon. Also available with 4 inch longer wheelbase.
Continental. Four-seat convertible with same wheelbase and mechanical features as the Brooklands. Special order only.
Continental R. Turbocharged, high performance four-seat coupé.

Return of the Flying Spur

When the Bentley Mulsanne Turbo was introduced in 1982 it was made abundantly clear that that development was a part of the revival of the Bentley marque which was then gathering momentum. It was not intended that any Rolls-Royce, as opposed to Bentley car, would have the benefit of turbocharging in the forseeable future. Since then, with the resurgence of the Bentley marque achieved to a degree that was unlikely to have been anticipated, we have seen the advent of the Turbo R and the spectacular, turbocharged Continental R. Until now, however, turbocharging has still been confined to Bentley models.

Now all that has changed. Enter the Flying Spur. This new addition to the Rolls-Royce range was announced on May 20th, 1994 with most being sold within a few days of the announcement.

Some may see this new model as merely another permutation of existing bodies, engines and drive trains; as a Silver Spur with a Bentley Turbo engine and drive train or perhaps as a long wheelbase Bentley Turbo R with a Rolls-Royce radiator, badges and interior details, depending on one's point of view. Whilst there would be a strong element of truth in this, the fact remains that the Flying Spur is the fastest and most powerful Rolls-Royce ever and exhibits genuinely distinct characteristics, providing a perfectly balanced blend of enhanced performance with true Rolls-Royce levels of refinement.

The Flying Spur's effortless 0–60 km/h) acceleration figure of 7.0 seconds is impressive by any standard, though a little slower than that of the latest version of the Bentley Turbo R, suggesting a slightly milder turbo boost. As Michael Donovan, Managing Director – Commercial, pointed out: 'It was essential that the enhanced performance was delivered while retaining the unmatched smoothness, silence and finesse of the unique Rolls-Royce driving experience. The exquisite balance of power and refinement achieved by our engineers in the Rolls-Royce Flying Spur, has created a motor car which is the epitome of Rolls-Royce excellence and finesse. These are values clearly held dear by those owners for whom Rolls-Royce Flying Spur motor cars are currently being built'.

Corniche – 'last orders please!'

The Company's London coachbuilding operation at Hythe Road, Willesden, is now closed. Once the London Repair Depot, then the home of the Mulliner Park Ward coachbuilding Division and more recently known somewhat ambiguously a 'H. J. Mulliner Coachworks', Hythe Road fell silent in August 1994, ending fifty-five years of history on the site. At the same time the Corniche and Bentley Continental convertible models, the body shells for which were built at Hythe Road, all but bowed out. A final, special batch of 25 cars marks the end of these models after 23 years – 28 years if you look further back to the Mulliner Park Ward Silver Shadows from which the Corniche was derived.

Actually it is not quite the end for these models. The Company has announced that they will continue to be available on a made-to-order basis – and priced accordingly. It is understood that any future convertible body shell requirement, as well as that for the Rolls-Royce Limousine, will be met by Park Sheet Metal of Coventry, a firm which at one time supplied body panels for the Camargue.

Bentley Turbo S

In October 1994 Rolls-Royce Motor Cars Ltd announced a new limited production, ultra-high performance version of the Bentley Turbo R, called the 'Turbo S', which combines super-car performance to match the world's fastest production cars with luxurious saloon car accommodation which no other car can match. It will have the most powerful engine ever fitted to a Rolls-Royce or Bentley car together with distinctive external and internal visual features.

The Turbo S has a governed top speed of 155 mph and is capable of accelerating from 0 to 60 mph in under 5.8 seconds. The 'Series S' version of the 6.75 litre turbocharged engine is re-engineered to incorporate a liquid-cooled intercooler, revised induction features and a new engine management system using Formula One technology.

'The Turbo S is thrilling to drive and its exterior has been styled to match that excitement', said Rolls-Royce Motor Cars Chairman and Chief Executive Peter Ward, adding that 'it offers a level of performance that is rarely found outside the race circuit. This is the most powerful car we have ever built, but also one of the most refined, comfortable and environmentally responsible'.

Fewer than 100 Bentley Turbo S cars will be built for selected European, Middle Eastern and Asian markets.

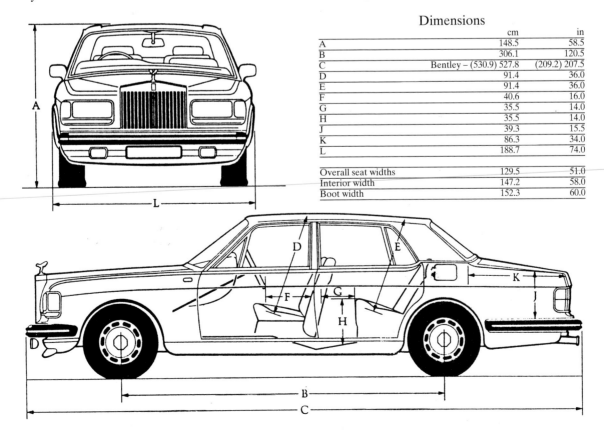

Dimensions

	cm	in
A	148.5	58.5
B	306.1	120.5
C	Bentley – (530.9) 527.8	(209.2) 207.5
D	91.4	36.0
E	91.4	36.0
F	40.6	16.0
G	35.5	14.0
H	35.5	14.0
J	39.3	15.5
K	86.3	34.0
L	188.7	74.0
Overall seat widths	129.5	51.0
Interior width	147.2	58.0
Boot width	152.3	60.0

TECHNICAL SPECIFICATION

Silver Spirit and derivative models 1980–present

Engine

Dimensions
Eight cylinders in 90 degree vee formation.
Bore 4.1 inches (104.1mm), stroke 3.9 inches (99.1mm), cubic capacity 412 cu. in. (6,750cc)
Compression ratio 9:1 (Cars for Nth America, Australia & Japan – 8:1.)

Cylinder block/Crankcase
Aluminium alloy monobloc casting with 'wet' cylinder liners. 1989 – cross-bolted crankcase.

Crankshaft
Nitride hardened chrome molybdenum steel. Integral balance weights. Five main bearings.

Pistons
Aluminium alloy with four rings.

Cylinder heads
Aluminium alloy with austenitic steel valve seat inserts.

Valve gear
Overhead valves operated through hydraulic tappets and push-rods. Monikrom cast iron camshaft driven by helical gears.

Carburetters and fuel injection
At introduction, all models (Except Nth America & Japan) – Two S.U. HIF.7 constant depression type. 1,875 in. bore.
Cars for Nth America & Japan – Bosch K-Jetronic continuous fuel injection system with 'closed loop' mixture control.
Bentley Mulsanne Turbo & Turbo R – Solex type 4A1 four barrel downdraught with partial throttle fuel economy device.
From 1987 Model Year, all models, all markets – fuel injection standard.
From 1989 Model Year – MK Motronic fuel injection and engine management system.

Ignition system
Lucas 35 DM8 Constant Energy Electronic. Bentley Turbo R fitted with knock sensing automatic retard system.

Cooling system
Coolant solution of 50% anti-freeze, 50% water pressurised at 15 psi, circulated by belt-driven centrifugal pump. Temperature regulation by thermostat.

Chassis

Monocoque construction with separate front and rear sub-frames:
Front – steel box-section construction mounted to car underframe by rubber mounts.
Rear – comprises the rear suspension and final drive cross-members connected by tubular members to form a rigid structure. Attached to car underframe by cylindrical rubber mounts. Short telescopic damper fitted to each front mount to dampen fore and aft movement.

Dimensions
Overall length 17' 3.42" (5,268mm)
Wheelbase, standard 10' 0.5" (3,061mm)
Wheelbase, long 10' 4.5" (3,162mm)
Front track 5' 1" (1,549mm)
Rear track 5' 1" (1,549mm)
Kerbside weight of car, between 4,950 lb (2,245 kg.) and 5,340 lb (2,420 kg.), depending on body type and country of domicile.

Suspension
Front – independent by coil springs with lower wishbones, compliant controlled upper levers, telescopic dampers and anti-roll bar mounted on the front sub-frame.
Rear – independent by coil springs with semi-trailing arms, gas springs in conjunction with suspension struts acting as integral dampers and height control rams. Anti-roll bar.

From 1990 Model Year, Silver Spirit II and derivatives (except Corniche III) – electronic 3-position automatic ride control system.

From 1992 Model Year, Corniche IV – electronic 3-position automatic ride control system.

Hydraulic system
Two camshaft-driven hydraulic pumps delivering Hydraulic Systems Mineral Oil under pressure (up to 2,500 p.s.i.) to a pair of hydraulic accumulators mounted on either side of the crankcase. Hydraulic pressure stored in the accumulators is used for the braking and height control systems. Two low pressure warning lights on the fascia, one for each hydraulic circuit.

Brakes
11 inch disc brakes on all four wheels. Each front wheel fitted with two twin cylinder calipers and each rear wheel with one four cylinder caliper. Two separate and independent hydraulic circuits from the high pressure hydraulic system operated by distribution valves connected to the brake pedal. Foot applied, hand release parking brake. Separate brake pads for parking brake.

1989 Model Year cars – anti-lock (ABS) brakes.

Height control system
Fully automatic hydraulic height control system to maintain the standing height of the car under all load conditions, by means of height control rams integral with the rear gas springs. The system operates at two speeds – slow levelling when driving and fast levelling with the gear selector lever in neutral or park.

Steering
Power assisted rack-and-pinion steering with centre take-off. Power assistance by hydraulic pressure from Saginaw engine-driven pump. Energy-absorbing collapsible steering column. Turns lock-to-lock: 3.25.

Transmission
At introduction – General Motors type GM400 3-speed torque converter automatic transmission.

Bentley Continental R and all models from 1992 Model Year – General Motors type 4L80-E 4-speed torque converter automatic transmission with overdrive top gear, electronically linked to the engine management system.

All cars have electrically operated gear selection with control mounted on right side of steering column (except Bentley Continental R, Bentley Brooklands and 4-speed Bentley Turbo R, which have a centre console mounted gear selector.)

Propeller shaft: dynamically balanced, single straight tube with rubber jointed coupling at front and rear.

Final drive ratio:
At introduction – 3.08:1
Bentley Mulsanne Turbo, Turbo R, Continental R and all models from 1992 Model Year – 2.69:1

Exhaust system
Cars not fitted with catalytic converter: Twin pipe system with six silencer boxes.
Cars fitted with catalytic converter: Twin downtake pipes from the engine merge into a single pipe prior to the catalytic converter, after which the system reverts to a dual system with twin intermediate and rear silencer boxes.

Road wheels and tyres
At introduction: 15" pressed steel wheels with 235/70 HR15 steel braced radial ply tyres.
Bentley Turbo R: 15" aluminium alloy wheels with 265/65 R15 low profile radial ply tyres.
Other Bentley models from 1986 (optional at first on Eight): 15" aluminium alloy wheels.
Silver Spirit II, Silver Spur II, Corniche III: 15" Aluminium alloy wheels with stainless steel covers.
Bentley Continental R and 1994 Model Year Bentley Turbo R: 16" alloy wheels with 255/60 ZR16 low profile radial ply tyres.
1994 Model Year Bentley Continental R: 17" aluminium alloy wheels with 255/55 R17 low profile radial ply tyres.

Coachwork

Saloon models: Four-door monocoque construction pressed steel saloon with aluminium doors, bonnet and boot. Long wheelbase saloon of similar construction. Corniche and Bentley Continental convertibles: Welded steel construction by Mulliner Park Ward on suitably reinforced base unit, with aluminium doors, bonnet and boot.
Limousine: Silver Spur body specially extended by H. J. Mulliner coachworks (London) and finished by Mulliner Park Ward at Crewe.

Chassis numbering system (Vehicle Identification Number) – Silver Spirit

Includes all derivative models and the Phantom VI from 1980.
In October 1980, when the Silver Spirit range of cars was introduced, an entirely new system of numbering was adopted. This was the 17-digit Vehicle Identification Number (VIN), an American device adopted by the International Standards Organisation for world use. Each of the first twelve digits has a specific meaning, detailed below. The remaining five digits made up the car's number. The sample VIN below is that of the first production Silver Spirit, followed by an explanation of the meaning of the 17 digits. It should be noted that the VIN was also adopted for models carried over from the previous range, i.e., Corniche, Camargue and Phantom VI.

Sample VIN   S C A Z S 0 0 0 0 A C H 0 1 0 0 1
Meaning *(see below)* 1   2   3   4   5   6   7   8   9   10   11   12   13   14   15   16   17

1 & 2   **World Manufacturer Identifier (country):**
S   Europe   C   England

3   **World Manufacturer Identifier (marque):**
A   Rolls-Royce   B   Bentley

4   **Chassis or underframe type:**
P   Phantom VI
Y   Camargue and early Corniche VINs*
Z   all other models

* Camargue and early 17-digit Corniche cars used a different underframe code because they used a 'half-way house' underframe, basically Silver Shadow (SY) but with Silver Spirit (SZ) type 'Rear Suspension Package', which had been developed for the 1979/80 Corniche and Camargue. Sufficient of these (DYZ) hybrid Camargue underframes were produced to see the model through until it was discontinued, but the Corniche eventually progressed from CYZ underframe to the full Silver Spirit specification (CZ) underframe.

5   **Body type:**
S   saloon   J   Camargue
L   long wheelbase with division   M   Phantom VI Limousine
N   long wheelbase, no division   T   Phantom VI Landaulette
D   Convertible

From the 1987 model year, L and T were dropped and the following new body type digits were phased in:
E   Bentley Eight* (1988 other than America)
F   Bentley Eight L (1988 other than America)

R   Bentley Turbo R (from 1989 model year)
P   Bentley Turbo RL (from 1989 model year)
X   Silver Spur and Mulsanne L Limousine
W   Silver Spur II Touring Limousine (1992)
B   Bentley Continental R (1992)
N   Long wheelbase (with or without division)
M   Phantom VI (all body types)
*E   Bentley Brooklands from 1993 model year.

6   **U.S. requirement.** Indicates engine type. Cars for all other markets initially had 0000 for the unused digits 6 to 9. Later, these digits came into use for all markets.

4	type L410 engine	8	Bentley Eight
0	other than America		

7   **Carburetters or fuel injection**

1	carburetters	T	Turbo
2	fuel injection	0	other than America

From the 1987 model year the following engine type codes were phased in for digits 6 and 7:

00 naturally aspirated, fuel injected
01 naturally aspirated, carburetters (Phantom VI only)
02 naturally aspirated, fuel injected, catalyst equipped
03 turbocharged, catalyst equipped
04 turbocharged

8   **Occupant restraint system**
A   Active belts
B   Passive belts – front (U.S.A. only)
C   Air bags
D   Driver-only air bag, passenger active belts
0   other than America (prior to 1987 model year)

9   **Check digit.**
A U.S. requirement. Used to ensure VIN is correct and to foil would-be VIN forgers. If the VIN is incorrect at any one digit, the check digit will show this. The check digit is 0 to 9 or X.

10   **Year**
Indicates the model year for which, not necessarily in which, a car was built (except in the case of the Phantom VI, the year letter of which indicated the year in which the chassis was laid down).

A	1980	F	1985	L	1990	S	1995	Y	2000
B	1981	G	1986	M	1991	T	1996		
C	1982	H	1987	N	1992	V	1997		
D	1983	J	1988	P	1993	W	1998		
E	1984	K	1989	R	1994	X	1999		

thence a numeral commencing with 1 for 2001 through to 9 for 2009, then re-commencing with A for 2010.

11   **Factory**   C Crewe   W Willesden

Note: this refers to the chassis, not the coachwork. The Phantom VI was the only chassis built at Willesden (Hythe Road) and was thus the only model to have the W digit at position 11 in the VIN.

12   **Steering position**

H   right-hand drive   X   left-hand drive

13-17   **Sequential identification number.**

These commenced at 01001 in 1980.

For the 1985 Model Year the numbers recommenced at 12001.

For the 1987 Model Year the numbers recommenced at 20001.

For the 1990 Model Year the numbers recommenced at 30001 (Corniche III and Bentley Continental) and 31001 (Silver Spirit II and other models).

For the 1992 Model Year, the numbers recommenced at 40001 (Corniche IV and Continental), 42001 (Bentley Continental R), 44001 (4-door saloon models) and 80001 (Silver Spur II Touring Limousine).

For the 1993 Model Year, the numbers recommenced at 40501 (Corniche IV and Continental) and 46001 (Silver Spirit III and other models).

For the 1994 Model Year, the numbers recommenced at 50001 (Corniche IV and Continental).

First and last Vehicle Identification Numbers, Silver Spirit range (including Phantom VI)

Firsts:

Silver Spirit	(pre-production, 1980)	SCAZS42A3BCX01011
Silver Spur	(pre-production, 1980)	SCAZN42A6BCX01012
Silver Spirit	(1980)	SCAZS0000ACH01001
Silver Spur	(1980)	SCAZN0000ACH01006
Bentley Mulsanne	(1980)	SCBZS0000ACH01009
17-digit no. Corniche Convertible	(1981)	SCAYD0009BCH01557
17-digit no. Camargue	(1981)	SCAYJ42A0BCH01570
17-digit no. Phantom VI	(1980)	SCAPM0000AWX01332
CZ underframe Corniche	(1982)	SCAZD0006CCH05037
Bentley Mulsanne Turbo	(1982)	SCBZS0T05CCH04233
Bentley Eight	(1984)	SCBZS8004ECH08862
Bentley Turbo R	(1985)	SCBZS0T04FCX12695
Bentley Continental	(1985)	SCBZD42A8GCX13412
Silver Spur Centenary	(1985)	SCAZN0004FCH14000
Bentley Mulsanne S	(1986)	SCBZS0007GCH14479
Corniche II (U.S.)	(1987)	SCAZD02A5HCX20011
Silver Spirit II	(1990)	SCAZS00A7LCH31001
Silver Spur II	(1990)	SCAZN02A7LCX31002
Corniche III	(1990)	SCAZD00AXLCH30001
Silver Spur Mulliner Park Ward	(1990)	SCAZN02D5LCX31347
'90 Model Year Bentley Mulsanne S	(1989)	SCBZS00A5LCX31006
'90 Model Year Bentley Eight	(1989)	SCBZE00A6LCH31008
'90 Model Year Bentley Continental	(1989)	SCBZD02A4LCX30002
'90 Model Year Bentley Turbo R	(1989)	SCBZR03DXLCX31004
Corniche IV	(1992)	SCAZD02A9NCX40001
'92 Model Year Bentley Continental	(1991)	SCBZD02A2NCH40002

Bentley Continental R	(prototype, 1990)	SCBZB03D5NCX42001
M.P.W. Limousine	(prototype, 1990)	SCAZW02D5NCX80001
Touring Limousine	(1992)	SCAZW02D9PCX80005
Bentley Brooklands	(1992)	SCBZE02D4PCX46004
'93 Model Year Silver Spirit II	(1992)	SCAZS02D7PCX46009
'93 Model Year Silver Spur II	(1992)	SCAZN02D3PCX46001
'93 Model Year Touring Limousine	(1992)	SCAZW02A8PCH80019
'93 Model Year Corniche IV	(1992)	SCAZD02D0PCX40501
'93 Model Year Bentley Turbo R	(1992)	SCBZR03D9PCX46003
'93 Model Year Bentley Continental	(1992)	SCBZD02DXPCX40503
'93 Model Year Bentley Continental R	(1992)	SCBZB03DXPCX42501
Silver Spirit III	(1993)	SCAZS02D5RCH54003
Silver Spur III	(1993)	SCAZN02D6RCX54001
'94 Model Year Touring Limousine	(1993)	SCAZW02C2RCX80101
'94 Model Year Corniche IV	(1993)	SCAZD02C5RCX50001
'94 Model Year Bentley Brooklands	(1993)	SCBZE02CXRCH54007
'94 Model Year Bentley Turbo R	(1993)	SCBZR03A9RCH54002
'94 Model Year Bentley Continental	(1993)	SCBZD02C4RCX50003
'94 Model Year Bentley Continental R	(1993)	SCBZB03C4RCX52001

Lasts:

Silver Spirit	(1989)	SCAZS00A4KCX27780
Silver Spur	(1989)	SCAZN00A1KCH27774
Bentley Mulsanne	(1987)	SCBZS0004HCX21999
CYZ underframe Corniche	(1982)	SCAYD42A7CCX05036
Corniche Convertible	(1987)	SCAZD0001HCH21668
Camargue	(1986)	SCAYJ42A7GCX10414
Bentley Mulsanne Turbo	(1985)	SCBZS0T08FCH14162
Corniche II	(1989)	SCAZD02A8KCX29289
Silver Spur Centenary	(1985)	SCAZN0004FCH14025
Corniche III	(1991)	SCAZD02A4MCX30636
Silver Spur Mulliner Park Ward	(1991)	SCAZN02A6MCH36065
Corniche IV*	(1992)	SCAZD02D3NCX40067
Bentley Continental*	(1992)	SCBZD02A8NCX40065
Mulliner Park Ward Limousine*	(1992)	SCAZW00AXNCX80004
Phantom VI†	(1992)	SCAPM01A2LWH10426
Bentley Eight	(1992)	SCBZE02A9NCH44562
Bentley Mulsanne S	(1992)	SCBZS05D5NCX44588
Silver Spirit II	(1993)	SCAZS00A6PCX46740
Silver Spur II	(1993)	SCAZN00AXPCX46781
Silver Spur II Touring Limousine	(1993)	SCAZW00AXPCH80056

* Indicates last cars built and finished at Mulliner Park Ward, Hythe Road, Willesden before painting, trimming and finishing operations for these cars were transferred to Crewe, January 1992.

† The year letter L indicates the year in which the chassis was laid down (1990). The coachwork took some 20 months to complete and the car was delivered in 1992.

Note: the Corniche Saloon was discontinued just prior to the introduction of the 17-digit VIN system. The first 17-digit Corniche Convertible and Camargue were 1981 cars, due to production of the previous 50001 series extending into that year.

Number of cars built, 1980–1992

Silver Spirit	8,129
Silver Spur	6,238
Bentley Mulsanne	482
Bentley Mulsanne L (long wheelbase)	49
Bentley Mulsanne Turbo	495
Bentley Mulsanne Turbo (long wheelbase)	24
Silver Spur Limousine (36" extension)	16
(42" extension)	84
Bentley Limousine (42" extension)	2
Silver Spur Centenary	1
Silver Spur Centenary replica	25
Rolls-Royce Corniche Convertible	1,301*
Bentley Corniche Convertible	12*
Rolls-Royce Corniche II	1,234
Rolls-Royce Corniche III	452
Corniche IV (1992–94)	114
Bentley Continental (1985–94)	405
Rolls-Royce Camargue	128*
Bentley Camargue	1*
Bentley Mulsanne S	970
Bentley Eight	1,736
Silver Spirit II	1,152
Silver Spur II	1,658

* The Corniche and Camargue models were carried over from the previous Silver Shadow range. These production figures refer only to those built after the introduction of the Silver Spirit range and the 17-digit VIN system. For pre-17-digit VIN Corniche and Camargue production figures refer to Silver Shadow chassis numbering system, page 256. For totals of these models, refer to Corniche and Camargue, total production figures, Appendix Four.

Annual production figures, 1982–93

1982	2,436	1988	2,968
1983	1,551	1989	3,254
1984	2,238	1990	3,274
1985	2,551	1991	1,620
1986	2,968	1992	1,244
1987	2,747	1993	1,264

Above The Silver Spirit saloon as introduced. The radiator shell is 1 inch (25mm) lower and 3.6 inches (93mm) wider than that of the Silver Shadow II and this formerly sharp-edged structure now has slightly radiused edges as a concession to safety. For the same reason the Spirit of Ecstasy mascot, at first for European markets only, was arranged to retract within the radiator shell on impact. The headlamp wash/wipe equipment – a neater arrangement than on the Silver Shadow II – may be seen in this photograph. The door mirrors are electrically adjustable from small buttons between the front seats.

Above The early Bentley Mulsanne was a Bentley radiatored and badged variant of the Silver Spirit. For the first time the Rolls-Royce and Bentley versions shared a common bonnet lid, its shape and that of the radiator shell having been carefully designed to avoid the need for separate pressings. However, the Bentley is 1.6 inches (40mm) longer overall due to its more prominent front bumper. No radiator mascots were fitted when these cars left the factory, though one is available as an accessory. This item comes with a warning that fitting it to the car would contravene type approval regulations and is the owner's responsibility.

Top right *The long wheelbase model in the Silver Spirit range was the Silver Spur. Recognition features, in addition to the extra four inches (10 cm) length aft of the centre pillar, included Camargue/Corniche pattern wheel trims, Silver Spur badging on the bootlid and normally, though not always, an Everflex-covered roof. A Bentley version of the long wheelbase model, the Mulsanne L was also offered but is a rare variant.*

Right *The fascia and controls standardised for the Silver Spirit range remained, at first, unchanged from those of the Silver Shadow II range except that a digital display for time of day, elapsed journey time and outside temperature as fitted to the Corniche from a year or so earlier, replaced the earlier models' analogue clock and outside temperature gauge. The parking brake was the American-style foot-applied, hand-released type for all markets.*

Bottom right *The seating, still in the familiar pleated-and-bolstered style that dates from the Bentley Mk VI, was normally in leather. However, leather with colour-keyed textile facings could be specified. For the first time in a standard saloon the rear seating consisted of two separate seats which were near duplicates of the front seats. Rolls-Royce and Bentley cars still have leather on the backs and sides of the seats and on the doors – even the carpet edging is leather – as opposed to the mere leather facings seen in other makes of car. The traditional vanity mirrors, or companions, in the rear quarters were retained, but the usual walnut veneered door cappings gave way, on early Silver Spirit model range cars, to simpler solid walnut finishers. Folding picnic tables in the backs of the front seats, which disappeared from Silver Shadows with a rush of safety consciousness in 1969, became available again, either leather-covered on their outer faces or all polished wood depending on the design requirements of the destination country.*

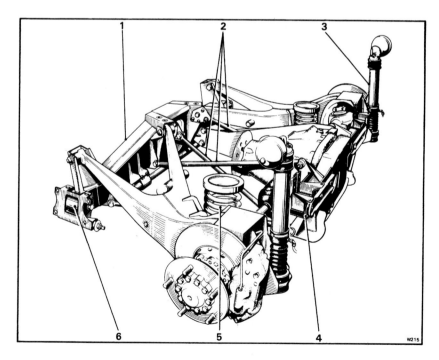

Above *Silver Spirit model range cars for the U.S. market were fitted with pairs of rectangular headlights of a type readily available in that country. The frontal appearance, seen here on a Bentley Mulsanne, was quite different as a result.*

Left *This is the modified rear suspension and final drive assembly that was first introduced without fanfare in May 1979 for the Corniche and Camargue models and standardised with the introduction of the Silver Spirit range in October 1980. Clearly shown are 1. rear crossmember, 2. diagonal bracing tubes, 3. the Girling gas springs/struts which replaced the shock dampers and levelling rams of the Silver Shadow range, 4. & 6. metalastic mounts and 5. the much shorter coil springs without levelling rams.*

306

Above & right *The hydraulic system (i.e., brakes and levelling) of the Silver Spirit and derivative models, as well as the 50,000 series Corniche and Camargue that preceded them, ran on Hydraulic Systems Mineral Oil. Because the introduction of even a minute amount of ordinary brake fluid into this system causes rapid deterioration and failure of the seals, elaborate precautions were taken against such an error being made. Brightly coloured warning labels on the engine compartment reservoirs and lead seals help guard against such a disastrous eventuality. Two dispensers of the correct mineral oil, together with the special nozzle required for the topping up operation, are provided in a compartment in the boot.*

Below right *The tools for the Silver Spirit series cars are fitted into a compartment between the boot lid hinges, above the fuel tank. Note the white gloves and red reflectorised hazard warning triangle.*

Below left *Battery isolating switch fitted in the boot. The battery itself, as has been the case in all Rolls-Royce and Bentley models since 1955, is fitted in a compartment in the boot.*

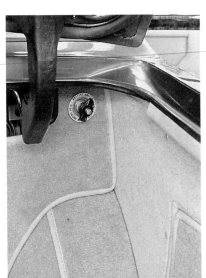

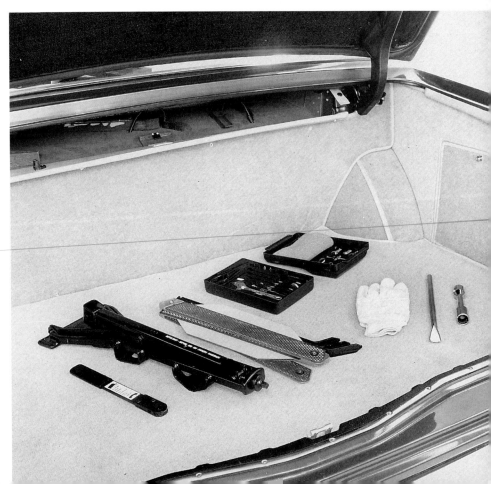

This page *The introduction of a new Bentley is always an exciting event but the announcement of the Mulsanne was eclipsed by that of the Mulsanne Turbo, which made its debut at the Geneva Motor Show in March, 1982. Such motoring press headlines as 'The Return of the Blower Bentley' and the like made plain the motoring world's astonishment and pleasure at the unexpected appearance of such an exciting new Bentley. The concept of a Bentley with even higher performance than the standard models had been tried before – W. O. Bentley's 4½ Litre model was supercharged in the late 'twenties for Le Mans. In the early 'fifties a rather different approach was taken for the R-type Continental, which achieved magnificent performance largely by means of lighter coachwork of streamlined shape and smaller cross-section and only slightly increased engine power. This time, however, the quest for higher performance was again approached through outright muscle in a standard body. Turbo recognition features normally included a radiator shell painted in the body colour rather than chrome plated, discrete 'TURBO' badging on the front wings and bootlid and twin exhaust pipes emerging together on the right-hand side.*

Right *A Bentley Turbo engine before installation in the car. The Garrett AiResearch turbocharger is visible behind its heat-shield at left. Note also the Citroën-type hydraulic accumulators for the braking and levelling systems below the nearside exhaust manifold. It is indicative of the rugged nature of Rolls-Royce machinery that few modifications were necessary to render the V-8 fit for the considerable additional stresses resulting from turbocharging. The only significant changes were strengthened pistons and an oil cooler to cope with the higher operating temperature.*

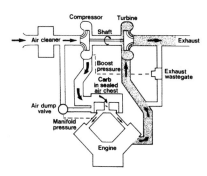

Above, right & below right
Before unleashing a turbocharged car on purchasers with such very high expectations as the customary clientele of Rolls-Royce Motors, the Company had to overcome a number of problems normally associated with turbocharging that would otherwise have rendered the entire concept unacceptable – in particular poor throttle response due to 'turbo lag'. The resultant engine package, was dauntingly complex, which explains why Mulsanne Turbos were at first largely confined to the home market where they could be kept under observation. This view of the Turbo engine installation shows, in the centre, the large cast aluminium air-box, or plenum chamber, which housed the Solex 4A1 four-barrel downdraught carburetter which was force-fed with air by the turbocharger, seen forward and to the right of the air-box. The Autocar cut-away drawing (right) shows the details and internals in a characteristically superb manner and the arrangement of the various components is clarified diagrammatically (above).

1	Crankcase breather fumes
2	Supercharged air delivery pipe
3	Recirculated air from air dump valve
4	'A' bank exhaust
5	Feed from 'B' bank exhaust
6	Exhaust outlet from turbine
7	Flow past wastegate valve
8	Exhaust to turbine
9	Filtered air in and breather fumes and recirculated air
10	Turbo oil drain
11	Four barrel two stage Solex down-draught carburetter
12	Air box with controls fixed to outside
13	Inlet manifold
14	Radiant heat shielding
15	New position for power steering pump
16	Oil cooler pipes
17	Oil feed to turbo

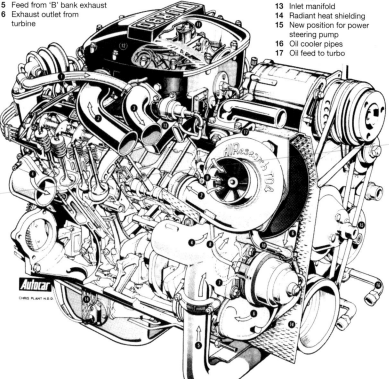

BENTLEY
MULSANNE · TURBO

The Guardian said of the Bentley Mulsanne Turbo that it is "almost indecently fast."

It travels from 0 to 60 m.p.h. in 7 seconds. It will travel from 60 to 90 just as quickly.

It will push you back in the seat even when accelerating through 100 m.p.h. to its top speed in excess of 135 m.p.h.

Such a remarkable performance is obtained by increasing the light alloy V8 engine's power output by 50% with a single turbocharger.

Consequently, Avon had to develop 235/70 VR rated tyres specifically for the Bentley Mulsanne Turbo.

And a unique electronic knock sensor, which listens continually to the engine, was specially engineered and fitted to the car to prevent detonation.

Yet for all its increased power, the engine runs not one revolution faster and the traditional refinement of the car has not been compromised.

It is as quiet to travel in as a Bentley has ever been.

It is also as comfortable at 135 m.p.h. as it is at 50.

To say the Bentley Mulsanne Turbo is rare is understatement. No more than 125 people in Britain will own one by the end of this year.

If it is standing still, you will recognise it by the famous radiator. This is the only Bentley ever to have its radiator painted the same colour as the body of the car.

It may also display discreet 'turbo' badges on the front wings. If not, rest assured, the Bentley Mulsanne Turbo will go just as fast without them.

Enthusiasts for the marque say this car truly reflects traditions created by Bentley at Le Mans, Brooklands and Montlhery.

The makers simply state that in the Bentley Mulsanne Turbo, the Silent Sports Car returns.

THE SILENT SPORTS CAR
R-E-T-U-R-N-S

BENTLEY MOTORS LIMITED · CREWE · CHESHIRE

A Vickers company

Below, left & right *A Mulsanne Turbo press demonstrator at its French namesake town, en route to the nearby racetrack at Le Mans in 1982.*

Inset *Speedometer 'off the clock' at 140 mph (225 km/h)-plus, another Mulsanne Turbo demonstrator at Le Mans...*

Below *...and at Goodwood.*

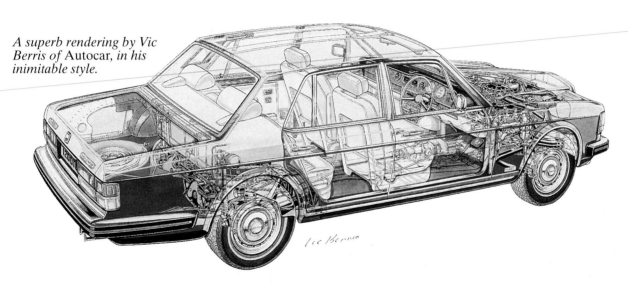

A superb rendering by Vic Berris of Autocar, in his inimitable style.

Above *The Bentley Eight was conceived as part of a strategy to build on the success of the Mulsanne Turbo and widen the appeal of the Bentley car to more fully exploit one of the greatest and most famous marques in the annals of motoring. Basically, the Eight as introduced in July, 1984 was a standard Mulsanne with stiffened front suspension to enhance the car's sporting characteristics, slightly reduced interior trim and, as its main external distinguishing feature, a handsome chrome wire mesh radiator grille reminiscent of the famous Bentley Le Mans winners of the 'twenties. Carefully priced below £50,000 at £49,497, some £5,743 less than the Mulsanne and £12,246 less than the Mulsanne Turbo, in order to attract the new customers that Company research showed would be attracted to Bentley driving with sporting performance and handling and traditional quality standards without the need for full Rolls-Royce luxury specification.*

Below *This interior view shows that the mirrors in the rear quarters, a feature of every other standard saloon model since 1946, were omitted for the Eight. Together with the straight-grained polished timber, this helped provide the slightly plainer interior that was sought, while in no way reducing the quality of materials or finish and without diminishing the traditional air of luxury.*

Above right *The fascia of the Eight, in straight-grained walnut, was a departure from the more traditional burr walnut veneer. An analogue (VDO) clock and outside temperature gauge were fitted in lieu of the digital display common to the other saloon models.*

Above & left *The Corniche Convertible, its appeal completely undiminished, was retained in the Silver Spirit model range. Serious consideration was given to re-styling the car to more closely resemble the four-door models. This proceeded beyond Peter Wharton's design drawing stage (above) to a full-size mock-up (left) before being abandoned in favour of retaining the existing, more traditional shape.*

Right *As part of the overall strategy to promote a resurgence of interest in the Bentley marque, the Bentley Corniche was, since August, 1984, marketed as the Continental – a shrewd revival of the evocative name applied to sporting Bentleys from 1952 to early 1966. New features for this model included new front seats with adjustable lumbar supports, a redesigned fascia with traditional Continental-type individual gauges in lieu of the four-in-one instrument and colour-keyed bumpers, side mirrors and radiator grille vanes.*

Above *The Camargue was retained in the Silver Spirit model range until 1986, when it was discontinued. Aside from the adoption of Silver Spirit technical specification, most components of which it received along with the Corniche some eighteen months before the introduction of the Silver Spirit range, the Camargue remained aloof and visually uninfluenced by the new models. The interior, including the special fascia, remained unchanged, as did the exterior except that the slim chrome moulding that followed the swage-line below the side windows had disappeared.*

Opposite *The Limited Edition Camargues were fitted with Bentley-style alloy wheels fitted with lockable R-R centres. These wheels have since become available as an accessory for fitting to Silver Shadow and early Silver Spirit and derivative cars.*

Opposite page bottom, This page left & below *Just before the Camargue was discontinued, a special run of a dozen Limited Edition Camargues was produced for the United States market. All twelve cars were finished in white with red coachlines. The interiors, in red hide piped in white, were particularly special, with silver inlays to the timber door cappings and rear waistrails and a number of luxury fittings provided by the Crewe Special Features Department. These included a R-R monogrammed silver vanity set, comprising a mirror, hair-brush, comb and clothes-brush fitted into the rear armrest, and a set of crystal glasses and silver-plated monogrammed hip flasks in a compartment between the seat cushions. The lid to this compartment was veneered on the inside and could be turned upside down to form a small table.*

This page *In order to combat unauthorised 'stretching' of Silver Spirits and Spurs, mainly in the United States, the Company decided to offer its own official lengthened version of the Silver Spur, called the Silver Spur Limousine, from 1984. Robert Jankel Design were commissioned to carry out the conversion work for two prototypes, one of which is shown here. Both cars were extended by 36 inches and had six doors. As may be gathered from the view of the amazingly comprehensively equipped rear compartment (left), the centre doors would be unlikely to serve any practical purpose, which led to their being omitted from 'production' versions (see Franco Britannic Autos advertisement). For maximum rear compartment comfort a second, independent air conditioning system was installed. A burr walnut centre console cabinet contained a video monitor and player as well as the latest type radio/cassette player with graphic equaliser, power amplifier and four speakers. There were also two forward-facing occasional seats and a two-way communication system between the front and rear compartments.*

This page *Improvements for 1985 included high-pressure headlamp washer jets which eliminated the need for headlamp wipers. This arrangement may be discerned on the Silver Spirit (above) and on the Bentley Mulsanne Turbo (below).*

Left & below *Interior changes for 1985 included a slightly revised fascia with air conditioning outlets occupying a higher position in the central console, a divided digital display and new, simpler controls for the cruise control. Most noticeable, though, was a reversion to the superb full burr walnut veneered and crossbanded door capping rails. These can be glimpsed in this interior view and through the windows of the 1985 Silver Spur (below).*

Above & left *The Silver Spur could be supplied with an electrically-operated glass division as seen here. Controls for the division, radio and air conditioning, together with air conditioning outlets, were fitted in the centre console, shown in close-up. Note the bench-type seat in the rear compartment of this variant, the modifications for which were carried out by the Mulliner Park Ward Division in London.*

This page *The Bentley Turbo R was announced in Geneva in March, 1985 and provided a decisive answer to criticisms that the Mulsanne Turbo's suspension was too soft for its 135 mph (217 km/h) performance. Roadholding (denoted by the 'R') and handling were dramatically improved by increased anti-roll bar stiffness (up 100% front, 60% rear), slightly stiffened dampers, improved rear subframe sideways location by means of its own hard-rate rubber-bushed Panhard rod, changes to the self levelling and slightly heavier steering. A special fascia was introduced for the Turbo R with a revolution counter alongside the speedometer, separate gauges reminiscent of those of the old Bentley Continentals and a full console between the front seats. Cast alloy wheels with Pirelli's safety rims carrying Pirelli low-profile (275/55VR15) tyres lent this model a distinctive external appearance. The fully leather covered steering wheel seen in the right-hand drive car (bottom right) quickly became standard for the Turbo R and was subsequently adopted for the other Bentley models. The Mulsanne Turbo was dropped from the range soon after the introduction of the Turbo R.*

Left *On August 2nd, 1985 Rolls-Royce Motors announced their 100,000th car. This special car, a 'Centenary' version of the Silver Spur, in Royal Blue, was unveiled at a motoring pageant at Crewe. All 3,800 employees were given time off from their normal duties to enjoy the hand-over ceremony in a specially built area. The two longest-serving employees, Mrs Margaret Green, 58, and Mr Jack Goodwin, 62, officially presented Chief Executive Richard Perry with the car's keys and registration documents for the Company's safe keeping. The Silver Spur Centenary took its place alongside the Company's 1904 10 h.p. two cylinder car and the original 1907 Silver Ghost demonstrator in the new customer reception centre and is now in the custody of the Rolls-Royce Enthusiasts Club. The name Silver Spur Centenary payed tribute to Britain's 1985 national celebration of a century of motoring. The figure of 100,000 represents the combined total of Rolls-Royce and post-1931 Bentley motor cars made by Rolls-Royce. The photograph depicts the Silver Spur Centenary car with, behind, some of the 25 Centenary 'replicars' – a select limited edition of twelve for the U.S.A., eight for the home market and five for Europe and the Middle East – all eagerly snapped up!*

Below, left & right *Among the distinctive items that add the 'Silver' qualities were silver inlaid, R-R monogrammed door capping rails, silver inlaid picnic tables, engraved door sill plates, a commemorative plaque on the inside of the glove compartment lid and matching spirit flasks in the front central cocktail compartment. Each owner received a radiator-shaped presentation case containing a silver key-ring, silver ball-point pen, note-pad and a silver engraved plate. The U.K. price for the Silver Spur Centenary 'replicar', at £77,740, was £9,995 more than that of the standard Silver Spur.*

Right *The 'production' version of the Silver Spur Limousine, built mainly for the U.S. market. The interior was all new and featured face-to-face rear compartment seating (the preferred configuration for 'stretch' limousines in the U.S.A.), revised positioning of the video and audio tape playing equipment and two telephones. The degree of 'stretch' was a huge 42 inches (106 cm). Note the U.S. market headlights on this car.*

Below *The Rolls-Royce and Bentley model ranges were improved for 1986 by a number of important modifications. All four-door models benefited from changes to the engine and body to give improved cooling performance and air flow through the engine compartment and modified suspension for improved roll resistance and smoother cornering performance. Note the revised positioning of the number plate on this Silver Spirit (Nth. American export cars retained their smaller licence plate mounting) and, less obvious, the smaller radiator badge.*

Above *The 1986 model year Corniche was fitted with the same new wheel trims as the Silver Spur and had colour-keyed bumpers and side mirrors. Note the narrower but deeper licence plate mountings of this U.S. market car.*

Above & right *The interior of the same Corniche shows the revised seats and fascia introduced in August, 1984. The front centre armrests were changed for 1986 to the type shown above. These formerly folded out of the seat squabs and were slimmer.*

Opposite page, top & bottom *The 1986 model year Silver Spur was distinguished by new stainless steel wheel trims and was fitted with a cellular telephone as standard equipment.*

This page *On September 19th, 1986 a Company press release announced that a Bentley Turbo R had broken no fewer than 16 speed and endurance records. The car concerned was the second 1987 model year specification car, Vehicle Identification Number SCBZR0409HCH20002. The most important title was the national one-hour endurance record which the Turbo R raised to 140 miles 1,690 yards (225.46 Km) despite a drama after 57 minutes when a pheasant struck the windscreen at 141 mph, causing several fractures in the glass. Company test driver Derek Rowland maintained speed and course while contending with another problem, fuel starvation, caused by the steep camber of the Millbrook circuit in Bedfordshire. Each two mile lap was completed consistently in around 51 seconds after a first lap of 67 seconds from a standing start. The record challenge was part of a concerted marketing plan to promote the Bentley marque strongly. The one-hour endurance title, previously held by a Lamborghini Countach, was taken without using the full performance potential of the car.*

This page *1986 model year Bentleys benefited from the fitting of a handsome variant of the distinctive alloy wheels of the Turbo R. These were standard for the Continental (right) and the Mulsanne (below) and available as an extra cost option for the Eight (bottom).*

Above, left & right *Silver Spirit model range cars for the U.S.A. and Japan featured fuel injection from the outset. For 1986 this version of the engine was introduced to the Australian market and became standard in all markets for the 1987 model year. The system used was Bosch K-Jetronic. Above left is the early fuel injection installation on a Camargue and above right the 1987 Model Year installation on a Silver Spur, Vehicle Identification Number SCAZN4OA7HCX20015. Also for the '87 Model year, a major revision of the engine design saw the number of engine components reduced by 40%, lower friction pistons, redesigned cylinder heads and a new, smaller, quieter but more powerful (Japanese) starter motor. Also for 1987, for cars sold in the U.K., European and Middle East markets, anti-locking (ABS) brakes were introduced. A programme of continuous improvement to the suspension system resulted in a tauter, better handling car.*

Above & below *1987 model year cars had slimmer, though still sumptuous front seats with new adjustable head restraints to provide improved lateral support and increased comfort, with an eight-way electric seat adjustment that included the squab rake adjustment for the first time. Another innovation was the provision of a memory switch for four preferred positions for each front seat. These photographs show the 1987 Silver Spur. The Silver Spirit and Bentley Mulsanne were similar, though with four inches less legroom for rear seat passengers. The picnic tables shown, in the backs of the front seats, were available at extra cost on the Silver Spirit and Bentley Mulsanne.*

Above *The 1987 model year Corniche, with the engine changes and new interior features such as memory seats, but initially without ABS brakes, was redesignated 'Corniche II' for the U.S. market only. This model designation was extended to other markets from the following year. Advantage was taken of the 14% increase in power output from the fuel-injected engine over the previous four-barrel Solex installation to raise the final drive ratio to 2.69:1 for even more effortless high speed cruising. This is a right-hand drive home market Corniche II.*

Below *In October, 1987 the Bentley Mulsanne S was introduced. This model featured the Turbo R style of centre console and instrumentation to give the Mulsanne a more distinctly sporting character. Straight-grain walnut interior woodwork was specified for this model, though burr walnut was available at extra cost. The Mulsanne S was successfully launched in the United States, where it was the first Bentley model available for more than a decade.*

This page *1989 model year Bentley saloons were further distinguished from their Rolls-Royce counterparts by a purposeful new frontal appearance with paired seven inch round headlights for all markets and colour-keyed door mirrors. Bright cantrail finishers were shared with the 1989 Rolls-Royce models. Above is the 1989 Bentley Eight and below the Mulsanne S.*

Above & right *The Bentley Turbo R for 1989, in addition to the seven inch round headlights and other visual changes, received a deeper front air dam, steel sill extensions and a rear skirt – all colour-keyed. The rear view (right) shows the new 'Winged B' badge on the bootlid. This was red for the Turbo R and black for the other models, and incorporated the boot lock.*

Below *The Rolls-Royce saloon models for 1989 retained their original headlamps but received a new front air dam and bright cantrail finishers. All models – both Rolls-Royce and Bentley – benefited from a ribbed and cross-bolted crankcase and stiffened THM400 gearbox for increased, smoother power. This is the long wheelbase Silver Spur.*

Left *For the 1990 model year the changes were considered sufficient to warrant a change of model names to Silver Spirit II, Silver Spur II and Corniche III. This is the Silver Spirit II, the main external distinguishing feature of which was the new alloy wheels with polished stainless trims.*

Below *From the rear, a new 'Silver Spirit II' bootlid badge identified the model.*

Below, left & right *The 1990 Silver Spirit II and Silver Spur II interior featured an inlaid and crossbanded burr walnut fascia. The new gear range selector indicator can just be seen in the warning light panel, while more obvious are the new leather covered steering wheel, two additional air conditioning outlets at the extremities of the fascia and the ignition/lighting switchbox of revised design at the right of the leather covered kneeroll. An extensive programme of ergonomics research has resulted in all controls and instruments being placed in a driver-friendly way. Rolls-Royce, quite rightly, steadfastly avoid fussy, multiple stalks on the steering column and still provide a proper switch for the windscreen wipers. The centre console now includes switches for seat heaters.*

Above *The micro-processor control unit at the heart of the 1990 saloon models' automatic ride control system which changes damper settings in 1/100th of a second in response to acceleration, deceleration, road surface condition and steering changes.*

Above right *The long wheelbase model became the Silver Spur II for 1990.*

Right *In order to take full advantage of the additional four inches (10 cm) of rear compartment legroom in the Silver Spur II, individually adjustable rear seats were introduced. A telephone jack was incorporated in the centre armrest so that the standard cellular telephone may be used in the rear as well as in the front. Note the neat recessed seat belt buckle stowage.*

Below *The Silver Spirit II and derivatives were the first Rolls-Royce cars fitted with alloy wheels other than the Limited Edition Camargue seen early in this chapter. On the left is the Silver Spirit II wheel with its chrome cover and, on the right, the Silver Spur II and Corniche III wheel with its painted trim-ring.*

Above *The 1990 Bentley saloons shared the new technical features of their Rolls-Royce counterparts but retained their own distinctive alloy wheel designs and did not receive the series II tag. The fascia layout changes also applied to the Bentleys but not the new inlaid woodwork style.*

Left *For 1990 the Corniche became 'Corniche III'. The new 1990 features applied with the exception of the automatic ride control, which was not fitted to either the Corniche or the equivalent Bentley Continental until 1992.*

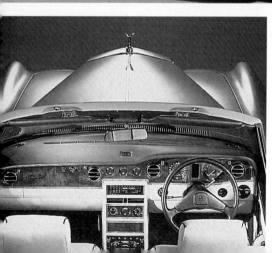

Left & right *Both the new inlaid woodwork and the leather covered steering wheel (for the U.S. market this was different and incorporated an airbag restraint system) were applied to the Corniche III. Note also the all-analogue instruments. The seat-shaped seat adjustment controls and memory buttons (introduced for the 1987 model year) are clearly visible in the centre console.*

Above *During 1991 a special batch of Silver Spur II saloons was dispatched to Mulliner Park Ward in London to be finished as Silver Spur II Mulliner Park Ward limited edition cars. All were finished in Bordeaux with twin magnolia coachlines. Unmistakable external recognition features included: hand-made 18-gauge stainless steel embellishers to the wheel arches, sills and lower rear wings, colour-keyed bumpers with polished stainless steel inserts and colour-keyed headlamp surrounds.*

Above right *The distinctive bootlid badge.*

Right *The specially selected burr walnut veneers were extended to all four door panels. Silver inlays, including R-R monograms on the waistrails and picnic tables, replaced the boxwood inlays of the standard Silver Spur.*

Left *The silver inlay theme was repeated throughout the woodwork, including the picnic tables in the backs of the front seats. Below these were cocktail compartments, each with two decanters and two glasses in a rack of solid black walnut.*

Below left *A miniature refrigerator between the rear seat squabs accommodates two 1-litre wine bottles. The outer lid forms a veneered tray.*

Below *Opening lids on the front centre armrests revealed a telephone and slots for rattle-proof coin storage. Upholstery was in magnolia hide with maroon hide for the fascia top roll, seat piping and carpet edges.*

Right *A compartment between the rear seat cushions contained a second telephone, a hide-covered notebook and a silver pencil.*

Right *A sliding lid on the right-hand picnic table revealed a cedar-lined cigar box, complete with cigar cutter and humidor. The other picnic table contained a green baize-lined storage compartment.*

Below *A plaque bearing the limited edition number of each car was recessed into the inner surface of the glove compartment lid. A magnolia hide pouch with silver R-R monogram was provided for the owner's handbook.*

Below right *Special stainless steel sill treadplates were fitted, with Mulliner Park Ward coachbuilder's plates enamelled in red in lieu of the usual black.*

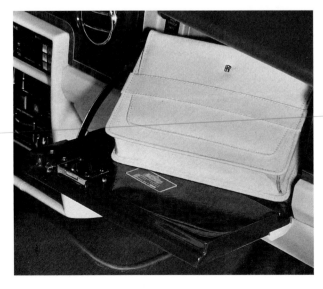

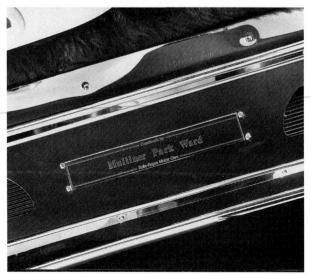

Left *'Project 90', a concept vehicle mock-up exhibited at the 1985 Geneva Motor Show, marked the start of the project which eventually produced the Bentley Continental R. In the background is an earlier Continental, an H. J. Mulliner-bodied Continental S-Type of around 1956.*

Below *On March 5th, 1991, at the Geneva Motor Show, the Bentley Continental R was launched, for deliveries commencing in the 1992 model year. In this view of one of the three prototypes it can be clearly discerned that the new, squatter radiator shell (painted in body colour like that of the Turbo R) has a slight rearward lean. For the first time there is no chrome moulding down the centreline of the bonnet and no provision for a radiator mascot.*

Above *The three-quarter rear view shows the distinctive shape of the boot and rear light clusters. With no front quarter-lights the traditional stainless steel door window frames would not have been sufficiently stiff for good sealing at the speeds of which the car is capable, so the doors are one-piece steel structures with heavy window frames extending into the roof, with slim stainless steel finishers to preserve the traditional appearance.*

Right *The Continental R's seating is similar to that of the Turbo R, but with a switch at the outside top of each front squab to motor the seat forward for access to the rear seats. The front centre armrest houses a compact disc player unit, a telephone and the owner's handbook. If the need arises to carry a third rear seat passenger the rear centre console and armrest can be lifted out and stowed in the boot. Note that the electric selector for the new four-speed, overdrive-top automatic gearbox is mounted in the centre console.*

Bottom right *The interior of the Continental R remains familiar in appearance, but with a new full-length centre console and fixed centre armrests. The instrumentation is the most comprehensive of any Bentley ever built and, like the R-type Continental of 1952, includes an oil temperature gauge.*

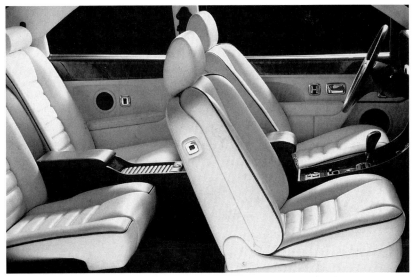

Above *In order to allow the Company to continue to offer a large, spacious limousine, a new limousine version of the Silver Spur was developed by Mulliner Park Ward in London as a successor to the Phantom VI, the final examples of which were completed early in 1992. At first this was to be called the Mulliner Park Ward Silver Spur II Limousine but following the virtual closure of Mulliner Park Ward's London operations, construction of this model was transferred to Crewe and the name Rolls-Royce Touring Limousine was adopted. Unlike the earlier Silver Spur Limousines, with an additional window between the doors and 36 inch or 42 inch 'stretch', the Touring Limousine retains much more elegant proportions with the classic six-light configuration, more modest 24 inch (61 cm) 'stretch' and a higher roofline.*

Below *The rear compartment is designed to cocoon two occupants in the absolute lap of luxury. The seats are individually adjustable. The switches for this and the two-level switches for the in-built seat heaters can be seen on the front of the centre seat cushion. There is a single rearward-facing occasional seat, making this a five-seater limousine. The electrically-operated glass division has a built-in privacy blind.*

Right *For 1992 the Corniche acquired the Automatic Ride Control that had been fitted to the saloon models since 1990, together with a new hood with heated glass rear window, becoming Corniche IV in the process. The Bentley Continental convertible acquired the same specification changes but remained unchanged in name.*

Above *1993 Bentley Brooklands saloon at speed on the famous banked Brooklands track near Byfleet, Surrey – the birthplace of British motor racing after which this Bentley was named. Note the radiator shell finished in the body colour and the absence of a chrome moulding along the bonnet centre-line.*

Right *Pleated inserts to the door panels are an attractive feature of the Brooklands interior. Though the Silver Spirit type seats shown were standard on the Brooklands as introduced the 'grippier' Bentley sports seats as fitted to the Turbo R were optional, as were picnic tables in the backs of the front seats.*

Left & below *The 1994 Silver Spirit III (left) and long wheelbase Silver Spur III (below) saloons are virtually unchanged in external appearance – save for the badges on the boot lid – from their predecessors the Silver Spirit II and Silver Spur II. However, interior and, particularly, technical changes are significant and the Silver Spirit III now shares the painted trim rings on the wheel covers with its long wheelbase counterpart. The small front licence plate bracket fitted to the Silver Spur III indicates that this is a North American car. The pairs of small rectangular headlamps once fitted for that market are no longer fitted, the home market pattern shown now being specified for all markets for the four-door Rolls-Royce models Mica paint technology enhances the external finish.*

Right *This view of the revised fascia of the Silver Spirit III and Silver Spur III provides a glimpse of the new seats. The driver's airbag is contained within the steering wheel while the passenger side airbag is installed in the area previously occupied by the glove compartment and is concealed behind a veneered, hinged flap. To compensate for the loss of the glove compartment, a new lockable stowage space is provided under the fascia. The driver information panel features revised illumination and graphics to improve clarity and visibility. A more comprehensive on-board diagnostic system enhances service diagnostics of complex electronic systems fitted to all the new models. Bentley models retain their more sporting and more comprehensively instrumented fascia, while incorporating all the new features.*

Above & inset *The Bentley
models retain their existing model
designations and remain
unchanged in external appearance
in all but detail. The Turbo R
(above) has lost its chrome bonnet
divider strip so that it is now even
more difficult to distinguish from
the naturally-aspirated Brooklands
(inset). The Turbo R gains subtly
re-styled 16 inch wheels. The keen-
eyed, particularly those who
attended R.R.E.C. Annual Rallies
when they were held at Castle
Ashby, Northants, will recognise
the location of this and other
photographs in this series.*

Right *The Corniche IV and
Bentley Continental convertibles –
both of which remained
unchanged in name for 1994
despite incorporating the new
technical innovations – acquired a
new hood. The heated rear window
is repositioned to improve the
rearward view while the hood and
its tensioning system have been
improved to assist in hood
operation.*

Left *Under the bonnet the new cars are visually improved by the fitting of smart new engine covers. Gone is the old cat's cradle appearance in favour of the 'clean' look seen in these two photos of the new engine installation in (above) the Rolls-Royce models and (below) the Bentley Turbo models. However, the improvements are by no means confined to the enhanced appearance. New heads and manifolding allow the 6.75 litre V-8 engine to deliver 20% more power with improved fuel economy and cleaner emissions.*

Below *The Bentley Continental R has completely re-styled 17 inch wheels for 1994. Both this model and the Turbo R benefit from new Electronic Transient Boost Control which temporarily overrides the turbocharger's normal maximum boost when full acceleration is called for, such as when overtaking. Despite weighing in at 2.4 tonnes, this ultimate supercar is capable of accelerating smoothly from standstill to 60 mph in an amazing 6.2 seconds.*

Above Bentley 'Concept Java', unveiled at the Geneva Motor Show on 8th March 1994. The specification includes a Cosworth-designed 3.5 litre twin-turbo V-8 engine and a five speed automatic transmission.

Right With its carbon fibre coupé roof attached, Concept Java shows an even closer family resemblance to the larger Continental R.

Below A mock-up of the Cosworth-designed engine, which will be a 3.5 litre, double overhead camshaft, 32-valve, twin-turbo V-8 with prodigious mid-range torque.

Below The interior incorporates all the features demanded by today's discerning Bentley owner. Leather and wood are used to create an atmosphere of sumptuous luxury. Four adults can be accommodated in complete comfort.

Left *The Rolls-Royce Flying Spur is essentially a Silver Spur III with turbo-charged engine. This is one of the 'niche' models that have enabled Rolls-Royce Motor Cars Ltd to keep sales up in difficult times.*

Below *Another, 'niche' model, the Bentley Turbo S saloon. Note the higher bumper, which is integral with the air dam, and the resultant lower profile grille shell. The 17 inch alloy wheels, with 255/55WR17 tyres, are the same as those of the '94 model year Continental R.*

On 7th March 1995, at the Geneva Motor Show, just as this book was going to press, Rolls-Royce Motor Cars Ltd unveiled a convertible version of the Bentley Continental R. Called the 'Azure', this is the first entirely new convertible since 1967, other than Concept Java (production of which is still some years away). The much acclaimed Continental R lines have been superbly adapted to convertible form by Crewe with the assistance of Pininfarina of Italy, arguably the world's leaders in convertible styling. Chris Woodwark, the recently appointed Chief Executive of Rolls-Royce Motor Cars Ltd, is delighted with this first new model since his appointment. "We have shown how we continue to develop new models that exceed the highest expectations of our customers and set new standards at the peak of the luxury and performance car market. Great credit is due to the Bentley design team at Crewe and our colleagues at Pininfarina. We believe this to be the most exciting product announcement in recent years. It represents another major step forward for this company, and one in which we can all take great pride". Mr Woodwark is also Chairman of fellow Vickers group company Cosworth Engineering and Executive Director of the parent company, Vickers PLC.

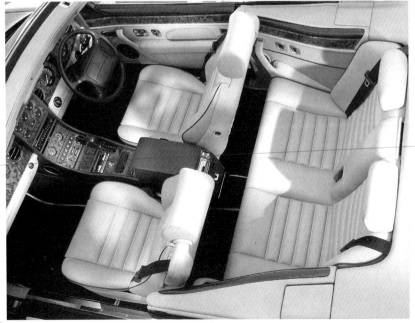

Appendix One

Chassis and engine numbering

Chassis numbers

Except in the case of the Phantoms IV and V, Rolls-Royce chassis numbers up to and including the Silver Cloud III comprised a prefix of three letters (four in the case of left-hand drive cars) followed by a one, two or three digit number. The Phantoms IV and V followed the pattern set by the pre-war Phantom III in having only two series letters, prefixed by the number 4 (Phantom IV) or 5 (Phantom V). Long wheelbase Silver Wraith and Silver Cloud chassis numbers always included the letter 'L'. This should not be confused with the 'L' prefix always added to the series letters of left-hand drive chassis.

Standard post-war Bentley chassis numbers up to and including the S3 followed the traditional pre-war pattern, i.e. a 'B' prefix, followed by a one, two or three digit number, with the series letters last. Bentley Continental chassis numbers were prefixed 'BC' and long wheelbase S

Series cars had three letters, one of which was always 'L', one 'B' plus a series letter, ahead of a one or two digit number.

Chassis series were numbered with either all even, all odd or consecutive numbers. The number 13 was never used in chassis numbers.

In all cases, left-hand drive cars were distinguished by the addition of the letter 'L' ahead of the regular series letters as in the following randomly chosen examples:

With the exception of the Phantom IV, all post-war models were offered with either right- or left-hand drive from 1949 onwards.

Engine numbers

Up to and including the Silver Cloud III, Bentley S3 and Phantom V, the engine number comprised letters broadly related to the chassis series letters and a number which, although not always obviously so at first glance, was closely related to the chassis number.

Use of letter 'L' to denote left-hand drive chassis

Model	Sample rhd chassis number	Sample lhd chassis number
Bentley Mk.VI	B89FU	B87LFU
R-type Continental	BC12D	BC16LD
Bentley S1 lwb	ALB4	LALB2
Silver Cloud II	SYD62	LSYD334
Phantom V	5AT8	5LAT4

Coachbuilt Silver Cloud IIIs from the 'G' series onwards were distinguished by a 'C' suffix – e.g. SGT585C.

The very early Silver Wraith and Bentley Mk.VI were allocated engines, and therefore engine numbers, more or less at random.

However, the system was quickly tidied up so that engine numbers ran in numerical order throughout each chassis series. Though the number 13 was traditionally omitted from chassis numbers, such was not the case with engine numbers, which meant that chassis and engine numbers fell out of alignment from chassis number 15 in each odd- and consecutively-numbered series.

A frequently resorted to practice was to divide cars within a series into two, or occasionally three sub-series, each with its own distinguishing letter but sharing the main series letter. This is made clear in the lists of chassis numbers. Except in the case of Silver Wraiths, which had consecutive chassis numbers, chassis thus grouped were numbered with either all odd or all even numbers within each sub-series. Since the engine numbers

always ran consecutively, this meant that in the first sub-series of a series numbered in this way the engine number was half the chassis number, after taking into account the omission of 13 from chassis numbering. For example, the Silver Cloud I 'A' series was divided into two sub-series, each of 125 cars. The first sub-series was numbered SWA2 to SWA250 (even numbers) and the second SXA1 to SXA 251 (odd numbers, omitting 13). The engine numbers in this series ran from SA1 to SA250, with engine numbers SA1 to SA125 corresponding with chassis numbers SWA2 to SWA250 (i.e. the engine number was the chassis number halved) and engine numbers SA126 to SA250 corresponding with chassis numbers SXA1 to SXA251.

Chassis series which were numbered consecutively had engine numbers

matching the chassis number up to and including number 12, after which the engine number ran one behind the chassis number due to the customary omission of 13 from chassis numbering. For example, Bentley S2 long wheelbase chassis LBA5 was allocated engine number LB5A, but chassis LBA24 corresponds with engine number LB23A.

Silver Shadow, Bentley T Series and derivative models had the same number for the engine as the car serial number, without the three-letter prefix. The Silver Spirit and derivative range broadly speaking continued this system, the engine number being the last five digits of the 17-digit Vehicle Identification Number, until 1989 from which time additional digits were added to engine numbers to convey extra information.

Appendix Two

Delivery dates by chassis series

(Models up to and including the Phantom V, Silver Cloud III & Bentley S3)

The dates in the following table are those on which complete cars were delivered to customers, retailers or, in the case of export cars, shippers. Delivery dates for coachbuilt cars indicated in coachbuilders' records sometimes conflict with those shown in Rolls-Royce records. In such cases the Company records have been given preference. There are instances of coachbuilt cars taking up to three years to be delivered to the customer after receipt of the chassis by the coachbuilder. Delivery dates of experimental cars eventually sold to customers are not included.

Delivery dates by chassis series

Silver Wraith

WTA	Sep. 46 to Jul. 47
WVA	Aug. 47 to Jan. 48
WYA	Oct. 47 to Aug. 48
WZB	Apr. 48 to Jul. 48
WAB	Jul. 48 to Sep. 48
WCB	Sep. 48 to Apr. 49
WDC	Dec. 48 to Jul. 49
WFC	May 49 to Nov. 49
WGC	Sep. 49 to May 50
WHD	Apr. 50 to Nov. 50
WLE	Nov. 50 to May 51
WME	Apr. 51 to Nov. 51
WOF	Oct. 51 to May 52
WSG	Apr. 52 to Dec. 52
WVH	Dec. 52 to Nov. 53
ALW	Jan. 52 to May 53
BLW	May 53 to Apr. 54
CLW	Mar. 54 to Aug. 54
DLW	Jun. 54 to Mar. 55
ELW	Oct. 55 to May 56
FLW	May 56 to Jun. 57
GLW	Jul. 57 to Jan. 58
HLW	Mar. 58 to Oct. 58

Silver Dawn

SBA	Apr. 49 to Jun. 50
SCA	Jun. 50 to Mar. 51
SDB	Nov. 50 to Aug. 51
SFC	Jul. 51 to Jul. 52
SHD	Mar. 52 to Sep. 52
SKE	Jul. 52 to Jan. 53
SLE	Nov. 52 to May 53
SMF	Dec. 52 to Sep. 53
SNF	Jul. 53 to Feb. 54
SOG	Feb. 54 to Aug. 54
SPG	Mar. 54 to Sep. 54
SRH	May 54 to Aug. 54
STH	Aug. 54 to Oct. 54
SUJ	Oct. 54 to Jan. 55
SVJ	Nov. 54 to Apr. 55

Bentley Mk. VI

AK	Nov. 46 to Jul. 47
AJ	Apr. 47 to Oct. 47
BH	Jun. 47 to Jan. 48
BG	Sep. 47 to Mar. 48
CF	Dec. 47 to Aug. 48
CD	Mar. 48 to Dec. 48
DA	Jul. 48 to May 49
DZ	Oct. 48 to Jun. 49
EY	Feb. 49 to Nov. 49
EW	Jun. 49 to Feb. 50
FV	Sep. 49 to Mar. 50
FU	Dec. 49 to Jul. 50
GT	Apr. 50 to Dec. 50
HR	Jul. 50 to Jan. 51
HP	Jul. 50 to Mar. 51
JO	Sep. 50 to Feb. 51
JN	Nov. 50 to May 51
KM	Jan. 51 to Jul. 51
KL	Feb. 51 to Aug. 51
LJ	Mar. 51 to Sep. 51
LH	May 51 to Dec. 51
MD	Jul. 51 to Jan. 52
MB	Sep. 51 to Feb. 52
NZ	Nov. 51 to May 52
NY	Feb. 52 to Sep. 52
PV	Apr. 52 to Jul. 52
PU	Jun. 52 to Aug. 52

DELIVERY DATES BY CHASSIS SERIES

Bentley R-type

RT	Jun. 52 to Apr. 53
RS	Sep. 52 to Apr. 53
SR	Sep. 52 to May 53
SP	Jan. 53 to May 53
TO	Apr. 53 to Sep. 53
TN	Jun. 53 to Dec. 53
UL	Oct. 53 to Dec. 53
UM	Nov. 53 to May 54
WH	Jan. 54 to May 54
WG	Mar. 54 to Jun. 54
XF	May 54 to Jun. 54
YA	Jun. 54 to Oct. 54
YD	Aug. 54 to Nov. 54
ZX	Oct. 54 to Jan. 55
ZY	Dec. 54 to Feb. 55

– Continental

A	Jun. 52 to Apr. 53
B	Apr. 53 to Sep. 53
C	Aug. 53 to Jul. 54
D	Jul. 54 to Mar. 55
E	Apr. 55 to May 55

Phantom IV

AF	Jul. 50 to Jun. 52
BP	Mar. 53 to Jul. 54
CS	Nov. 55 to Oct. 56

Silver Cloud I

SWA	Apr. 55 to Jan. 56
SXA	Jan. 56 to May 56
SYB	Mar. 56 to Jun. 56
SZB	Jun. 56 to Sep. 56
SBC	Aug. 56 to Oct. 56
SCC	Oct. 56 to Apr. 57
SDD	Feb. 57 to May 57
SED	Apr. 57 to Aug. 57
SFE	Aug. 57 to Jan. 58
SGE	Dec. 57 to Jul. 58
SHF	Jul. 58 to Nov. 58
SJF	Oct. 58 to Jan. 59
SKG	Jan. 59 to Feb. 59
SLG	Feb. 59 to Apr. 59
SMH	Mar. 59 to Jun. 59
SNH	May 59 to Jul. 59

– Long Wheelbase

ALC	Nov. 57 to Jun. 58
BLC	Feb. 58 to Jan. 59
CLC	Dec. 58 to Jul. 59

Bentley S1

AN	Apr. 55 to Nov. 55
AP	Sep. 55 to Feb. 56
BA	Dec. 55 to Mar. 56
BC	Feb. 56 to Apr. 56
CK	Apr. 56 to Jul. 56

CM	Jul. 56 to Nov. 56
DB	Sep. 56 to Nov. 56
DE	Oct. 56 to Jan. 57
EG	Jan. 57 to Jul. 57
EK	Jul. 57 to Dec. 57
FA	Nov. 57 to Jun. 58
FD	Jun. 58 to Mar. 59
GD	Feb. 59 to Apr. 59
GC	Mar. 59 to May 59
HB	May 59 to Jun. 59
HA	May 59 to Jun. 59

– Long Wheelbase

ALB	Nov. 57 to Jul. 59

– Continental

AF	Mar. 55 to Feb. 56
BG	Feb. 56 to Jan. 57
CH	Jan. 57 to Jul. 57
DJ	Jul. 57 to Jan. 58
EL	Oct. 57 to Jun. 58
FM	Jun. 58 to Jan. 59
GN	Dec. 58 to Apr. 59

Silver Cloud II

SPA	Aug. 59 to Dec. 59
SRA	Nov. 59 to Mar. 60
STB	Feb. 60 to Apr. 60
SVB	Apr. 60 to Sep. 60
SWC	Jun. 60 to Dec. 60
SXC	Nov. 60 to Feb. 61
SYD	Feb. 61 to Aug. 61
SZD	Jun. 61 to Dec. 61
SAE	Dec. 61 to Aug. 62

– Long Wheelbase

LCA	Sep. 59 to Aug. 60
LCB	Aug. 60 to May 61
LCC	Apr. 61 to Jul. 62
LCD	Jun. 62 to Sep. 62

Bentley S2

AA	Aug. 59 to Dec. 59
AM	Nov. 59 to Jan. 60
BR	Jan. 60 to May 60
BS	May 60 to Aug. 60
CT	Sep. 60 to Nov. 60
CU	Nov. 60 to May 61
DV	Apr. 61 to Dec. 61
DW	Dec. 61 to Aug. 62

– Long Wheelbase

LBA	Jan. 60 to Dec. 60
LBB	Jan. 61 to Sep. 62

– Continental

AR	Jul. 59 to Jun. 60
BY	Jun. 60 to Jul. 61

CZ	Feb. 61 to Aug. 62

Phantom V

AS	Sep. 59 to Jul. 60
AT	Aug. 60 to Feb. 61
BV	Feb. 61 to Jul. 61
BX	Aug. 61 to Jan. 62
CG	Nov. 61 to Nov. 62
VA	Sep. 62 to Mar. 64
VB	Nov. 63 to Apr. 64
VC	Apr. 64 to Oct. 64
VD	Sep. 64 to Sep. 65
VE	Sep. 65 to Mar. 66
VF	Mar. 66 to Apr. 68

Silver Cloud III

SAZ	Oct. 62
SCX	Sep. 62 to May 63
SDW	May 63 to Oct. 63
SEV	Sep. 63 to Jan. 64
SFU	Dec. 63 to Jul. 64
SGT	Jun. 64 to Nov. 64
SHS	Oct. 64 to Feb. 65
SJR	Dec. 65 to Apr. 65
SKP	Apr. 65 to Sep. 65
CSC-B	Apr. 65 to Dec. 65
CSC-C	Sep. 65 to Feb. 66

– Long Wheelbase

CAL	Oct. 62 to Jan. 63
CBL	Jan. 63 to Jun. 63
CCL	Jun. 63 to Feb. 64
CDL	Feb. 64 to Aug. 64
CEL	Sep. 64 to Jun. 65
CFL	Jun. 65 to Aug. 65
CGL	Aug. 65 to Sep. 65

Bentley S3

AV	Oct. 62
CN	Sep. 62 to Oct. 63
DF	Sep. 63 to Dec. 63
EC	Nov. 63 to Jun. 64
FG	May 64 to Dec. 64
GJ	Oct. 64 to Jan. 65
HN	Jan. 65 to Jul. 65
JP	Jul. 65 to Sep. 65

– Long Wheelbase

BAL	Nov. 62 to May 63
BBL	Jun. 64 to Jan. 65
BCL	Feb. 65 to Sep. 65

– Continental

XA	Sep. 62 to Jul. 63
XB	Jun. 63 to Sep. 63
XC	Nov. 63 to Nov. 65
XD	Feb. 65 to Apr. 65
XE	Mar. 65 to Apr. 66

Appendix Five

Steering wheel controls, 1946–59

The early post-war Rolls-Royce and Bentley cars had controls on the steering wheel boss for the hand throttle, ride and mixture controls as applicable to each model. These controls were laid out as shown in the following illustrations.

Below left *THROTTLE and RIDING*

Silver Wraith with manual gearbox. Phantom IV with manual gearbox. Silver Dawn to chassis SHD60. Left-hand drive Bentley MkVI.

Below right *THROTTLE, MIXTURE and RIDING*

Right-hand drive Bentley MkVI including very early (R-type) Continental.

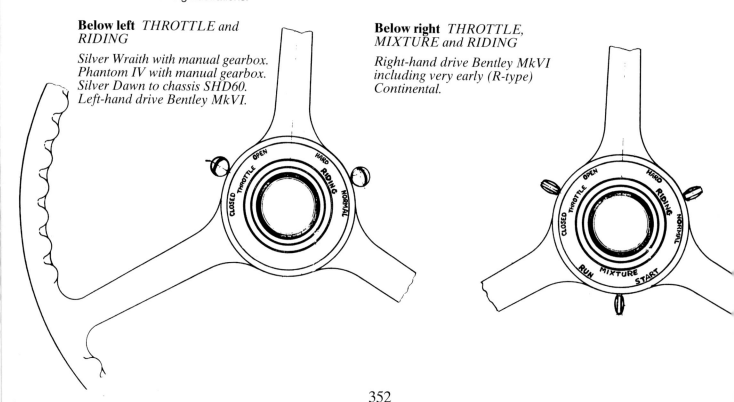

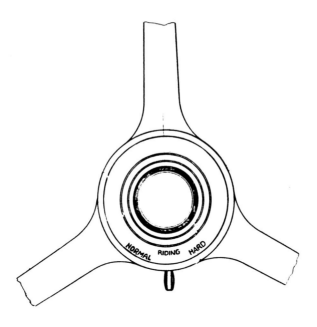

Above *RIDING*

Bentley R-type including all but earliest Continental.
Silver Dawn from chassis SKE2.
Silver Wraith with automatic gearbox.
All left-hand drive Silver Wraith from chassis LWVH15.
Early long wheelbase Silver Wraith with automatic gearbox, without power-assisted steering.
Phantom IV with automatic gearbox.

Below *NO CONTROLS, boss turns with wheel (electrically controlled rear dampers, switch on side of steering column).*

Silver Cloud.
Bentley S Series.
Late long wheelbase Silver Wraith with power-assisted steering.

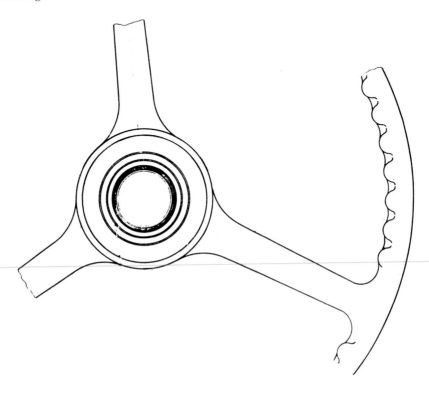

Appendix Six

Switchboxes

The traditional Rolls-Royce and Bentley 'switchbox' changed completely only twice during the post-war period to date. The early post-war cars continued the switchbox design on the last pre-war models.

Above *Lighting switch and ignition lock with key-operated starter, warning lights for generator and low fuel. Introduced 1955 for the Silver Cloud and Bentley S Series. With detail changes, this switchbox was by far the longest lasting design and continued on the Silver Shadow, Bentley T Series and derivatives, with an oil pressure warning light in place of the low fuel warning. The lighting switch had three (illustrated) or four positions depending upon whether or not the car was fitted with fog lights. Essentially the same design then continued on the Silver Spirit range of cars until the introduction of the Silver Spirit II and derivatives.*

Silver Cloud I, II & III; Bentley S1, S2 & S3; Phantom V; Phantom VI; Silver Shadow, Bentley T Series and derivative models; Silver Spirit and derivative models to 1989.

Above *Separate master/lighting switch, ignition switch, starter button and lock.*

Silver Wrath; Silver Dawn; Phantom IV; Bentley Mk VI; Bentley R-type.

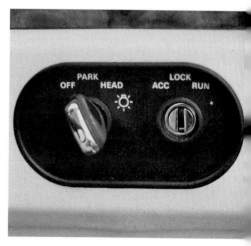

Above *For the 1990 Model Year, a completely new switchbox was introduced, with the lighting switch and ignition lock side by side and no warning lights. There are two variations, one round as before, the other a flattened oval shape as illustrated.*

Round: Silver Spirit II & III, Silver Spur II & III including Limousine; Bentley Continental, 1990 and later; Bentley Continental R.

Oval: Bentley 4-door models, 1990 and later

Appendix Seven

Mascots

Rolls-Royce models are fitted with a Spirit of Ecstasy radiator mascot. Bentley models were customarily fitted with a winged 'B' radiator mascot until the introduction of the Mulsanne in 1980, after which it continued to be available as an accessory. Mascots fitted during the post-war period have varied in design, as follows:

Left *'Kneeling' type Spirit of Ecstasy. Introduced 1934 as an option and continued as standard for the early post-war models.*

Silver Wraith (short wheelbase).
Silver Dawn.
Long wheelbase Silver Wraith to 'D' series.
Phantom IV 'A' & 'B' series.

Below *Standing type Spirit of Ecstasy. A revival of the original 1911 Charles Sykes design.*

Silver Cloud I, II & III.
Long wheelbase Silver Wraith from 'E' series.
Phantom IV 'C' series.
All subsequent models with mounting cap variations.

Above *Spring-loaded Spirit of Ecstasy. Sometimes wired to car horn as an anti-theft device.*

Late Silver Shadow; Corniche; SilverShadow II; Silver Wraith II. Early Silver Spirit and Silver Spur not fitted with retractable type (see next page).

Left *Late kneeling type Spirit of Ecstasy. Oil-rich Arabs have had an enduring love affair with the Rolls-Royce car, but somehow the proud lady on the radiator 'revelling in the freshness of the air and the musical sound of her fluttering draperies' infringed upon Arab sensibilities sufficiently to bring about a revival of the 1935-55 'kneeling' type lady for the middle east market.*

Silver Spirit (Middle East and special order).
Silver Spur (Middle East and special order).

Above, left & right *Retractable Spirit of Ecstasy. For safety reasons the radiator mascot is now arranged to retract into the radiator shell on impact. It may be drawn back out into its normal position and latched into place by hand.*

Silver Spirit (for certain markets, later extended to cars for all markets except U.S.A.)
Silver Spur (for certain markets, later extended to cars for all markets except U.S.A.)

Left *Rearward-leaning Winged 'B'. This was mounted on a dummy radiator filler cap.*

Early Bentley Mk VI.

1980 Rolls-Royce Motors Ltd merged with Vickers. Silver Spirit range of cars introduced. Bentley version called Mulsanne. Long wheelbase model called Silver Spur.

1981 Last deliveries of Corniche two-door Saloon.

1982 Bentley Mulsanne Turbo introduced.

1983 Company name changed to Rolls-Royce Motor Cars Ltd.

1984 Bentley Eight introduced.

1985 Bentley Turbo R introduced.

Bentley Corniche renamed Bentley Continental.

1986 Bentley Mulsanne specification upgraded to become Mulsanne S.

1989 Silver Spirit II (and long wheel-base Silver Spur II) introduced for 1990 Model Year. Bentley saloons share new specification but model names unchanged.

1990 Bentley Continental R introduced.

1992 Last deliveries of Phantom VI, Bentley Mulsanne S and Bentley Eight.

Bentley Brooklands saloon introduced.

1993 Silver Spirit III (and long wheelbase Silver Spur III) introduced for 1994 Model Year. Bentley models share new specification but model names remain unchanged.

1994 Bentley Concept Java unveiled at Geneva Motor Show. Limited edition Rolls-Royce Flying Spur introduced. Limited edition Bentley Turbo S introduced.

Appendix Nine

The Clubs

Rolls-Royce and Bentley owners and enthusiasts are extremely well served by a number of very active clubs in several countries. The following clubs are those which accept into membership owners of all Rolls-Royce and Bentley cars dealt with in this book.

UK and EUROPE
Rolls-Royce Enthusiasts' Club
Headquarters:
The Hunt House,
High Street,
Paulerspury,
Northamptonshire NN12 7NA,
England

The Rolls-Royce Enthusiasts' Club was formed in 1957. The headquarters of the Club, the Hunt House, is shared with the Sir Henry Royce Memorial Foundation and is the sole repository for Rolls-Royce and Bentley archival material recognised by the Company. The Club has Sections in 16 areas of the United Kingdom, 11 other European countries and Canada, with a total of around 7,000 members. Each

Section holds its own events throughout the year and the Club holds numerous technical seminars at the Hunt House and an Annual Rally and Concours which is by far the biggest gathering of Rolls-Royce and Bentley cars in the world. The R.R.E.C. publishes an excellent journal, the *Bulletin*, six times per year.

NORTH AMERICA
Rolls-Royce Owners' Club Inc.
Headquarters:
191 Hempt Road,
Mechanicsburg,
Pennsylvania 17055
United States of America

Formed in 1951, the Rolls-Royce Owners' Club is the oldest all-model Rolls-Royce club in the world. It has since flourished and has a total membership approaching 7,000. The Club has 33 active Regions in the United States and Canada, each of which organises its own activities in addition to national activities which include tours in various parts of the country, technical sessions and the

Annual Meet, which is held in various parts of the U.S. and Canada. The journal *Flying Lady* has been published six times per year since the Club's inception.

AUSTRALASIA – AUSTRALIA
Rolls-Royce Owners' Club of Australia
Registered office:
Malcolm Johns & Company,
Level 12,
Skygarden,
77 Castlereagh Street,
Sydney,
New South Wales 2000
Australia

The Rolls-Royce Owners' Club of Australia was formed in 1956 and has Branches in six States and Territories of Australia, each of which holds events throughout the year, with a total membership around 1,100. Each Branch in turn hosts the annual Federal Rally which is thus held in a different part of the country each year. The Club publishes six editions of its journal *Praeclarum* per year.

NEW ZEALAND
New Zealand Rolls-Royce &
Bentley Club Inc.
Secretary:
Tom Williams,
78 Kesteven Avenue,
Glendowie,
Auckland,
New Zealand

The New Zealand Rolls-Royce &
Bentley Club has an enthusiastic and
active membership in three Regions of
the country, each of which holds its
own events in addition to the Club's
Annual Rally. The Club publishes a
magazine six times per year.

Right *The Hunt House,*
Paulerspury, England,
headquarters of the Rolls-Royce
Enthusiasts' Club. Built in 1865 by
Lord Grafton as headquarters of
the Grafton Hunt, it was purchased
by the Sir Henry Royce Memorial
Foundation in 1977. It is a Grade
II Listed Building and houses a
priceless collection of Rolls-Royce
and Bentley archival material.

Below *Part of the Hunt House ground floor display area. Exhibits in this*
photograph are, from left to right, a 40/50h.p. 'Silver Ghost' engine, a
20/25h.p. chassis and a sectioned Silver Wraith engine.

Top right *The Royce Room at the Hunt House, where the great man's drawing board, drawing instruments and other personal effects are displayed. To the right of the drawing board are three late 1920s colour wash design drawings by Royce's colleague Ivan Evernden, who went on to take a leading role in designing the first post-war standard steel saloon and the Bentley R-type Continental.*

Right *Archive storage in the C. S. Rolls Wing at the Hunt House.*

Bottom right *The auditorium in the C. S. Rolls Wing. This photograph gives some idea of the standard of the facilities at the Hunt House. Note the engines displayed along the far wall.*

Index